**SIR THOMAS WYATT
A LITERARY PORTRAIT**

WITHDRAWN

SIR THOMAS WYATT
A LITERARY
PORTRAIT

Selected Poems, with Full Notes,
Commentaries and a Critical Introduction by

H. A. Mason

Published by Bristol Classical Press
English Editors: David Hopkins and Tom Mason

Cover illustration: Sir Thomas Wyatt
from *Wyatt Resteth Here* 1542, Huntington Library.

Printed in Great Britain

First published (1986) by
BRISTOL CLASSICAL PRESS
Department of Classics
University of Bristol
Wills Memorial Building
Queens Road
BRISTOL BS8 1RJ

© H.A. Mason, 1986

British Library Cataloguing in Publication Data

Wyatt, *Sir* Thomas
Sir Thomas Wyatt : a literary portrait : selected
poems.
I. Title II. Mason, H.A.
821'.2 PR2401

ISBN 0-86292-086-8
ISBN 0-906515-65-3 Pbk

Printed in Great Britain by
Short Run Press Limited
Exeter

ACKNOWLEDGEMENT

To Richard Bates, John Mason, Tom Mason, for dedicating so much of their time to checking and cheering me in the labours of commentary and annotation.

Much of the credit for any success must be laid to their account. All the blame for errors and shortcomings must go to mine.

HOW TO USE THIS BOOK

This book is an edition of some of Thomas Wyatt's best poems. It is also an introduction to the world he lived in. The book may be dipped into for help with particular poems or read through as an account of Wyatt's essential poetic character. The poems have been made as easy to read as possible. They are printed one to a page unencumbered by comment and form the centre of the book.

An attempt has been made in the commentaries to provide within the covers of a single volume all the materials and information needed for a full understanding of each poem. The notes are introduced by a general essay on the problems and pitfalls of reading early Tudor literature and a descriptive list of useful books (List A). The notes themselves are interspersed with short essays on some of the larger questions raised by the poems – such as Wyatt's real or literary relations with Ann Boleyn, Savonarola, Luther, Cromwell, and his King. Wyatt's religious poems are accompanied by a list of contemporary versions and commentaries on the psalms (List B).

CONTENTS

CRITICAL INTRODUCTION

The assumption from which this essay starts is that the kind of pleasures which readers of selected poems by Sir Thomas Wyatt have been getting since the early years of the nineteenth century can be increased and refined for readers of this century by considering all the possible connections *between* the poems. It may have been too ambitious to expect to derive from them a conviction that Wyatt had a poetic *career* such as we find with poets who had no public business or occupation and could therefore devote their time exclusively to cultivating their gift and literary talents. Wyatt's extant poems bear so many signs of having been the products of hours of enforced leisure such as fell to the lot of all sixteenth-century servants from the king's close advisers down to Shakespeare's Joan when not keeling the pot that the usual device of making connections by reference to the poet's biography is less illuminating for Wyatt than for some other poets who have left few poems behind. (It is, however, a tantalising part of the attempt to 'connect' that there is such a high proportion of Wyatt's poems which we think of as clearly *circumstantial* and would therefore give us heightened pleasure if we knew in greater detail how Wyatt was placed when he composed each of them.) But it does not seem too ambitious to enquire whether Wyatt was the same poet in all the different kinds of poems he wrote, and therefore set on all his best poems a mark which stamps them as his own. (Here again we have a tantalising glimpse from the impression Wyatt made on his contemporaries of a powerful 'character' and a strong 'personality' which might lead us to expect some correlation of the man and the poet.)

The hope which goes along with this assumption is that one result of looking for connections between the poems would be that a kind of poetical unity would emerge to compose a twentieth-century portrait to be placed alongside the literary

1

portraits drawn by Leland and, above all, that drawn by Surrey, which I have placed first *honoris causa* to serve both as a model and a challenge. We can all become draughtsmen of our own poetical portraits of Wyatt, once we believe that there is an underlying unity to be found in the poems. So why write an essay? Why not leave the selected poems to the mercies of the reader, who must in any case be the final judge whether the poems shape themselves into a picture of the poet? The reason is that, while over the years I have acquired a powerful conviction that Wyatt for all his variety was *semper idem*, one and the same in the poems which bear his mark, I do not expect that a reader who has just found himself enjoying all the selected poems severally will consent to any formula which would make the variety a true unity unless he were presented with a fairly powerful argument in favour of specific unifying terms. Still less could I hope to convince by a mere 'say-so' the hardened reader who has long ago made up his mind that Wyatt can be seen as *semper idem* only in his 'lyrics', and finds all the other poems a sad falling-off.

Many of those who quite like Wyatt's 'non-lyric' poems nevertheless feel that their author is a different man from the poet who, they suppose, wrote love poems to be sung. An extreme view is that there was an actual break in Wyatt's career, and that the supposedly abrupt change in style and subject matter followed immediately on a tragic crisis in Wyatt's life. The word 'traumatic' is often abused nowadays, but Wyatt himself used the language of 'wound' and 'scar' when he looked back on the first twenty days of May 1536, when he himself was arrested and put in the Tower, when Anne Boleyn was beheaded and some of his close friends and acquaintances were also put to death as her lovers and therefore as traitors to the King. Since Wyatt's career as a poet has to be fitted into a life-span of less than forty years, 1503–1542,[1] it is plausible to suppose that this year, 1536, was indeed climacteric. But ought we to accept the following interpretation of the events?

> Wyatt remained a prisoner for several weeks longer; and when he was finally released he was a changed man. The experience of 'these bloody days' had broken his heart, he tells us in the poem: 'my youth did then depart'. We can see

---

1 For a list of some of the principal dates in Wyatt's career, see page 96.

the change brought about by these events by comparing the two Holbein portraits — one of a handsome man in the prime of life, the other of a prematurely aged man. The fashionable courtier and writer of ballets was superseded by the hard-working diplomat, by the writer of satires and penitential psalms.[1]

It may seem a merely flippant reply to point out that an admiring description of the later portrait is given by Leland in one of the commendatory poems written to commemorate the poet's death. (The text will be found on a later page in the commentary on Surrey's Epitaph.) Leland considered that Wyatt's beard more than compensated for the disappearance of hair on the top. But it was not merely to protest against the confusion of premature baldness and premature old age that I have dragged in this remarkable version of the main crisis in Wyatt's life. Nobody can now provide clinching evidence of what really happened. This interpretation, however, gains all its plausibility from one way of reading the poems. If you ground your general view of what is characteristic of Wyatt at his best on the 'lyrics', and read them in a vaguely 'romantic' way, such an interpretation seems to square best with the literary evidence. My main reason for considering this view is that, as Macbeth said, 'in my way it lyes'. It is also a widely-held view, and perhaps the view that has prevailed through the last fifty years. My counter-view starts from the opposite end. It is a claim that the unity of Wyatt's best poetry can be seen only after we have appreciated the poems in *terza rima*,[2] Wyatt's chief literary occupation from 1533 to his death. It will again be a mere 'say-so' to remark that, so far from finding a broken-down, 'burnt-out case' in them, I see a more powerful expression of the talents first revealed in what we suppose to be the verse of Wyatt's early years.

1 *Life and Letters of Sir Thomas Wyatt*, by Kenneth Muir, 1963, p. 35. The author of a poem in a Dublin manuscript beginning *Who lyst* wrote:

> These blodye Dayes have brokyn my hart;
> My lust, my youth dyd them departe
> And blynd desyer of astate . . .

The full text is printed in *Collected Poems of Sir Thomas Wyatt*, ed. Muir and Thomson, pp. 187–188.

2 An Italian form of iambic verse, consisting of sets of three lines, the middle line of each set rhyming with the first and last of the succeeding (aba, bcb, cdc, etc.).

But something can be done by commenting in detail on the *terza rima* poems to establish a point that is often overlooked, that Wyatt did not *suddenly* become a Christian Humanist in 1532. We have printed evidence that Wyatt was interested in Plutarch's *Moralia* by 1527. I think the references in the later poems make it plausible to suppose that he read all the great works of Erasmus as they became available. It is equally implausible to suppose that Wyatt never gave religion and religious controversy a thought until the day when he determined to 'translate' the Seven Penitential Psalms. Our historical records are heavily weighted in favour of religious *extremists*, and by and large confine themselves to the views of those in power about those who fell into their hands. It is therefore impossible to estimate the proportion of all active-minded men of Wyatt's age who, while substantially retaining their Catholic tradition, took a sufficient interest in the 'new' doctrines of Luther, Zwingli and others to bring themselves under suspicion of heresy, yet not sufficient to bring them to trial or public exposure. We do not know whether Wyatt read forbidden religious books as soon as did the members of the White Horse Inn group,[1] that is, before he composed any of his extant poems. But it seems to me reasonable to think of him collecting some of this underground 'literature' long before the texts he used for his translations.

Equally obviously, it cannot be maintained that the number of lines and passages from the Chaucerian *corpus* (for Wyatt, like all his contemporaries, would think of several non-Chaucerian pieces as the work of the master) which we can detect in the *terza rima* poems show that Wyatt suddenly came under Chaucer's influence in his thirties. Lastly, on the human level, Wyatt was never a mere lute-twanging hanger-on in the court, a member of the silly set, but a responsible court official who showed potential ability as a diplomat as soon as he came of age.

Nevertheless, it would be flying in the face of the facts to declare that unity is more immediately perceptible than variety in Wyatt's poems, and to deny that, if we look only at subject-matter, there is a gulf between the love poems and those dealing with religion or society. I shall be trying by shifting attention over to 'form' to make my up-hill task lighter, but before setting

---

1 From about 1521 a group of Cambridge scholars, some of whom became notable figures in the Reformation of religion in England, began to meet at the White Horse Inn.

out, it might predispose the sceptical in my favour if I were to instance a striking parallel which occurred in this century. Far greater than the disappointment expressed by those who regretted that Wyatt turned away for every from 'lyrics', although still in his prime, was the cry of pain from the many admirers *W.B. Yeats* had acquired by 1898, when they gradually discovered that the Yeats they loved was never going to re-appear. Both memoirs and contemporary reviews confirm that there was a wide-spread lament that by 1900, that is, when he was 35, Yeats had become a prematurely aged poet who had given his all, and that the living man of the years 1900–1920 had nothing in common with the bard of the Celtic Twilight. It was not until Yeats published his own memoirs that the public learnt that the topics which began to crop up in his mid-twentieth-century poems had pre-occupied him ever since he was a boy. As he lived on past Wyatt's span, almost the reverse occurred, and Yeats had to assure us that the 'new' author of *The Tower* and *The Winding Stair* had never parted company with the poet of *Poems*, 1899:

> Though leaves are many, the root is one . . .

All such analogies will inevitably limp, but this will serve to present the general form of my contention.

A strong 'hint' or 'tip' was given me by starting out from the poems in *terza rima*, namely, that it was characteristic of Wyatt's whole career to develop from translation in a brutally literal sense to an activity which would not normally go under that name. The paradoxical conviction which came over me was that the original, personal stamp which signs Wyatt's poems for us and tells us that he has triumphed in and over a literary form was in part a consequence of a power one might think incompatible with the striking formula Dante gave for his own compositions:

> *I' mi son un che, quando*
> *Amor mi spira, noto, e a qual modo*
> *ch' e' ditta dentro vo significando.*
> (As for me, I am one who makes a note when Love
> inspires me, and proceeds to turn into meaning-
> ful verse what He dictates inside me.)

— a power, I mean, to select and combine materials drawn from many sources so that a *dédoublement* occurs in which the author is both inside and outside his poem, both actor and observer of the action.

   So little has this to do with translation in the vulgar sense
that, rather than copy out from the commentary the evidence of
Wyatt's drawing on the experience of many predecessors in order
to present his own when he was writing moral, reflective verse
in *terza rima*, I will take as the most striking illustration, the
poem that I have put at the front, that beginning *They flee from
me*. How many readers have observed what might be called the
combining process in this poem? I say, rhetorically, 'none', but
lapse for safety into the first person singular to record my resis-
tance in 1935 to a scholar's suggestion that the line about taking
bread was lifted from a much earlier poem. My quick reaction was,
'Impossible; if ever a poem was a direct transcript from life . . .',
and I refused to open my mind to the possibility that the poem
is in part the result of much collecting and concentrating of dis-
parate literary material. I therefore challenge the reader who has
a similar impression of the relation of composition to experience,
to turn to the commentary on this poem and ask himself whether
the perspective opened up there does not set his mind off on a
truer course. I use the word 'perspective' or 'avenue of suggestive speculation', since the commentary has not succeeded in
bringing home any more than a little of the range of mind involved
in putting this poem together. (I expect that before long someone
will turn up earlier poems with a similar ironic twist on 'kindly'
and 'deserved'.)

   Need I say that, if I call this way of composing 'translation',
no translation can be a success in which the translator does not
draw on his own stock of *direct* experience? It seems to me
perverse to suppose that the dramatic success of this poem was
achieved without *any* knowledge of what Hawes called 'chamber
work' in his *Passetyme*:

> What the man is and what he can do
> Of chambre werke as nature will agre.
> Though by experience ye knowe nothynge therto
> Yet ofte ye muse and thynke what it may be.
> Nature prouoketh of her stronge decre
> You so to do as hath ben her olde guyse . . .

I therefore thought that the reader of these poems might be glad
to have in the same volume an account (however fictitious) of

Wyatt stalking in Anne Boleyn's chamber.[1]

One consequence of following up the thought that Wyatt does not become himself until the translating process has gone a considerable way beyond the literal, that Wyatt is characteristically the *maker* rather than the passive translator, is that very few of his translations of Petrarch can claim a place in a selection of the best. When we are looking for the characteristic among his translations, we should turn rather to his versions of the *strambotti* of Serafino. But here, too, we find that mastery of this form of an eight-line epigram consisted in leaving behind the external wit of the Italian, usually applied to Petrarchan commonplaces, and filling the eight lines with application to concrete situations, usually drawn from his own life, and adding a bitter tang, where the wit rests on facts of life and human behaviour. Serafino gave him the opportunity but Wyatt took it in order to create a tight, original form.

I would there be happy to throw out as a covering formula for Wyatt's successes that they are all *formal poems whose formal virtues impress on us some truth of nature and experience*. This assertion is in the first place intended as a flat denial of all that is implied in the consecrated formulation, 'the songs which came to him as naturally as the leaves to a tree'. Given the general banality of all the lyric verse written during Wyatt's youth, I should have thought it was the hardest and therefore the greatest of his triumphs to have written one or two poems that will never be dropped (I should imagine) from any anthology of our finest lyrics.

To establish this claim, it is necessary to distinguish *merely* formal triumphs from great poems. There is such a thing as 'formal beauty', just as there is elegance in the solution of problems in mathematics or in chess. But if we can detect nothing more than formal beauty, and, above all, if we are conscious of no power forcing the mind to reconsider and revalue matters commonly thought to be of human importance, it is hard to move from admiration to love. A fair example of a merely formal beauty seems to me the following reconstruction. (I must describe it so, since some of the formal beauty is the result of editorial labour. The details are given in *Editing Wyatt* p. 87.)

1 See page 147.

*A proper new ballet wherein the lover doth
request her friend to continue his truth
until she deserve the contrary:*

Disdain me not without desert
Ne pain me not so suddenly
Sith well ye wot that in my heart
I mean it not but honestly.[1]
    Refuse me not.

Refuse me not without cause why
Ne think me not to be unjust
Sith that by lot of fantasy
The careful knot needs knit I must.
    Mistrust me not.

Mistrust me not though some there be
That fain would spot my steadfastness.
Believe them not sith well ye see
The proof is not as they express.
    Forsake me not.

Forsake me not till I deserve
Ne hate me not till I offend.
Destroy me not till that I swerve
Sith well ye wot what I intend.
    Disdain me not.

Disdain me not that am your own,
Refuse me not that am so true.
Mistrust me not till all be known.
Forsake me not now for no new.
    Thus leave me not.

And yet, perversely, it refuses to be confined to the
description, 'merely formal beauty', for I find that the moment
I allow this poem to 'work', it ceases to be a simple, flat, pattern
made by spacing and grouping and repetition of phrases. The
repetitions of '. . . me not' begin to toll like a bell. But there

---

1 *cf.* Queen Katherine in her appeal to Henry VIII against the case for divorce:
. . . ayenst me that neuer entendyd but honestie . . .
    (Cavendish in his Life of Wolsey, p. 81);
cf. in *I am as I am* the line:
    I mene no thing but honestly . . .

comes a limit, and eventually the word 'tinkle' offers itself, or if 'chime', then one heard far-off. Yet are we English people so cut off from the world of Wyatt and Elyot? I am sure that at the age of eleven I did not know that *Myosotis palustris* was the scientific name of a flower with magical properties. But when one sunny Sunday morning I found the flower laid on my window sill, I instantly got the message. Of course this delicate act may have been (unknown to me) a Victorian revival of a lapsed country ritual, yet the phrase *Forget me not* did not then strike me as archaic or requiring re-phrasing.

Yet, however much we are willing to respond to the charm of the poem, we could never, I contend, rank it with Wyatt's supreme lyrics, where similar patterning gives rise to so very much more powerful effects. On the defective diamond, *What should I say*? (p. 42) a definitive comment was made many years ago by Miss A.K. Foxwell, who, in her edition of Wyatt's poems, wrote:

> This lyric stands amongst the few poems which have earned for Wiat a place amongst the chief English lyrists; there is an airiness and lightness of touch about it which is amazing when we contrast it with some of the most conceited translations of the Sonnets. But combined with the lightness of structure there are depths of underlying feeling, culminating in the last line, "Farewell unkiste."[1]

I call it 'definitive' since it praises the poem as much for the sound as for the sense, and in fact we can be taken with the sound and movement and know the rhythm is not banal long before we recognize its strictness to be functional for controlling an otherwise unbearable pain that left to itself would sprawl over. But the best remark was to speak of 'depths'. I should like to add 'subtlety', and to prove its propriety by noting how impossible it has turned out to get the defective third stanza restored satisfactorily. I have put in 'Your cruel kind' merely as a fill-up, but it offends against the whole poem, which, though always coming near it, never is so flat and blatant in reproach as that.

I hope I have made some small amends for this in my

1 But see the commentary (p. 140) for this phrase.

commentary by reminding the reader of the many echoes in the poem of the English words pronounced in the Roman Catholic marriage service of Wyatt's day. These permit us to speculate that the poem had a 'real' occasion in the early infidelity of his wife, Elizabeth Brooke. At the age of seventeen Wyatt married above him into a noble neighbouring family, the Cobhams. How deeply he was offended by his wife's adultery may be guessed from his stubborn opposition to the powerful family, who kept pressing him to take the lady back. An obvious conclusion can be drawn from remarks he made in a letter written to his son when he in turn was marrying:

> Love well and agree with your wife, for where is noise and debate in the house, there is unquiet dwelling. And much more where it is in one bed. Frame well yourself to love, and rule well and honestly your wife as your fellow, and she shall love and reverence you as her head. Such as you are unto her such shall she be unto you . . . And the blessing of god for good agreement between the wife and husband is fruit of many children, which I for the like thing do lack, and the fault is both in your mother and me, but chiefly in her.

The beauty of the poem seems to be concentrated in the compression of the reproach by an underlying tenderness, which follows each epigrammatic point against the partner by the large expressive exclamation. This underlying pattern is itself right, so right that each small variation is as telling as possible. The poem seems much larger and freer than a marriage break-up, yet the promise to *obey* surely refers to the marriage vows?

The most rigorous test my general claim has to face is whether the common style detected in the otherwise known poems by Wyatt enables us to include in the canon poems only weakly attributed to Wyatt or, in one case, never before named as his. The first of such identifications in the selection is *Quondam was I* (p. 38). Here I think it is the 'tang' which distinguishes it as Wyatt's and marks it off from the similar poem (printed in the commentary on page 130) *Once in your grace*. It may be a mere fancy that there is a humorous self-deprecation, as in our 'has-been', (and a happy effect of *dédoublement*) in the very word *quondam* so used that it alerts a reader of the Dublin manuscript to a *prima facie* possibility that this is Wyatt's characteristic humour and distance from personal calamity. *Dédoublement*, however, is what most helps us to differentiate the Wyatt poem from the imitation. If Wyatt ever felt as sorry for himself as the lover who lamented 'once I was', he has got over, in *Quondam was I*, the embarrassed isolation created by the distress. You feel that he can well bear to be contemplated by his successor, and even that in some way Wyatt has the last laugh. The *Quondam* poem is also better for being shorter (and would have been even better if the scansion were stricter).

I hope that 'tang' will not appear inappropriate as a word for the dry phrases in each stanza, *e.g.*:

And when that you have trod the trace . . .

I take it that Wyatt had the same thing as Hawes had in mind when he wrote of 'her olde guyse' to describe the power driving men and women to 'chamber work', and that it was the same phrase as Chaucer's 'dance the olde daunce'.

That 'ever' lasted but a short while

might have been written yesterday, and is well capped by

I thought she laughed. She did but smile.
Then quondam was I . . .

which is as dramatic as Browning's

Then all smiles stopped together

in his *My Last Duchess*. By the time we come to

what though she had sworn,
Sure quondam was I

we are convinced that we have been hearing the authentic voice of a man of much experience and humanity. *Aut Viatus aut Diabolus*, if that is not Wyatt himself, it must be the devil impersonating him!

The case for the inclusion of *The bird that sometime* (p. 41) among Wyatt's poems will require a longer argument, and perhaps at the end will fail to produce general agreement. Where there would, however, be general agreement is in the proposition that one of Wyatt's best self-portraits is to be found in his first poem addressed to Poyntz (p. 67), where he invited his friend to visit him in Kent:

> This maketh me at home to hunt and hawk
> And in foul weather at my book to sit,
> In frost and snow then with my bow to stalk . . .
> But here I am in Kent and Christendom
> Among the Muses where I read and rhyme . . .

This is one of the many reminders that Wyatt combined the rôles of a literary and a sporting man, that he balanced indoor and outdoor activity. My claim is that with Wyatt the outdoors sometimes penetrates the indoors, and in more subtle ways than the intrusion of references to hunting and hawking in his poems.

The suggestion I would make is that feelings Wyatt no doubt absorbed while watching and enjoying field sports entered deeply into his understanding of the non-rational sides of human nature. I would even go so far as to say that Wyatt had in his own terms a thesis like that we find in Freud's *Das Unbehagen in der Kultur* (*Civilisation and its Discontents*), that our natures are imprisoned in the cage of civilisation. But Wyatt was also on the side of reason. After all, one of his objects in running away from the pressure of court life was that he might wrap himself in his own virtue:

> To will and lust learning to set a law.

Nevertheless, it is his apprehension of the elemental freedom of untamed animal nature that enables him to write so subtly about love and lust.

That this is a strong *motif* in several of his poems will be at once admitted. Although *They flee from me* is concerned with human behaviour, we are invited to contemplate the relevant aspects by using animal analogies. We cannot miss the animal analogy in *Whoso list to hunt* (p. 40). Yet here, too, it seems significant that Wyatt finally decides that his nets were trying to catch, not a deer, but the *wind*. An example of the subtlety of Wyatt's feelings comes to us in *What no, pardie!* (p. 39). I have no doubt that a modern reader's time would be well spent in participating imaginatively, as he goes through a handbook on the training of falcons and similar birds, in all that *in the field* would be understood by

> Think not to make me to your lure.

For it is just as important to feel that love itself imposes a constraint on the free, proud spirit, and constitutes its own form of servitude. Although the whole training of these birds was based on *hunger*, and the falcon swooped down on the lure for *flesh*, the handbooks insist that the successful falconer must love his bird, and that bird and man must learn to know each other by the human cries uttered to encourage the bird in its different tasks. This opens up depths and subtleties into the crude power image in 'make' in

Think not to make me to your lure.

It seems to me suggestive to consider what I take to be an instance where the emphasis is rather on love than power, though the question to be put to the episode in the Fifth Canto of Dante's *Inferno*, where the dramatic hero seems to have power to draw down the two lovers, Paolo and Francesca, out of the sky and subject them to his interrogation, is, what was the bird call he used, and what were the two pigeons hearing?

> *Quali colombe dal disio chiamate*
>   *con l'ali alzate e ferme al dolce nido*
>   *vegnon per l'aere, dal voler portate;*
> *cotali uscir de la schiera ov' è Dido,*
>   *a noi venendo per l'aere maligno,*
>   *sì forte fu l'affettuoso grido.*

(They broke ranks, and left Dido and her troop,
like pigeons borne loving to their nest on steady
wingspread, called by desire. So powerful was
my feeling cry that they came down to us through
the evil air.)

I trust that the reader will not find it an all-too-fanciful suggestion that poets who wished to bring out the mysteries in the attractions of love were consciously drawing on the experience of all falconers that the relations between man and bird in the successful execution of their art contained inexplicable and mysterious features. One such feature was the mixture of certainty and uncertainty. Birds were often stable and reliable, but you could never count on them or predict when they would fly off for ever. I fancy I catch something of this in all Wyatt's poems where love and friendship are the principal topic, and in particular in these lines from *What no, pardie!* (p. 39):

> shall still that thing
> Unstable, unsure, and wavering
> Be in my mind without recure?

It is because of this complexity that my main argument for including *The bird that sometime* among Wyatt's poems would not be the overt similarity of bird imagery with that in *Luck, my fair falcon* (p. 64), but a hidden affinity with the most disturbing 'animal' reference in all Wyatt's poetry. It seems to me very probable that *Some time I fled* (p. 44) is one of Wyatt's strictly autobiographical poems in which the metaphorical language is to be reduced to literal fact. I therefore suppose that at the moment of composition Wyatt's earlier feelings for Anne Boleyn were far-off, and that the surface of his mind was not greatly removed from the coarse feeling of a poem such as that beginning

> Tangled I was in love's snare

and ending

> Was never bird tangled in lime
> That brake away in better time
> Than I that rotten boughs did climb
>> And had no hurt but scapéd free.
>> Now ha ha ha, full well is me,
>> For I am now at liberty!

An alert reader might have detected a ripple from a different world in the line:

> Lo, how desire is both sprong and spent!

For partridge and other forms of wild life are driven from covert when dogs or hawks 'spring' them. The poem seems about to close on the same note it struck in the first lines when there comes a shock I can only liken to that felt by a swimmer near the shore who ventures a little way out from a stone promenade at high tide. He breasts the steady but not formidable incoming wave, thinks all is well, until he is almost drowned by a heavy backwash rebounding from the seawall. A more complex account must be given of the last two lines of the poem:

> And all his labour now he laugh to scorn,
> Meshed in the briers that erst was all to-torn.

because they force us to reinterpret the whole experience Wyatt was so coolly and drily reporting on. We must now believe that the weary and perhaps disgusted ex-lover was once a bleeding victim. What sends this thought, however, to depths of feeling is the implied story in the last line. For I take it that this was a regular experience of the hunting field. The hunters laid their snares or nets but the animal evaded them. When the men closed in on it, the beast plunged blindly into the undergrowth and was crucified to death in the thorns of the closely inwoven bushes.

The 'turn' or movement from calm to disturbance is a much slighter affair in *The bird*. The mysterious laws of change governing both the instinctive moves of free animal behaviour and the tides of love are so quietly drawn on that right up to the last line we are at best only mildly engaged. There is an agreeable reminder of the warm feelings that led to the application of 'nestle' to human actions. There is a vein of affable courtliness in the use of terms of hospitality, as Wyatt, the deserted lover, greets 'mine host', him who has become master of the inn where the beloved now lodges.

But all suddenly changes in the last line. The shock is not so great, of course, but in kind is like that of suddenly leaving the heavenly mind of Shakespeare's Desdemona for the inferno in which Othello was confined. What a concentrated image of pathetic male possessiveness are those silken strings tied to the hawk's legs to prevent her flying for the 'wrong' prey!

> Though that her lesses were my deere heart-
> strings . . .

That, surely, is a case of 'what oft was thought . . .'. Wyatt's point is Othello's. The 'faucon gentle' is never thoroughly tamed. For a time it may respond 'fair', almost as if it were tame, and come down out of the air when the falconer showed the lure. But you never knew when it would 'check', that is, instead of hunting down the game desired by her master, pursue baser game that crossed her flight, and never return.

> If I do proue her Haggard . . .

Perhaps there is now less of a compliment in Wyatt's warning to his successor.

There is another line of argument which could be used to support the case for including the poem among Wyatt's. It is that we do not know that any English poet save Wyatt ever translated a *strambotto* from Serafino or used the *strambotto* form for quasi-autobiographical purposes. There are three such poems in the Dublin manuscript which I would quite cheerfully admit to the Wyatt canon. But it is impossible for us to know for certain that Wyatt was in fact the only practitioner of this form. Nor, of course, do we know that anybody just after Wyatt's death was aware that Wyatt alone could be the author of poems of this form. There are so many things we do not know about what could happen to detached poems by Wyatt and others that it is impossible to draw any conclusions from the late inclusion of this poem (the only one in the group that could be Wyatt's) in the second edition of Tottel's Miscellany.

* * * * * * * * * * * * * * * * * * *

At one time, when the topic came up of the merits of the poems Wyatt wrote from paraphrases of the 'penitential' psalms and incorporated in a 'love story' involving David and Bathsheba, it was a fair reply to those who would dismiss them out of hand to ask, 'have you ever read them?'. Now what has to be said to those who have eyed them and found them cold is to ask, 'have you ever *heard* them?' But perhaps an even more important question to put is 'have you discovered what Wyatt was trying to do?' He was consciously in a tradition that must go back to the early days of monasteries, when seven psalms were chosen as specially fitted for the penitent sinner. Often the repetition of these psalms was itself imposed as a penance. This situation provides the framework of the earliest surviving verse paraphrase of the seven psalms in English, which was composed in 1414 by Thomas Brampton. In the prologue the author describes how he rose at midnight and prayed to Jesus for forgiveness of his sins. He went to his confessor, who imposed the repetition of the Seven Psalms as a penance:

> And ferthermore, for thi trespace,
> That thou hast don to God of hevene
> Gif God wille sende the lyif and space,
> Thou shalt seyn thise Psalmes sevene:
> The bettyr with God thou mayst ben evene,
> Or ever thi soule passe fro the

Begynne and seye with mylde stevene[1]
Ne reminiscaris, Domine![2]

It is clear that merely reciting these words of the Bible could easily become a vain repetition, a mechanical act, what Luther and his followers branded 'an outward deed'. Wyatt was trying to turn the outward, inward, to re-enact the whole business of confession and forgiveness. In general the following account (taken from Thomas More) might have been his model:

> [After auricular confession] Let him ... choose himselfe some secret solitary place in his owne house, as far from noise & companie as he conueniently can, and thither let him sometime secretly resort alone, imagining himself as one going out of the world, euen straight vnto the giuing vp of his reckening vnto God of his sinneful liuing: than let him there before an Altar, or some pitiful Image of Christes bitter Passion (the beholding whereof may put him in remembrance of the thing, and mooue him to deuout compassion) knele downe or fal prostrate, as at the feete of Almightie God, verily beleuing him to be there inuisibly present, as without any doubt he is. There let him open his heart to God, and confesse his faultes such as he can cal to mind, and pray God of forgiuenes. Let him also cal to remembrance the benefites that God hath giuen him, either in general among other men, or priuately to himself, and giue him humble harty thankes therefore. There let him declare vnto God the temptations of the diuel, the suggestions of the flesh, thoccasions of the world, & of his worldly frindes, much worse many times in drawing a man from

1 voice
2 O Lord, be not mindful [of my sins]

God, than are his most mortal enemies...[1]
There let him lament and bewaile vnto God his
owne frailte, negligence, and slouth in resisting
and withstanding of temptation, his readines and
pronitie to fal therevnto. There let him beseche
God of his gracious aide and helpe, to strength
his infirmitie withal, both in keping him from
falling, and whan he by his owne fault misfor-
tuneth to fal, than with the helping hand of his
merciful grace to lift him vp & set him on his fete
in the state of his grace againe, and let this man
not doubt, but that God heareth him, and graun-
teth him gladly this boone . . .

But, as the poem developed, Wyatt wanted us to see David going
through all the stages that Luther thought were necessary for
every sinner who wishes to escape from the intolerable burden
of sin created by the Law.

In this respect we may say that Wyatt's task was like that
of a dramatist. His words are those that Shakespeare would have
had to write if the sinful Claudius had been a true penitent, as
Hamlet feared, when he surprised his uncle at prayer. Wyatt's
words had to be like those presupposed by Thomas More, those
men use when they think they are alone but believe that God is
listening. We judge their effectiveness by the degree to which that
silent listener takes on consistency. He vanishes if the speaker
begins to think of his own performance or of being overheard by
an eavesdropper. For this reason the speech cannot be stage speech.
This can be seen from a comparison of Wyatt's lines:

> Then if I die, and go whereas I fear
> To think thereon . . .

and Claudio's in *Measure for Measure*:

---

1 This passage is taken from The Second Booke of his *A Dialogue of Cumfort* (1573)
p. 112. On an earlier page More, speaking of the temptations of the devil, said:
> he tempteth vs by our owne frindes, and vnder colour of kindred, he maketh many
> times our next frindes our most foes. For as our Sauiour saith, *Inimici hominis,
> domestici eius.* A mans owne familiar frindes are his enemies.
This is like what Wyatt wrote when translating Psalm 38:
> And when mine enemies did me most assail
> My friends most sure, wherein I set most trust,
> Mine own virtues, soonest then did fail
> And stand apart . . .

I, but to die, and go we know not where . . .

It would have been shocking if David had gone on to develop the theme as was proper for Claudio talking not only at his sister but at the audience.

But once we attempt to come closer to Wyatt's set of seven prologues and seven psalms, it is far from easy to make out convincingly exactly what Wyatt was doing, and, especially, whether he adhered throughout to a plan conceived in advance. I trust that an unprejudiced reader will obtain satisfaction from the effect made upon him by the bare text. Whether he will then wish to go behind the scenes, as it were, and see from what a variety of sources the poems were made up is far from certain. Unworthy thoughts, such, for instance, as that Wyatt supposed he was improving on the Authorised Version of the Bible may be quenched by reference to the various forms of extended paraphrase he was translating from. It is convenient to have so much 'hard' evidence of Wyatt's good taste and his instinct for finding the inner lines of power in a wishy-washy original. Since I have catered so generously in the commentary for the interests of learned readers, and have afforded what may coarsely be called the translation 'buff' a field-day he is not likely to experience again until he comes to Dryden, it becomes all the more necessary in this essay to return to the proper business of the enquiry, which, after all, is not into what Wyatt was trying to do, but what he has done.

Here the language of Ben Jonson in his protest against *the adulteries of art*:

They strike mine eyes but not my heart.

will guide us to the right question, which is, if we detect the best of Wyatt by the impact on the heart, in what way do we feel Nature is speaking to us in this religious context? Jonson, too, has formulated the question which will settle the fate of these Psalms with the non-pious lover of poetry:

Language most shewes a man: speake that I may
    see thee.
It springs out of the most retired and inmost parts
    of us . . .

Does Wyatt in fact embody the best that the age had to offer?

Is he the poetic voice of the religious revival which can be discerned in all shades of Christian belief? Has he embodied what the finest religious spirits cared for, as expressed in his line:

For, lo, thou lovest the truth of inward heart . . .?[1]

There is no doubt that these words do declare the core of sixteenth-century religious feeling; they name what was felt to be the new thing in the traditional central psalm of penitence, *Miserere mei*. The two elements, *truth*, and *inward*, are separate but their force comes from their joint application. *True* religion is felt *only* when the heart is open to the depths. From a multitude of prose expressions of this belief I choose the following sentence from Bucer:

> . . . *sapientiam quae in penetrali cordis resideret*
> . . . *in intimis cogitationibus & affectibus . . . in*
> *operto penetrali cordis . . .* (the wisdom which is
> seated in the secret chamber of the heart . . . in
> its intimate thoughts and feelings . . . in the hidden,
> secret places of the heart . . .)

The lay reader does not need help when asked whether Wyatt has in this sense turned the outward celebration of the penitential act into an inward colloquy, so that while David is praying and pleading for all men, we hear one man speaking alone. But when passing from *inward* to *truth*, he may wonder whether a decent hesitation is not in place. We can say whether we think Wyatt was feeling deeply, but can we determine whether his contemporaries were justified in claiming that in these Psalms Wyatt also showed himself *deep-witted*? Does he think justly as well as feel truly? Are these poems also evidence of Wyatt's intellectual force?

It is when faced with this question that I would rather start by looking at the other poems in *terza rima*, the three epistles to his intimate friends, Poyntz and Bryan. The poem I would turn to as easily the most illuminating, if we wish to define in what sense Wyatt might be called *wise*, is the second epistle to Poyntz (p. 72), in which Wyatt was inspired to follow Horace in approaching his sense of right and wrong in human behaviour by telling a

1 Wyatt first wrote: *the hertes trowgh in Inward place*

tale of two mice. For here Wyatt blended his mediaeval and classical inheritance in such a way that each strengthens the other. Almost everybody has felt that, although the mouse fable bears a *functional* resemblance to the tale told by Horace in *Sat.* II/6, the presentation of Wyatt's little creatures was a gift from Chaucer. It may therefore be worth noting that Wyatt has not only caught the spirit of Chaucer but has drawn extensively on the letter. He must have been familiar with the whole contents of the volume collected by Thynne in 1532. What has not been noticed is the richness of his sources in the second half of the poem. Here Wyatt had at his disposal a wealth of moralists mediated to him by Erasmus and his fellow Christian Humanists. It seems proper to begin with the Bible. The moral theme opens with a quotation from the New Testament:

> And blind the guide, anon out of the way
> Goeth guide and all in seeking quiet life.

It seems reasonable to suppose that behind these lines there lies, not Tyndale's powerful phrase:

> Let them alone, they be the blynde leaders of the blynde

but a version of the *hodēgoi* of *Matt.* 15/14 which had the contemporary synonyms for the man who leads the traveller on his way, 'guide' or 'conductor' [conduytour]. It is characteristic both of Wyatt's mode of moral thinking and that of his Christian Humanist mentors that he should go for the proverb or the apophthegm in the New Testament:

> None of you all there is that is so mad
> To seek for grapes on brambles or on briers . . .

Which Wyatt would find in *Matt.* 7/16:

> *Numquid colligunt de spinis uuas, aut de tribulis ficus?*

or, as Wyclif put it:

> Whether men gaderen grapis of thornys or figgis of breris?

On the other hand, we could just as well say that here Christ is being assimilated to the heathen moralists, for they figure in almost every line.

These moralists, too, however, figure as authors of pithy sayings, so much so indeed that we may sometimes suspect that Wyatt knew their sayings from collections of *Sententiae*, drawn from the Greek and Roman moralists. An exception might be made for Seneca's *Moral Epistles*. The same spirit that led Wyatt to relish *inward* truth as he found it stressed in the paraphrases of the Psalms may have directed him to phrases in these Epistles for these lines:

> Then seek no more out of thy self to find
> The thing that thou has sought so long before
> For thou shalt find it sitting in thy mind . . .

At any rate the claim that the theatre of good and evil is inside us is a regular topic in Seneca's Epistles, as this contrasting pair of sentences will show:

> *Non est extrinsecus malum nostrum, intra nos*
> *est, in uisceribus ipsis sedet . . .*
> *prope est a te deus, tecum est, intus est . . . sacer*
> *intra nos spiritus sedet . . .*
> (Evil does not lie outside us, it is in us, it is sitting
> in our very guts . . .
> God is near you, he is with you, inside . . . the
> Holy Ghost is sitting inside us . . .).

What Wyatt may have possessed is something that every scholar from the Middle Ages down to the time of Dryden constructed for himself, a commonplace book, in which all the great topics of man's contemplation were set down as headings, and pithy illustrations entered beneath them, drawn as much from the Bible and the Fathers, as from the Classics. It is out of such a book that Montaigne must have fashioned his first Essays. Wyatt, it seems clear, had arranged topics occurring in his translation from Plutarch under several such headings, though the arrangement of one of these topics, *examples of mad behaviour*, may have been supplied by Erasmus. For Wyatt goes immediately from the New Testament instance of such behaviour to these lines:

> Nor none (I trow) that hath his wit so bad
> To set his hay[1] for conies [2] over rivers,
> Ne ye set not a drag-net for an hare . . .

It seems to me highly significant that Wyatt went over Budé's head back to Erasmus for his translation of this part of Plutarch:

> we accuse wicked fortune and our desteny whan
> rather we shulde dam our selfes of foly as it were
> to be angry with fortune that thou canst nat
> shote an arowe with a plou or hunt an hare with
> an oxe and that some cruell god shulde be agaynst
> them that with vayn indeuour hunt an hart with
> a dragge net and nat that they attempt to do these
> impossibilytes by their own madnesse and folyssh-
> nesse . . .

This epistle at any rate is the one which best exemplifies the merits of Wyatt which impressed Surrey when he was writing the poet's epitaph. The tone of the close, where these lines of Persius:

> *magne pater diuum, saeuos punire tyrannos*
> *haut alia ratione uelis, cum dira libido*
> *mouerit ingenium feruenti tincta ueneno:*
> *uirtutem uideant intabescantque relicta* . . .
> (Great Father of the Gods, when, for our Crimes,
> Thou send'st some heavy Judgment on the Times;
> Some Tyrant-King, the Terrour of his Age,
> The Type, and true Viceregent of thy Rage;
> Thus punish him: Set Virtue in his Sight,
> With all her Charms adorn'd; with all her Graces
> bright:
> But set her distant, make him pale to see
> His Gains out-weigh'd by lost Felicity.
> Dryden)

are boldly Christianized:

> These wretched fools shall have nought else of me,
> But to the great God and to his high doom

1 net
2 rabbits

> None other pain pray I for them to be
>> But when the rage doth lead them from the right
>> That, looking backward, virtue they may see
> Even as she is, so goodly fair and bright,
>> And, whilst they clasp their lusts in arms across,
>> Grant them, good Lord, as thou mayest of thy
>>> might,
> To fret inward for losing such a loss . . .

rightly gives Surrey the comment:

> A Visage stern and mild, where both did grow
> Vice to contemn, in virtues to rejoice . . .

The reminder is needed here, for the poem is not just a collection of wise observations culled from pagan and Christian sources and folk sayings. Wyatt might have himself printed his 'sources' *in extenso* in the form of notes, and the effect could only have been to direct our attention to his own unique contribution as a poet and as a man. The merit of the poem is all in the *savour*; it is the *use* which Wyatt makes of collective wisdom that convinces us that he was wise. No doubt the ability to bring together such mutually strengthening moral materials is a precondition for success, for by such means all time is brought into the present and all insights are harmonised and the total vision becomes more comprehensive than any one man's enlightenment, yet, such are the laws of poetry, this potentially powerful content cannot release its power until it is made to seem the voice of the poet speaking personally.

Wyatt is not to be *identified* with the poor mouse, yet if he had not lost himself in her situation, he could not have made it seem so 'real'. The play of empathy runs over the whole situation as well as the actual plight of the little animal. To take one *trait*:

>> in France
> Was never mouse so feared . . .

there is poetic energy in the fancy that the quality of the whole French nation extends to the very mice of the country. By it we are rivetted even more to the steaming eyes under the stool. Similarly, we might not be able to kindle to the second part of the epistle if we did not feel that, just as Wyatt had been caught like the mouse, so he had to fight against the same folly on the human plane. The poem will not work unless we feel the tension in the string of imperatives (make plain . . . see . . . content . . . seek . . . gape . . . deep) flung at the external enemy. They seem more powerful to me because I suspect that Wyatt had first hurled them all at himself. That is why I turn to Surrey's picture of Wyatt's stern face. I should turn away if I though the moralising came easy from a calm consciousness of moral superiority.

Surrey also suggests a point about this epistle when he says that Wyatt's

> piercing look did represent a mind
> with virtue fraught, reposed, void of guile . . .

and

> But to the heavens that simple soul is fled . . .

but, I am bound to say, it was a point which did not impress me until I had appreciated the great advance Wyatt had made in his third epistle, *A spending hand* (p. 77), in which he both writes to and brings on the scene, his friend, Sir Francis Bryan. For after digesting that poem it came over me that it was a defect in *My mother's maids* that we could so easily distinguish the mediaeval and the classical parts, and that all the humour lay in the behaviour of the mice, while Wyatt was monotonously in earnest in denouncing vice. *A spending hand* shows that Wyatt could master irony, even if it is something broader and coarser than the gloriously fine *malice* of Horace's Fifth Satire in his Second Book.

It is by reference to the development of this precious moral gift in the work of Montaigne that we can become aware that in *My mother's maids* Wyatt shared in a form of naivety characteristic of the moralising of his contemporaries, which diminishes the interest in Montaigne's first essays. In an earlier work I tried to sum up the criticism as follows:

> Real thinking implies a close relation between the general truth and the particular fact. This weakness lies at the heart of Humanism. At best the scholars did little but possess the wisdom of the past as we might possess a set of copy-book maxims. The maxims certainly make us aware of a difference between the actual and the ideal, but they do not of themselves enable us to penetrate

the actual; still less do they show us how to bring
the actual nearer to the ideal. It is pathetic to see
the Humanists in all walks of life supposing that
the mere writing up on the wall of a wise saying
will make a difference to those who read the writing
on the wall.

I cannot believe that Wyatt was writing without irony in these
opening lines:

"A spending hand that alway poureth out
   Had need to have a bringer-in as fast."
And "on the stone that still doth turn about

There grows no moss." These proverbs yet do last,
   Reason has set them in so sure a place
   That length of years their force can never waste.

Nobody can fail to see that Wyatt in this third poem has
had his eye on the real forms of corruption in the court of his day.
Yet just where everybody finds him speaking with all his force in
the dramatic repudiation of *auri sacra fames* (what Dryden called
'sacred hunger of my gold'):

Wouldest thou I should for any loss or gain
Change that for gold that I have ta'en for best
   Next godly things, to have an honest name?
   Should I leave that, then take me for a beast!

there he is translating, and there, surely, we can say that it is
because he was translating that he was able to rise to such heights?
His raw material was, characteristically, both Biblical and Classical,
a passage from *Proverbs* and a passage from Plutarch:

Melius est nomen bonum, quam diuitiae multae:
super argentum & aurum, gratia bona . . .
(A good name is rather to be chosen than great
riches, and loving favour rather than silver and gold).

Wyatt would have found the Plutarch in a translation by Erasmus,
Quo pacto quis efficere possit ut capiat utilitatem ab inimicis?
(How to derive advantage from one's enemies). But, to clinch the
argument, I offer a rough translation:

Whenever our enemies appear to have succeeded by

flattery or base tricks, by bribery or corruption in
acquiring disgraceful and tyrannical power at court
or in government, they shall not annoy us. Rather
shall they put heart into us as we oppose to their
vices our antithetical virtues of true liberty, political purity and decency. All the gold in the earth
and on the earth, said Plato, cannot pay the price
of virtue. And let us always have at our elbows
that saying of Solon's, 'we shall never take their
wealth in exchange for virtue'.

But if, as is highly likely, Wyatt had these pieces before his mind,
and we persist in calling Wyatt's activity *translation,* would this
not be a case for drawing the distinction between 'the mere
Humanist, who, as it were, has the Classics in his head', and 'the
true Humanist who has translated the Classics into the only form
in which they can still live'?

* * * * * * * * * * * * * * * * * * *

The well-disposed reader, who would readily grant that a
case has been made out for judging that Wyatt in this difficult
terza rima form of verse has shown himself capable of expressing
true religious feeling and reproducing the moral sentiments of a
good Christian Humanist, would just as fairly object that, if these
concessions are made, they will all at the same time have been
granted in deference to information supplied in the commentary.
It must be admitted that, even when the notes supply valid point
to flat lines, we at best still stand at a distance, take in some information, and then nod assent. This is not how we take in poetry.
The poems which have made Wyatt's reputation carry us away
with them almost at once. They are admired even when some
points in them are missed. Much as I have been impressed by
Wyatt's poem in *terza rima*, I do not find that any one poem
makes such an impression *throughout*. For it is only for short
runs in the long poems that everything works together to produce the characteristic *singing* quality which distinguishes Wyatt.
I borrow the word 'singing' to indicate that it is the ear which
is gratified, and marks the difference between Wyatt the respec-
table man and Wyatt the poet who has mastered his verse form.
This singing quality is never offered for and by itself as

a separate enjoyment. But no good line is without it. Which leads me to suppose that what is giving the gratification is a resultant of several forces. In all the successful runs we are, I think, made aware of an urgent flow but of an urgency that has not cluttered the lines. It is also noteworthy that they are runs of *speech*. At his best Wyatt sweeps us along with him, and we find him convincing us by his very manner, as here:

> My wit it nought, I cannot learn the way.
> . . .
> To press the virtue that it may not rise:

As drunkenness good fellowship to call,
    The friendly foe with false and double face
    Say he is gentle and courteous therewithal,

And say that Favell hath a goodly grace
    In eloquence, and cruelty to name
    Zeal of justice and change in time and place:

And he that suffers offence without blame
    Call him pitiful, and him true and plain
    That raileth reckless to every man's shame:

Say he is rude that cannot lie and feign,
    The lecher a lover, and tyranny
    To be the right rule of a prince's reign.

> I cannot, I, no, no, it will not be.

If we take that as a fair specimen, we can add the further point that it is as much the variety of tones, starting from almost prosaic argument, the progressive urgency and culminating in the final explosion which marks the passage off as poetry. In this case it has the further advantage of preparing for the calm of the remainder of the poem.

* * * * * * * * * * * * * * * * *

If I now consider whether in fact it helps to look back on Wyatt's poetry from this final achievement, it comes over me that one common note has emerged which certainly did not consciously guide my choice of poems. It is the common note of protest, though protest of many different kinds. But what I take this to be a symptom of is the fact that Wyatt from first to last was ever a tilting, a pulsing, energetic poet, whose energy is best felt when there is something for him to master or resist. In terms of language, he is clearly almost exclusively a subject-verb-object writer. His verbs tell more than his adjectives. Consequently, the pleasure he gives is largely of well-defined action and certainty of aim and effect. This clarity is that of a subject doing, and his doing is almost exclusively of the I–you, You–me, form. Wyatt is the master of the imperative, just as much in religious as amorous poems. It is on looking back that we feel we have the right to say how much of Wyatt is packed into the 'lyric' *And wilt thou leave me thus*? (p. 37).

One of the powerful reasons for treating this as the quintessential Wyatt poem is that it provides the perfect counter-pull if we are inclined to think of Wyatt's linguistic spareness in negative terms. (There is a similar difficulty that, if we say that his religious outlook resembled Sir Thomas More's *Christianae uitae simplicitas, temperantia, frugalitas*, the simplicity, temperance and frugality of the Christian way of life, we may be led to over-stress the hairshirt and the note of *abstention*. But Wyatt also shared in the warm plenitude of Erasmus' *Enchiridion militis Christiani*, which Tyndale translated with the title 'the Manuall of the Christen knyght'.) Wyatt's poem *is* sparse, the terms are confined to those simple vows of the marriage service. Yet there is never a limp syllable; wherever we press on a line, it presses back. But if we call the poem tight, this does not imply a lack of ease. The personal urgency is not allowed to pain us, for the graceful turn given to the whole makes it possible to feel that the situation hurts the dramatic speaker far more than the poem hurts us. It is just as long as we can bear.

The jump this essay is hoping the reader will make is from a too-exclusive delight in the chime of the recurrent rhymes in this 'lyric' to the singing quality this poem shares with all Wyatt's good poems. My claim at bottom is that what predominates is the *chime of sense*, it is the pleasure in the choice of words that strike home to our heads and hearts which gives the common note. It is therefore impossible to distinguish the sound made to the ear from the response in the heart. It is because of this that I think it fair to sum up my claim for Wyatt by saying that at his characteristic *best* he is a shining, singing, author; his sense sings, and what he sings is sense. And to this I would couple a remark thrown out more than two centuries ago by David Lloyd:

> His phrase was clean and clear, the picture of his
> thoughts and language.

POEMS

¶An excellent Epi=
taffe of syr Thomas Wyat, with two
other compendious dytties, wherin are
touchyd, and set furth the state
of mannes lyfe.

 Yat resteth here, that quicke coulde
neuer rest.
whose heuenly gyftes, encreased by
dysdayne
And vertue sanke, the deper in his
brest
Suche profyte he, of enuy could optayne

¶ A head, where wysdom mysteries dyd frame
Whose hammers beat styll in that lyuely brayne
As on a styth, where some worke of fame
Was dayly wrought, to turn to Brytayns gaine

¶ A Uysage sterne and mylde, where both dyd groo
Uyce to contempne, in vertues to reioyce
P.t.   Amyd

SURREY'S TRIBUTE

An excellent epitaph of Sir Thomas Wyatt

Wyatt resteth here, that quick could never rest,
    Whose heavenly gifts, increased by disdain
And virtue, sank the deeper in his breast,
    Such profit he of envy could obtain.

A Head where wisdom mysteries did frame,
    Whose hammers beat still in that lively brain
As on a stithy where some work of fame
    Was daily wrought to turn to Britain's gain.

A Visage stern and mild, where both did grow
    Vice to contemn, in virtues to rejoice,
Amid great storms whom grace assured so
    To live upright and smile at fortune's choice.

A Hand that taught what might be said in rhyme,
    That reft Chaucer the glory of his wit,
A mark the which (unparfited for time)
    Some may approach but never none shall hit.

A Tongue that served in foreign realms his King,
    Whose courteous talk to virtue did inflame
Each noble heart, a worthy guide to bring
    Our English youth by travail unto fame.

An Eye whose judgement no affect could blind
    Friends to allure and foes to reconcile,
Whose piercing look did represent a mind
    With virtue fraught, reposed, void of guile.

A Heart where dread yet never so impressed
    To hide the thought that might the truth advance,
In neither fortune lift nor so repressed
    To swell in wealth nor yield unto mischance.

A valiant Corps where force and beauty met,
    Happy, alas, too happy but for foes,
Lived, and ran the race that Nature set,
    Of manhood's shape where she the mould did lose.

But to the heavens that simple soul is fled,
    Which left with such as covet Christ to know
Witness of faith that never shall be dead,
    Sent for our wealth but not received so.

Thus for our guilt this jewel have we lost.
The earth his bones, the heavens possess his ghost.

Amen.

Henry Howard, Earl of Surrey.

THE LOVER

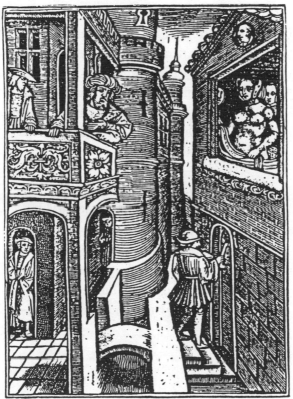

David and Bathsheba: from a woodcut used extensively in Wyatt's lifetime to illustrate the Seven Penetential Psalms

They flee from me that sometime did me seek
　With naked foot stalking in my chamber:
I have seen them gentle, tame, and meek,
　　That now are wild, and do not remember
　　That sometime they put themselves in danger
　　　To take bread at my hand; and now they range
　　　Busily seeking with continual change.

Thanked be fortune, it hath been otherwise,
　Twenty times better, but once in especial:
In thin array after a pleasant guise
　　When her loose gown from her shoulders did fall,
　　And she me caught in her arms long and small,
　　　And therewithal sweetly she did me kiss,
　　　And softly said, "Dear heart, how like you this?"

It was no dream, for I lay broad waking.
　But all is turned thorough my gentleness
Into a strange fashion of forsaking,
　And I have leave to go of her goodness,
And she likewise to use newfangleness.
　　But since that I so kindly am served,
　　What think you by this that she hath deserved?

And wilt thou leave me thus?
    Say nay! Say nay, for shame,
    To save thee from the blame
    Of all my grief and grame.
And wilt thou leave me thus?
    Say nay! Say nay!

And wilt thou leave me thus,
    That hath loved thee so long
    In wealth and woe among?
    And is thy heart so strong
As for to leave me thus?
    Say nay! Say nay!

And wilt thou leave me thus,
    That hath given thee my heart
Never for to depart
    Neither for pain nor smart?
And wilt thou leave me thus?
    Say nay! Say nay!

And wilt thou leave me thus,
    And have no more pity
    Of him that loveth thee?
Alas, thy cruelty!
And wilt thou leave me thus?
    Say nay! Say nay!

Quondam was I in my lady's grace,
   I think as well as now be you:
And when that you have trod the trace,
   Then shall you know my words be true,
     That quondam was I.

Quondam was I. She said, "for ever".
   That 'ever' lasted but a short while,
A promise made not to dissever;
   I thought she laughed, she did but smile.
     Then quondam was I.

Quondam was I that full oft lay
   In her arms with kisses many a one.
It is enough that I may say,
   Though 'mong the more now I be gone,
     Yet quondam was I.

Quondam was I: she will you tell
   That since the hour she was first born
She never loved none half so well
   As you. But what though she had sworn,
     Sure quondam was I.

What no, pardie! ye may be sure,
Think not to make me to your lure
  With words and cheer so contraring,
  Sweet and sour counterweighing.
Too much it were still to endure.
Truth is trayed where craft is in ure.
But though ye have had my heart's cure,
  Trow ye I dote without ending?
    What no, pardie!

Though that with pain I do procure
For to forget that once was pure
  Within my heart, shall still that thing
  Unstable, unsure, and wavering
Be in my mind without recure?
    What no, pardie!

Whoso list to hunt, I know where is an hind,
  But as for me, alas, I may no more.
  The vain travail hath wearied me so sore
  I am of them that farthest come behind.

Yet may I by no means my wearied mind
  Draw from the deer, but as she fleeth afore
  Fainting I follow. I leave off therefore,
  Since in a net I seek to hold the wind.

Who list her hunt, I put him out of doubt
  As well as I may spend his time in vain,
  And graven with diamonds in letters plain
There is written her fair neck round about:

"Noli me tangere, for Caesar's I am,
And wild for to hold, though I seem tame."

The bird that sometime built within my breast
    And there as then chief succour did receive
Hath now elsewhere built her another nest,
    And of the old hath taken quite her leave.
To you, mine host, that harbour mine old guest,
    Of such a one as I can now conceive,
        Since that in change her choice doth chief consist,
        The hawk may check that now comes fair to fist.

What should I say
  Since faith is dead
And truth away
  From you is fled?
  Should I be led
    With doubleness?
    Nay, nay, mistress!

I promised you,
  You promised me
To be as true
  As I would be.
  But since I see
    Your double heart,
    Farewell, my part!

You for to take
  Is not my mind
But to forsake
  Your cruel kind,
  And as I find
    So will I trust.
    Farewell, unjust!

Can ye say nay
  But that you said
That I alway
  Should be obeyed?
  And thus betrayed
    Ere that I wist!
    Farewell, unkissed!

Madame, withouten many words,
    Once, I am sure, ye will or no;
And if ye will, then leave your bourds
    And use your wit and show it so,

And with a beck ye shall me call,
    And if of one that burns alway
Ye have any pity at all,
    Answer him fair with yea or nay.

If it be yea, I shall be fain,
    If it be nay, friends as before.
Ye shall another man obtain,
    And I mine own, and yours no more.

Some time I fled the fire that me brent
  By sea, by land, by water and by wind,
And now I follow the coals that be quent
  From Dover to Calais against my mind.
Lo, how desire is both sprung and spent!
   And he may see that whilom was so blind,
    And all his labour now he laugh to scorn,
    Meshed in the briers that erst was all to-torn.

Now farewell, Love, and all thy laws for ever!
  Thy baited hooks shall tangle me no more.
  Senec and Plato call me from thy lore
To perfect wealth my wit for to endeavour.

In blind error whilest I did persever,
  Thy sharp repulse, that pricketh aye so sore,
  Hath taught me to set in trifles no store,
But scape forth since liberty is liefer.

Therefore farewell, go trouble younger hearts
  And in me claim no more authority.
  With idle youth go use thy property
And thereupon go spend thy brittle darts,

    For hitherto though I have lost my time,
    Me list no longer rotten boughs to climb.

THE CHRISTIAN

The burning of William Tyndale

Psalm 6 *Domine, ne in furore tuo*

O Lord, since in my mouth thy mighty name
    Sufferth itself my Lord to name and call,
    Here hath my heart hope taken by the same,

That the repentance which I have, and shall,
    May at thy hand seek mercy as the thing,
    Only comfort of wretched sinners all.

Whereby I dare with humble bemoaning,
    By thy goodness, of thee this thing require:
    Chastise me not, Lord, for my deserving

According to thy just conceived ire.
    O Lord, I dread, and that I did not dread
    I me repent, and evermore desire

Thee, thee to dread. I open here and spread
    My fault to thee; but thou, for thy goodness,
    Measure it not in largeness nor in breadth,

Punish it not as asketh the greatness
    Of thy furor, provoked by my offence.
    Temper, O Lord, the harm of my excess

With mending will that I for recompense
    Prepare again, and rather pity me
    For I am weak and clean without defence.

More is the need I have of remedy,
    For of the whole the leech taketh no cure.
    The sheep that stray'th the shepherd seeks to see.

I, Lord, am strayed, I, sick without recure,
    Feel all my limbs, that have rebelled, for fear
    Shake, in despair unless thou me assure.

My flesh is troubled, my heart doth fear the spear,
    That dread of death, of death that ever lasts,
    Threateth of right, and draweth near and near.

Much more my soul is troubled by the blasts
    Of these assaults, that come as thick as hail,
    Of worldly vanities that temptation casts

Against the weak bulwark of the flesh frail,
    Wherein the soul in great perplexity
    Feeleth the senses with them that assail

Conspire, corrupt by vice and vanity,
    Whereby the wretch doth to the shade resort
    Of hope in thee in this extremity.

But thou, O Lord, how long after this sort
    Forbearest thou to see my misery?
    Suffer me yet, in hope of some comfort,

Fear and not feel that thou forgettest me.
    Return, O Lord, O Lord, I thee beseech,
    Unto thine old wonted benignity,

Reduce, revive my soul, be thou the leech
    And reconcile the great hatred and strife
    That it hath ta'en against the flesh, the wretch

That stirred hath thy wrath by filthy life.
    See how my soul doth fret it to the bones,
    Inward remorse so sharp'th it like a knife,

That, but thou help the caitiff that bemoans
    His great offence, it turn'th anon to dust.
    Here hath thy mercy matter for the nonce,

For if thy rightwise hand that is so just
    Suffer no sin or strike with damnation,
    Thine infinite mercy want needs it must

Subject matter for his operation,
    For that in death there is no memory
    Among the damned, nor yet no mention

Of thy great name, ground of all glory.
    Then If I die and go whereas I fear
    To think thereon, how shall thy great mercy

Sound in my mouth unto the world's ear?
    For *there* is none that can thee laud and love,
    For that thou nilt no love among them there.

Suffer my cries thy mercy for to move,
    That wonted is an hundred years' offence
    In a moment of repentance to remove.

How oft have I called up with diligence
    This slothful flesh, and long afore the day,
    For to confess his fault and negligence,

That to the down, for ought that I could say,
    Hath still returned to shroud itself from cold,
    Whereby it suffer'th now for such delay.

By nightly plaints instead of pleasures old
    I wash my bed with tears continual
    To dull my sight that it be never bold

To stir my heart again to such a fall.
    Thus dry I up among my foes in woe,
    That with my fall do rise and grow withal

And me beset, even now where I am so,
    With secret traps to trouble my penance.
    Some do present to my weeping eyes, lo,

The cheer, the manner, beauty and countenance
    Of her whose look, alas, did make me blind.
    Some other offer to my remembrance

Those pleasant words now bitter to my mind,
    And some show me the power of my armour,
    Triumph and conquest, and to my head assigned

Double diadem, some show the favour
    Of people frail, palace, pomp and riches.
    To these mermaids and their baits of error

I stop mine ears with help of thy goodness,
  And, for I feel it com'th alone of thee
  That to my heart these foes have none access,

I dare them bid, "Avoid, wretches, and flee,
  The Lord hath heard the voice of my complaint,
  Your engines take no more effect in me,

The Lord hath heard, I say, and seen me faint
  Under your hand, and pitieth my distress.
  He shall do make my senses by constraint

Obey the rule that reason shall express,
  Where the deceit of your glozing bait
  Made them usurp a power in all excess."

Shamed be they all that so lie in wait
  To compass me, by missing of their prey!
  Shame and rebuke redound to such deceit!

Sudden confusion's stroke without delay
  Shall so deface their crafty suggestion
  That they to hurt my health no more essay,

Since I, O Lord, remain in thy protection.

Psalm 50 (A.V.51) *Miserere mei*

Rue on me, Lord, for thy goodness and grace,
 That of thy nature art so bountiful,
 For that goodness that in the world doth brace

Repugnant natures in quiet wonderful,
 And for thy mercies' number without end
 In heaven and earth perceived so plentiful

That over all they do themselves extend,
 For those mercies, much more than man can sin,
 Do way my sins that so thy grace offend.

Again wash me, but wash me well within,
 And from my sin that thus mak'th me afraid
 Make thou me clean, as aye thy wont hath been.

For unto thee no number can be laid
 For to prescribe remissions of offence
 In hearts returned, as thou thyself has said.

And I beknow my fault, my negligence,
 And in my sight my sin is fixed fast,
 Thereof to have more perfect penitence.

To thee alone, to thee have I trespassed,
 For none can measure my fault but thou alone,
 For in thy sight I have not been aghast

For to offend, judging thy sight as none
 So that my fault were hid from sight of man,
 Thy majesty so from my mind was gone.

This know I and repent. Pardon thou than,
  Whereby thou shalt keep still thy word stable,
  Thy Justice pure and clean, because that whan

I pardoned am, then forthwith justly able,
  Just I am judged by justice of thy grace.
  For I myself, lo, thing most unstable,

Formed in offence, conceived in like case,
  Am nought but sin from my nativity.
  Be not this said for my excuse, alas,

But of thy help to show necessity.
  For, lo, thou loves the truth of inward heart,
  Which yet doth live in my fidelity,

Though I have fallen by frailty overthwart.
  For wilful malice led me not the way
  So much as hath the flesh drawn me apart.

Wherefore, O Lord, as thou hast done alway,
  Teach me the hidden wisdom of thy lore,
  Since that my faith doth not yet decay.

And as the Jews to heal the leper sore
  With hyssop cleanse, cleanse me, and I am clean.
  Thou shalt me wash and more than snow therefor

I shall be white, how foul my fault hath been.
  Thou of my health shalt gladsome tidings bring.
  When from above remission shall be seen

Descend on earth, then shall for joy up spring
    The bones that were afore consumed to dust.
    Look not, O Lord, upon mine offending,

But do away my deeds that are unjust.
    Make a clean heart in the midst of my breast
    With sprite upright, voided from filthy lust.

From thine eyes' cure cast me not in unrest,
    Nor take from me thy sprite of holiness.
    Render to me joy of thy help and rest,

My will confirm with sprite of steadfastness.
    And by this shall these goodly things ensue:
Sinners I shall into thy ways address,

They shall return to thee and thy grace sue.
    My tongue shall praise thy Justification,
    My mouth shall spread thy glorious praises true.

But of thyself, O God, this operation
    It must proceed by purging me from blood,
    Among the just that I may have relation,

And of thy lauds for to let out the flood
    Thou must, O Lord, my lips first unloose.
    For if thou hadst esteemed pleasant good

The outward deeds that outward men disclose,
    I would have offered unto thee sacrifice.
    But thou delightest not in no such gloze

Of outward deed as men dream and devise.
 The sacrifice that thee, Lord, liketh most
 Is sprite contrite: low heart in humble wise

Thou dost accept, O God, for pleasant host.
 Make Sion, Lord, according to thy will,
 Inward Sion, the Sion of the ghost,

Of heart's Jerusalem strength the walls still.
 Then shalt thou take for good these outward deeds
 As sacrifice thy pleasure to fulfil.

Of thee alone thus all our good proceeds.

Of deep secrets that David here did sing,
 Of mercy, of faith, of frailty, of grace,
Of God's goodness and of Justifying,
 The greatness did so astone himself a space,
As who might say, "Who hath expressed this thing?
 I, sinner, I, what have I said, alas,
  That God's goodness would with my song entreat?
  Let me again consider and repeat".

Psalm 129 (A.V.130) *De profundis clamaui*

From depth of sin, and from a deep despair,
　　From depth of death, from depth of heart's sorrow,
　　From this deep cave, of darkness deep repair,

Thee have I called, O Lord, to be my borrow.
　　Thou in my voice, O Lord, perceive and hear
　　My heart, my hope, my plaint, my overthrow,

My will to rise, and let by grant appear
　　That to my voice thine ears do well entend.
　　No place so far that to thee is not near,

No depth so deep that thou ne mayest extend
　　Thine ear thereto. Hear then my woeful plaint,
　　For, Lord, if thou do observe what men offend

And put thy native mercy in restraint,
　　If just exaction demand recompense,
　　Who may endure, O Lord? Who shall not faint

At such account? Dread, and not reverence,
　　Should so reign large. But thou seeks rather love,
　　For in thy hand is mercy's residence,

By hope whereof thou dost our hearts move.
　　I in thee, Lord, have set my confidence.
　　My soul such trust doth evermore approve.

Thy holy word of eterne excellence,
　　Thy mercy's promise, that is alway just,
　　Have been my stay, my pillar, and pretence.

My soul in God hath more desirous trust
    Than hath the watchman looking for the day
    By the relief to quench of sleep the thirst.

Let Israel trust unto the Lord alway,
    For grace and favour are his property.
    Plenteous ransom shall come with Him, I say,
And shall redeem all our iniquity.

THE COURTIER

Tagus, farewell, that westward with thy streams
    Turns up the grains of gold already tried,
With spur and sail for I go seek the Thames,
    Gainward the sun that showeth her wealthy pride,
And to the town which Brutus sought by dreams
    Like bended moon doth lend her lusty side.
      My King, my Country, alone for whom I live,
      Of mighty love the wings for this me give.

In court to serve, decked with fresh array,
  Of sugared meats feeling the sweet repast,
The life in banquets and sundry kinds of play
  Amid the press of lordly looks to waste
  Hath with it joined oft times such bitter taste
That whoso joys such kind of life to hold
In prison joys, fettered with chains of gold.

Throughout the world if it were sought,
　　Fair words enough a man shall find,
They be good cheap, they cost right nought,
　　Their substance is but only wind,
　　　　But well to say and so to mean,
　　　　That sweet accord is seldom seen.

Stand whoso list upon the slipper top
    Of court estate, and let me here rejoice
And use me quiet without let or stop,
    Unknown in court that hath such brackish joys.
In hidden place so let my days forth pass
    That, when my years be done, withouten noise
I may die aged after the common trace.

For him death grippeth right hard by the crop
    That known of all, but to himself, alas,
    Doth die unknown, dazed with dreadful face.

Luck, my fair falcon, and your fellows all,
How well pleasant it were your liberty.
Ye not forsake me that fair might ye fall,
But they that sometime liked my company
Like lice away from dead bodies they crawl.
Lo, what a proof in light adversity!
But ye, my birds, I swear by all your bells,
Ye be my friends, and so be but few else.

The pillar perished is whereto I leant,
    The strongest stay of mine unquiet mind,
    The like of it no man again can find
    From East to West still seeking though he went:

To mine unhap, for hap away hath rent
    Of all my joy the very root and rind,
    And I, alas, by chance am thus assigned
    Daily to mourn till death do it relent.

But since that thus it is by destiny,
    What can I more but have a woeful heart,
    My pen in plaint, my voice in careful cry,

My mind in woe, my body full of smart,
    And I my self my self always to hate
    Till dreadful death do ease my doleful state?

Sighs are my food, my drink are my tears,
    Clinking of fetters such music would crave.
Stink and close air away my life it wears:
    Innocency is all the hope I have:
Rain, wind or weather I judge by mine ears:
    Malice assaults that righteousness should save.
Sure I am, Bryan, this wound shall heal again,
But yet, alas, the scar shall still remain.

To John Poyntz (I)

Mine own John Poyntz, since ye delight to know
　　The causes why that homeward I me draw,
　　And flee the press of courts whereso they go

Rather than to live thrall under the awe
　　Of lordly looks, wrapped within my cloak,
　　To will and lust learning to set a law:

It is not for because I scorn or mock
　　The power of them to whom Fortune hath lent
　　Charge over us of right to strike the stroke,

But true it is that I have always meant
　　Less to esteem them than the common sort
　　Of outward things that judge in their entent

Without regard what doth inward resort.
　　I grant sometime that of glory the fire
　　Doth touch my heart; me list not to report

Blame by honour, and honour to desire;
　　But how may I this honour now attain
　　That cannot dye with colour black-a-lyre?

My Poyntz, I cannot frame my tune to feign,
　　To cloak the truth for praise without desert
　　Of them that list all vice for to retain.

I cannot honour them that sets their part
　　With Venus and Bacchus all their life long,
　　Nor hold my peace of them although I smart.

I cannot crouch nor kneel to do such wrong
    To worship them like God on earth alone
    That are as wolves these silly lambs among.

I cannot with my words complain and moan
    And suffer nought nor smart without complaint
    Nor turn the word that from my mouth is gone.

I cannot speak with look right as a saint,
    Use wiles for wit, and make deceit a pleasure,
    Call craft counsel, for profit still to paint.

I cannot wrest the law to fill the coffer,
    With innocent blood to feed myself fat,
    And do most hurt where most help I offer.

I am not he that can allow the state
    Of him, Caesar, and damn Cato to die,
    That with his death did scape out of the gate

From Caesar's hands (if Livy do not lie)
    And would not live where liberty was lost,
    So did his heart the common wealth apply.

I am not he such eloquence to boast
    To make the crow in singing as the swan,
    Nor call the lion of coward beasts the most

That cannot take a mouse as the cat can;
    And he that dieth for hunger of the gold
    Call him Alexander, and say that Pan

Passeth Apollo in music many fold,
    And praise Sir Thopas for a noble tale
    And scorn the story that the Knight y-told;

Praise him for counsel that is drunk of ale;
    Grin when he laughs that beareth all the sway,
    Frown when he frowns and groan when he is pale;

On others' lust to hang both night and day:
    None of these points will ever frame with me,
    My wit is nought, I cannot learn the way.

And much the less of things that greater be,
    That asken help of colours of device,
    To join the mean with each extremity,

With the next virtue cloak always the vice,
    And as to purpose likewise it shall fall,
    To press the virtue that it may not rise:

As drunkenness good fellowship to call,
    The friendly foe with false and double face
    Say he is gentle and courteous therewithal,

And say that Favell hath a goodly grace
    In eloquence, and cruelty to name
    Zeal of justice and change in time and place.

And he that suffers offence without blame
    Call him pitiful, and him true and plain
    That raileth reckless to every man's shame.

Say he is rude that cannot lie and feign,
 The lecher a lover, and tyranny
 To be the right rule of a prince's reign.

I cannot, I, no, no, it will not be.
 This is the cause that I could never yet
 Hang on their sleeves that weigh, as thou mayest see,

A chip of chance more than a pound of wit.
 This maketh me at home to hunt and hawk
 And in foul weather at my book to sit,

In frost and snow then with my bow to stalk.
 No man doth mark whereso I ride or go,
 In lusty lees at liberty I walk,

And of these news I feel nor weal nor woe,
 Save that a clog doth hang yet at my heel.
 No force for that, for it is ordered so

That I may leap both hedge and ditch full well.
 I am not now in France to judge the wine,
 With savoury sauce the delicates to feel,

Nor yet in Spain, where one must him incline,
 Rather than to be, outwardly to seem.
 I meddle not with wits that be so fine,

Nor Flanders cheer lets not my sight to deem
 Of black and white, nor takes my wit away
 With beastliness these beasts do so esteem.

Nor I am not where Christ is given in prey
 For money, poison, and treason at Rome,
 A common practice used night and day.

But here I am in Kent and Christendom,
 Among the Muses where I read and rhyme,
 Where, if thou list, my John Poyntz, for to come,

Thou shalt be judge how I do spend my time.

To John Poyntz (II)

My mother's maids, when they did sew and spin,
    They sang sometime a song of the field mouse,
    That for because her livelihood was but thin,

Would needs go seek her towny sister's house.
    She thought herself enured to much pain.
    The stormy blasts her cave so sore did souse

That when the furrows swimmed with the rain
    She must lie cold and wet in sorry plight,
    And worse than that, bare meat there did remain

To comfort her when she her house had dight,
    Sometime a barley corn, sometime a bean,
    For which she laboured hard both day and night

In harvest time whilst she might go and glean.
    And when her store was stroyed with the flood,
    Then – wellaway! – for she undone was clean.

Then was she fain to take instead of food
    Sleep, if she might, her hunger to beguile.
    "My sister," quod she, "hath a living good,

And hence from me she dwelleth not a mile.
    In cold and storm she lieth warm and dry
    In bed of down. The dirt doth not defile

Her tender foot. She labours not as I;
    Richly she feeds, and at the rich man's cost,
    And for her meat she needs not crave nor cry.

By sea, by land, of delicates the most
   Her cater seeks and spareth for no parail.
   She feedeth on boiled, baken meat and roast,

And hath thereof neither charge nor travail,
   And when she list, the liquor of the grape
   Doth glad her heart till that her belly swell."

And of this journey she makes but a jape.
   So forth she goes, trusting of all this wealth
   With her sister her part so for to shape,

That, if she there might keep herself in health,
   To live a lady while her life doth last.
   And to the door now is she come by stealth,

And with her foot anon she scrapes full fast.
   T'other for fear durst not well scarce appear,
   Of every noise so was the wretch aghast.

At last she asked softly who was there,
   And in her language as well as she could,
"Peep," quod the other, "sister, I am here."

"Peace," quod the town mouse, "why speak'st thou so loud?"
   And by the hand she took her fair and well.
   "Welcome," quod she, "my sister, by the Rood!"

She feasted her that joy it was to tell
   The fare they had. They drank the wine so clear,
   And, as to purpose now and then it fell,

She cheered her with, "How, sister, what cheer?"
    Amidst this joy befell a sorry chance,
    That – wellaway! – the stranger bought full dear

The fare she had. For as she looked askance
    Under a stool she spied two steaming eyes
    In a round head with sharp ears: in France

Was never mouse so feared, for though th'unwise
    Had not yseen such a beast before,
    Yet had nature taught her after her guise

To know her foe and dread him evermore.
    The towny mouse fled; she knew whither to go.
    The other had no shift, but wondrous sore

Feared of her life. At home she wished her tho.
    And to the door, alas, as she did skip,
    The heaven it would, lo, and eke her chance was so,

At the threshold her silly foot did trip,
    And ere she might recover it again
    The traitor cat had caught her by the hip

And made her there against her will remain,
    That had forgot her poor surety and rest
    For seeming wealth wherein she thought to reign.

Alas, my Poyntz, how men do seek the best
    And find the worst by error as they stray!
    And no marvel, when sight is so oppressed

And blind the guide, anon out of the way
    Goeth guide and all in seeking quiet life.
    O wretched minds! There is no gold that may

Grant that ye seek, no war, no peace, no strife.
    No, no, although thy head were hooped with gold,
    Sergeant with mace, with halberd, sword, or knife

Cannot repulse the care that follow should!
    Each kind of life hath with him his disease.
    Live in delight even as thy lust would

And thou shalt find, when lust doth most thee please,
    It irketh straight, and by itself doth fade.
    A small thing is it that may thy mind appease.

None of ye all there is that is so mad
    To seek for grapes on brambles or on briers,
    Nor none (I trow) that hath his wit so bad

To set his hay for conies over rivers,
    Nor ye set not a drag-net for an hare.
    And yet the thing that most your heart desires

Ye do mislike with more travail and care.
    Make plain thine heart that it be not knotted
    With hope or dread, and see thy will be bare

From all affects, whom vice hath ever spotted.
    Thy self content with that is thee assigned,
    And use that well that is to thee allotted.

Then seek no more out of thy self to find
    The thing that thou hast sought so long before,
    For thou shalt feel it sitting in thy mind.

Mad if thee list to continue thy sore,
    Let present pass, and gape on time to come,
    And deep thyself in travail more and more.

Henceforth, my Poyntz, this shall be all and some.
    These wretched fools shall have nought else of me,
    But to the great God and to his high doom

None other pain pray I for them to be
    But when the rage doth lead them from the right
    That, looking backward, Virtue they may see

Even as she is, so goodly fair and bright,
    And, whilst they clasp their lusts in arms across,
    Grant them, good Lord, as thou mayest of thy might,
To fret inward for losing such a loss.

To Sir Francis Brian

"A spending hand that always poureth out
    Had need to have a bringer-in as fast."
    And "on the stone that still doth turn about

There grows no moss." These proverbs yet do last,
    Reason hath set them in so sure a place
    That length of years their force can never waste.

When I remember this and eke the case
    Wherein thou stands, I thought forthwith to write,
    Brian, to thee, who knows how great a grace

In writing is to counsel man the right.
    To thee, therefore, that trots still up and down
    And never rests, but running day and night

From realm to realm, from city, street, and town,
    Why dost thou wear thy body to the bones,
    And might'st at home sleep in thy bed of down

And drink good ale so noppy for the nonce,
    Feed thyself fat, and heap up pound by pound?
    Lik'st thou not this? "No." Why? "For swine so groans

In sty and chaw turds moulded on the ground
    And drivel on pearls with head still in the manger.
    So of the harp the ass doth hear the sound,

So sacks of dirt be filled up in the cloister,
    That serves for less than do these fatted swine.
    Though I seem lean and dry withouten moisture,

Yet will I serve my Prince, my lord, and thine,
    And let them live to feed the paunch that list,
    So I may live to feed both me and mine."

By God, well said! But what and if thou wist
    How to bring in as fast as thou dost spend?
    "That would I learn". And it shall not be missed

To tell thee how. Now, hark what I intend.
    Thou know'st well, first, whoso can seek to please
    Shall purchase friends where truth shall but offend.

Flee therefore truth. It is both wealth and ease.
    For, though that truth of every man hath praise,
    Full near that wind goes truth in great misease.

Use virtue as it goeth nowadays,
    In word alone to make thy language sweet,
    And of the deed yet do not as thou says,

Else, be thou sure, thou shalt be far unmeet
    To get thy bread, each thing is now so scant.
    Seek still thy profit upon thy bare feet.

Lend in no wise, for fear that thou do want,
    Unless it be as a chalk for a cheese,
    By which return be sure to win a cant

Of half at least. It is not good to lose.
    Learn at Kitson, that in a long white coat
    From under the stall without lands or fees

Hath leapt into the shop, who knows by rote
    This rule that I have told thee here before:
    Sometime also rich age begins to dote.

See thou when there thy gain may be the more.
    Stay him by the arm whereso he walk or go.
    Be near always, and if he cough too sore,

When he hath spit, tread out, and please him so.
    A diligent knave that picks his master's purse
    May please him so that he, withouten mo,

Executor is, and what is he the worse?
    But if so chance thou get nought of the man,
    The widow may for all thy charge deburse.

A rivelled skin, a stinking breath, what than?
    A toothless mouth shall do thy lips no harm.
    The gold is good, and though she curse or ban,

Yet where thee list thou mayest lie good and warm.
    Let the old mule bite upon the bridle
    Whilst there do lie a sweeter in thine arm.

In this also see that thou be not idle:
    Thy niece, thy cousin, thy sister or thy daughter,
    If she be fair, if handsome be her middle,

If thy better hath for her love besought her,
    Advance his cause, and he shall help thy need.
    It is but love, turn thou it to a laughter.

But ware, I say, so gold thee help and speed,
    That in this case thou be not so unwise
    As Pandare was in such a like deed,

For he, the fool, of conscience was so nice
    That he no gain would have for all his pain.
    Be next thyself, for friendship bears no price.

Laughest thou at me? Why, do I speak in vain?
    "No, not at thee, but at thy thrifty jest.
    Would'st thou I should for any loss or gain

Change that for gold that I have ta'en for best
    Next godly things, to have an honest name?
    Should I leave that, then take me for a beast!"

Nay then, farewell, and if thou care for shame,
    Content thee then with honest poverty,
    With free tongue what it thee mislikes to blame,

And for thy truth sometime adversity.
    And therewithal this gift I shall thee give:
    In this world now little prosperity,
And coin to keep as water in a sieve.

Fortune doth frown,
    What remedy?
I am down
    By Destiny.

The louer sheweth how he is forsaken of such as he somtime enioyed.

They flee from me, that somtime did me seke
With naked fote stalkyng within my chamber.
Once haue I seen them gentle, tame, and meke,
That now are wild, and do not once remember
That sometyme they haue put them selues in danger,
To take bread at my hand, and now they range,
Busily sekyng in continuall change.

Thanked be fortune, it hath bene otherwise
Twenty tymes better: but once especiall,
In thinne aray, after a pleasant gyse,
When her loose gowne did from her shoulders fall,
And she me caught in her armes long and small,
And therwithall, so swetely did me kysse,
And softly sayd: deare hart, how like you this?

It was no dreame: for I lay broade awakyng.
But all is turnde now through my gentlenesse,
Into a bitter fashion of forsakyng:
And I haue leaue to go of her goodnesse,
And she also to vse newfanglenesse.
But, sins that I vnkyndly so am serued:
How like you this, what hath she now deserued?

A page from Tottel's *Songes and Sonettes*

TEXTUAL NOTES

So far as we know, Wyatt never prepared his poems for publication. During his life-time manuscript copies were in circulation of versions he later modified. Even in the few cases where his autographs have survived, we cannot be sure that they represent his final versions. It is therefore always a legitimate presumption that the surviving texts may not be exactly what Wyatt wrote.

The principal manuscript collection, the only one which we know Wyatt handled, is now in the British Library. In these notes it will be referred to as E, because it is listed as Egerton Ms. 2711. All my departures from E are given in these notes. Other manuscript collections can be used to help editorial restoration of lost originals. Among these the chief are, in the British Library, Add. Ms. 17492, which will be referred to as D, and, in Arundel Castle Library, a manuscript designated A. For the printed *Songes and Sonettes* (1557), edited for R. Tottel, I have accepted the convenient symbol, T. Other 'sources' will be mentioned where relevant.

This is in no sense a critical edition of the selected poems, since the problem of making out what Wyatt wrote and what he did not write is a long way from being solvable. Even the simplest task, that of transcribing what can be found in our extant manuscripts, has not yet been performed to complete satisfaction. Consequently, all my conjectures must be regarded in the light of desperate remedies, temporary stop-gaps; even if one or two eventually find favour, they will have to find proper textual-critical grounds first.

My main difficulty, as the sheer number of emendations caused by it will confirm, is over scansion. There is as yet no general agreement among editors on the principles of scansion in Wyatt's mind on each poetical occasion. Even if we assume, as some do not, that the poet had an ear, we cannot get away from the fact that Wyatt's poems do not 'scan' in every line. For example, in the poems in *terza rima*, there are long stretches of regular 'pentameters', or lines with ten syllables and five stresses, which are interrupted by single lines which cannot be read in this way. And these 'irregular' lines do not conform to any rule of their own. While it is occasionally possible to think of satisfactory emendations to smooth the lines out, there remain several lines written out by the poet himself which defy such treatment. Such lines, however, do not justify the view, which used to be common, that Wyatt cultivated metrical irregularity. Wyatt is not a poet who was deliberately 'rough'.

Even though nobody at the moment can offer a truly critical text, the alternative of unprincipled anarchy remains disagreeable, and every departure from our received texts, though made in the name of good sense or good metre, is bound to strike some readers as re-writing rather than emending faulty copies. I have therefore felt bound in every case to let the reader know what I was departing from, although I did not think that he would want to know of the long debate, and the weighing of possibilities that occurred while I was making up my mind what to print. Even here I have not been consistent: once or twice I have passed a phrase I do not believe was written by Wyatt. The number of confident conjectures, as distinct from desperate guesses, is equally small.

So that, given all these circumstances, if we set aside the one text I think badly corrupt, that of *Mine own John Poyntz*, the total number of new departures may be regarded as not excessive.

I have been driven to similarly unprincipled behaviour in the matter of spelling. My basic rule was to avoid creating difficulties for a reader who was coming to sixteenth-century verse for the first time. Many such readers cannot read old spellings with the necessary speed to obtain the impression of easy flow which, I believe, characterises Wyatt's best verse. On the other hand, a number of difficulties for the unwary reader must accompany the great convenience of a modernised text of the poems which is as easy to grasp now as Wyatt's poems were to his first readers. The chief difficulty is that all the words are unconsciously promoted from the meanings they had for Wyatt to those current to-day. Such is the continuity of our civilisation that with very little tact and historical imagination we can comprehend the slight changes that all these words have undergone since the early sixteenth century. But experience shows that readers have trouble where the modern meanings are quite different. Two examples occur so often that they may be mentioned here. 'Wealth' often means 'spiritual welfare' or 'well-being', and 'still' is commonly used where we might put 'always' or 'continually'. I have therefore drawn attention in the Commentary to other words presenting this and similar difficulties.

Lines may lose a whole syllable if a plural noun, such as Wyatt's *heartis* is written *hearts*. Another characteristic difficulty occurs when the rhyme word is one of those which we now pronounce differently. Wyatt, for example, often ends a line with *than* where a modernised text would like to have *then*. Sometimes a modern spelling changes the meaning completely, as to print *all in fear* where Wyatt wrote *all in fere*, meaning 'all together'. Yet, irrational and illogical as my modernising may appear, I know from experience that such a text has the effect of bringing out the beauty of Wyatt's lines, which a transcript of Wyatt's own spelling could not have for many of those who will be reading Wyatt in the next twenty years.

Wyatt resteth here

The text is based on the version in a rare pamphlet, published in 1542, (here designated H) reproduced here from the unique copy in the Huntington Library, and corrected by comparison with a manuscript version in the British Library (Harl. 78) and the printed copy in Tottel's *Songs and Sonettes* of 1557.

of envy]	*So* H, Harl. 78 T by enuy
As on a stithy where some]	Harl. 78 H As on a styth, where some T As on a stithe: where that some
H readings	
beat]	Harl. 78, T bet
in virtues]	*So* Harl. 78 T in vertue
no affect]	Harl. no effecte T none affect
yet never so impressed]	Harl. 78 yet neu*er* so opprest T was neuer so imprest
lift]	*So* Harl. 78 T loft
nor so repressed]	*So* Harl. 78 T nor yet represt
in wealth]	*So* T Harl. 78 at welthe
nor yield]	*So* Harl. 78 T or yeld
The heavens]	*So* Harl. 78, T H the heuen

AMEN]   *Only in* H.

They flee from me

Extant in E, D, and T. Reputable scholars have maintained that when we find, as here, a poem in the Egerton manuscript with the signature 'Tho.' in the margin, we may safely conclude that the text represents Wyatt's last thoughts and careful revision of all scribal errors committed by those who transcribed his 'foul papers', that, in fact, it has the authority of an autograph, and an autograph specially revised by Wyatt himself. So secure have some literary critics felt in this scholarly ruling, they have grounded Wyatt's system of scanning on lines in E which have no parallel in the rest of his work. And, lastly, some of these anomalies have been regarded by amateurs as among the best lines in this poem, *e.g.*

> It was no dreme I lay brode waking.

The minimum permissible doubt concerns spelling. The E scribe consistently spells in his own way words which Wyatt never wrote, such as *helas* for *alas*. So here, *stalking* for Wyatt's *staulkyng*. May we proceed further to wonder whether the E scribe also left little words out? For instance, can any parallel be found for the way the verb *kysse* is related to the other verbs in the sequence *fall, caught, saide*? Whereas the second and fourth actions are linked by *and*, the third begins abruptly with *therewithalll*. If we look for examples of how Wyatt used this word in his other poems, we find that it nowhere begins a line and everywhere follows *And*. Several small inaccuracies of this sort lead me to wonder whether the E scribe was any more careful than the D scribe, who has occasionally left out a word or words. When the D scribe does it, nobody tries to find a new principle of scansion to justify the odd appearance of a line of eight syllables in a poem where all the other lines each have ten!

I have therefore played the conjectural game of trying to reconstruct the poem each of our three scribes had before him, and have come up with the conjecture that what seems to be behind a corrected D text might be close to a genuine Wyatt original. But this conjectured original forces me to suppose that Wyatt had later thoughts and retouched the poem. The line in D (f. 70*r*.)

> but sins that I so gentilly am servid

sounds like the Wyatt who wrote

> She fleith as fast by gentill crueltie

In *Suche vayn thought*. But the more ironic *kyndely* of the E text is so like Wyatt that I cannot believe a lesser man could have inserted this word for *gentilly*. A complication arises if we now turn to the version printed in Tottel. The line

> But, sins that I vnkyndly so am serued:

suggests that the editors had the E text before them, and smoothed out the line to get an easier sense and scansion. Yet in the following line the Tottel editors have:

> How like you this, what hath she now deserued?

which suggests that there was a stage in the history of the poem where Wyatt was satisfied with no further changes from the version which eventually reached the D scribe. This is the stage I have tried to present. But the reader will find in the notes which now follow all the significant variants of our E text, and one or two references to Tottel which I thought supported my reconstruction. One instance is the odd use of *especiall* in the line:

> Twenty tymes better: but once especiall

which suggests to me that Wyatt **may have** written (perhaps in one word) *inespeciall,* which the D scribe carelessly misread as *inesspiall* and the E scribe as *in speciall.*

I have seen them]	*So* E
	D I have sene them both
	T Once haue I seen them [This evidence suggests that our three 'sources' all had the line as found in E and that both the D scribe and the Tottel editors found it defective. My emendation would, on rhythmical grounds alone, favour *And I have seen . . .*]
do not remember]	T do not once remember
they put]	T they haue put
with continuall]	E with a continuall
	T in continuall
	D contynuall
in especial]	D in esspiall
	E in speciall
	T especiall
from her shoulders did]	T did from her shoulders
And therewithall]	D But therewithall
	E therewithall
	T And therwithall
she did]	E dyd
for I lay]	E I lay
	T for I lay
strange]	T bitter
to go]	D to parte
	E,T to go
likewise]	E, T also
so kindly]	*So* E
	D so gentillye
	T vnkyndly so
What think you by this that]	E I would faine knowe what
	T How like you this, what hath she now deserued?

And wilt thou

Only in D.

Alas]	D Helas

Quondam was I

Only in Trinity College, Dublin MS. D.2.7 (Dub).

I have introduced the following changes to regularise the metre:

A promise]	Dub Promis
was I that]	Dub was I he that
many a one]	Dub many whon
that I may]	Dub that thys I may
'mong the more]	Dub amonge the moo
) 'e]	Dub I yet she
what though]	Dub what altho

What no, pardie

Extant in E and D

contraring]	E contrarieng D contraryng
trayed]	E tryed D trayde

Whoso list

Extant in E, A and Dub

alas]	E helas (*corrected to* alas) A,Dub alas
fleeth]	*So* E, A Dub flyth
Since]	E sethens (*corrected to* Sins) A Sithens Dub sens

The bird

One of the poems added to the second edition of Tottel's Miscellany, July 31, 1557, with the title: "The louer to his loue: hauing forsaken him, and betaken her self to an other."

What should I say

Extant only in D

The following are my attempts to regularise the metre

	D. fol. 77 *recto*
You promised]	& you promisid
You for]	Though for
Is not]	yt ys not
Your cruel kind]	[a conjecture to fill a line omitted by the scribe]

But that you]   but you

Ere that]   [in this place and others in D the spellings *or* and ore
                                       are preferred. Wyatt used *ere* in his prose writings.]

Madame, withouten

Extant in E, T and Dub

Madame, withouten]   *So* E, T
                                       Dub Mestris what nedis

ye will]   *So* E, Dub
                                       T you

And with]   *So* E, Dub
                                       T For with

ye shall]   *So* E
                                       T you shall
                                       Dub ye may

burns]   *So* T
                                       Dub borns
                                       E burneth

any pity]   *So* E, Dub
                                       T pity or ruth

with yea]   *So* T
                                       Dub with ye
                                       E with &

be yea]   *So* T
                                       Dub be ye
                                       E be &

Some time I fled

Extant in E, D, Harl. 78 (lines 1–4), A, T

Meshed]   All manuscripts ha⋁ .All manuscripts have *mashed*
                                       T Meashed

Now farewell, Love

Extant in D, E, T, A.

The text is based on D (with two obvious omissions supplied) on the assumption that
the poem existed in two forms. The point of the version in D is carried in the reason for
giving up love:

> too sore a proof hath called me from thy lore
> to surer wealth my wittis to endeavour.

The point of the second version is given in the substitution of these lines:

Senec and Plato call me from thy lore
to perfect wealth my wit for to endeavour.

It is worth noting that the Tottel editors, who print this version, the one now found in
E, nevertheless retain readings we find in D. In these notes I record variants from D and
the E readings I have rejected in favour of D's.

Now farewell]	E, T, A Farewell
whilest]	*E, T, A when*
prick eth aye]	*So* E, T, A D *om.* ay
But scape]	*So* T E, A and scape
since]	*So* E, A D for T thence; since
And thereupon go]	E, T, A And theron
thy brittle]	E, T, A thy many brittle
hitherto though]	*So* E, T, A D *om.* though
lost my]	*So* T E, A lost all my
Me list]	*So* T E, A me lusteth

O lord, since

Wyatt wrote his versions of the Seven Penitential Psalms into E. This is his version of
Psalm 6, *Domine, ne in furore.*

Chastise me not, Lord]	Wyatt did not write *Lord*
breadth]	Wyatt wrote *bred*
My flesh is troubled]	At this point a folio is missing in E. The text has to be restored from A, together with a manuscript in the British Library, Royal Ms. 17 A xxii (here designated Roy) and a printed book, *Certayne psalmes* 1549–1550 (here designated PC).
worldly vanities]	*So* PC Roy worlds vanitie A worldlye vanytie
by vice]	Roy, A by use PC by pleasure
shade]	*So* Roy, PC A shadowe
thine]	*So* Roy A thie PC thy
rightwise]	*So* Roy A rightuous PC righteouse

ground]	Since the line does not scan, *grounder* or *the ground* might be considered.
In a moment]	*So* PC. A, Roy in moment
and long]	Roy, PC, A long
And me beset]	*Here we return to Wyatt's autograph*
beauty]	*Wyatt wrote* bealte

Rue on me

This version of the psalm, beginning in the Vulgate *Miserere mei* (Psalm 51 in the Authorised Version) is also in Wyatt's hand in E.

than . . . whan]	*Wyatt's forms for then . . . when*
midst]	*Wyatt corrected* mydes *to* myddes

Of deep secrets

These lines are also in Wyatt's hand in E.

With my song]	*In the manuscript* in *has been inserted after* with. *The phrase* within my song *is found in the first line of a poem in D and Dub.*

From depth

This is Wyatt's version of a psalm beginning in the Vulgate *De Profundis*, Psalm 130 in the A.V.

Tagus, farewell

Written into E by Wyatt himself. Some interesting variants in T.

With spur and sail for I go seek]	T For I with spurre and saile go seke
doth lend her]	T that leanes her
alone]	T I seke
Of mighty love]	T O mighty Ioue
wings]	T windes

In court to serve

Extant in Tottel (with the title "The courtiers life") immediately after *Stand whoso* and on the page on which *Tagus, farewell* appears.

Throughout the world

Extant in Tottel (with the title "Of dissembling wordes") immediately before

Stand whoso

Extant in A. There is a much altered version in T. I have followed A with the following emendations:

court estate]	A courtes estates
For him]	A Ffrom him
That known of all, but to]	A that is moche knowen of other/ and of
	T That knowen is to all: but to
Doth die]	T He dyeth

Luck, my fair

The poem was printed in *Nugae Antiquae*, 1769, Vol. II p. 196. Ruth Hughey in *The Arundel Harington Manuscript of Tudor Poetry*, 1960, Vol. I, p. 23 suggests that this was one of the epigrams which stood in the manuscript now at Arundel Castle, and was torn out to supply the printer of *Nugae Antiquae*. She conjectures that the place was in the missing folios 69–74.

The poem is extant in a related Harington manuscript, now in the British Library, Add. Ms. 36529 fol. 32 *verso*. [Here referred to as P.] It was printed among other Wyatt poems in Tottel's Miscellany, 1557.

Variants

Luck]	NA Lucke P Luckes T Lux
might ye fall]	NA, P might ye befall T mought you fall
bodies they crawl]	NA boddies crall P, T bodies thei crall

The pillar

Extant in A and T.

very root]	A vearye bark T very bark
Daily]	*So* T. A Dearlye
in careful cry]	*So* T. A in wofull crye
ease]	*So* T. A cause

Sighs are

Extant in the British Library Ms Harl. 78 (H) and T. I have followed H except where stated;

my drink]	*So* T. H drynke
life it wears]	*So* T. H lyf wears
assaults]	*So* T. H assaulted
save]	H, T. have

Mine own John

The most reliable text is found in Ms 168 item 22 of Corpus Christi College, Cambridge (Co). There is a good text of lines 52–103 in E. There are other copies in D, T, P, A. There is a poor text in Ms ff. 5.14 in the Library of Cambridge University (Cul).

causes]	*So* Co, T. *All other versions* cause
with colour]	*All versions have* the colour
tune]	*So* D, T, Cul. Co tonge
to do such wrong]	D, P, A to do so grete a wrong Co nor do suche wrong T to such a wrong Cul to doo so mych wronge
as wolves]	Co like wolues
with my words]	*So all versions except* Co with my worde
with . . . as]	*So* Co with Loke ryght as D, Cul look like T loke like as
Call craft]	*So* T. *All other versions* And call
of him]	*So* D, Co, Cul. T, P, A of high
in singing]	*So* T *All other versions* singing
of coward beasts]	*So* Co, T, A D of cowardes Bestes P coward of bestes
And praise]	*All versions* prayse
y-told]	*All versions* told
when he is]	*All versions save E, which omits* he
will]	*So* Co, P, A. E, D, Cul, T would
with me]	*So* Co, Cul. E, D, T, P, A in me
next]	*All versions* nearest
cloak]	*All versions* to cloke
false and double]	T faire double *All other versions* with his double
right rule]	*All versions* right
hawk]	*So* Co, A, D E to hawke
these beasts]	E, D they bestes Co, Cul those beastes P, A the beastes
John Poyntz]	E, D, Co, Cul Poyntz T myne owne John Poyns P, A J.P.

My mother's maids

Extant in E, D (1–18), T, A.

towny]	*All versions* townish

enured]	*All versions* endured
delicates]	*So* T, A E the delicates
baken]	E bacon T, A bake
of this]	E, T, A at this
there might]	E might T, A might there
town]	*So* T, A E townysshe
for though th'unwise]	E for tho T, A for the vnwise
towny]	*So* E T, A towne
whither]	*So* T, A E whether
forgot]	*So* T, A E forgotten
with halberd]	*So* T, A E hawbert
or]	*So* A E, T nor
is it]	*So* T, A E it is
seek for]	*So* T, A E seke
on brambles or on]	*So* T, A E vpon brambles or
Nor ye set not]	*So* T, A E ne ye se not
your heart desires]	E, T, A is your desire
mislike]	*So* T(1559), A E, T mysseke
that well]	E, T, A it well
thee list . . . thy sore]	E, T, A ye list . . . your sore
thyself]	*So* T(b), A E your self

A spending hand

Extant in E, T, A.

groans]	*So* T(D I) E, T, A groyns
turds]	E the turds T, A dung
with head]	*So* A, T E the hed
So of]	*So* T. A So, on E then of
doth hear]	*So* T, A E to here
withouten]	*So* T, A E withoute

live to feed]	*So* T, A E fede to lyve
nowadays]	*So* T, A E now a daye[s] so
a chalk for]	E to a dogge T, A to a calfe
thou get]	*So* T, A E you get
see that thou]	*So* T (second edition), A E se you
see that thou]	*So* T (second edition), A E se thou *corr. to* you
be her middle]	*So* T, A E by her myddell
for her]	E, T, A her
thou it]	*So* T (second edition), A E it
if thou]	*So* T, A E if you
it thee]	E, T, A thee
gift]	*So* T (second edition), A E, T thing

Fortune doth

Extant in D.

SOME PRINCIPAL DATES IN THE LIFE OF
SIR THOMAS WYATT

1503   Born at Allington Castle, Kent.
1516   Appointed Sewer Extraordinary.
1520? Married Elizabeth Brooke, daughter of Lord Cobham.
1521   Son, Thomas, born.
1524   Clerk of the King's Jewels.
1525? Separated from his wife.
1526   Accompanied Sir Thomas Cheney on mission to King of France.
1527   Accompanied Sir John Russell on a mission to the Papal court.
1527   Translated essay by Plutarch from a Latin version by G. Budé.
1528-30 Marshal of Calais.
1532   Crossed to Calais with other members of the Court when Henry VIII
         and Anne Boleyn visited Francis I.
1533   Served at Coronation of Anne Boleyn.
1535   March 18? Knighted.
1536   May 5   Arrested and placed in the Tower.
         May 19 Anne Boleyn executed.
         June 14 Sent to Allington Castle.
         Made Sheriff of Kent.
1537   Appointed ambassador at the court of the Emperor, Charles V.
1539   Returned to England via Lisbon.
         Visited the Emperor in France and the Netherlands.
1540   July 28 Witnessed the execution of Cromwell on Tower Hill.
1541   Imprisoned and charged with treason.
         June 12 Made will with provision for his mistress, Elizabeth Darrell,
         and their son, Francis.
1542   Sent to Falmouth to welcome Spanish envoy.
         Died, and buried at Sherborne, October 11.

Erasmus, from Holbein's marginal sketch in his copy of *The Praise of Folly*

READING WYATT. A GUIDE TO THE COMMENTARY

It would be a natural mistake for a reader coming fresh to this selection of poems to suppose that Wyatt meant exactly what he said, and that all his words were in current use. To a surprising extent this assumption proves correct, but as the reader goes back over the poems or the passages he likes, he is bound to feel that there is something odd about Wyatt's use of certain words which are in current use but are clearly given a quite different meaning by Wyatt. One or two of them were mentioned in the Notes on the Text, but there are several others, such as *allow, among, borrow, cure, deface, depart, fret, reduce, recompence, trace*, for which the reader will need a gloss. This is the main trap for the unwary reader, since the number of words used by Wyatt which have dropped out of our every-day speech is remarkably small.

Another hidden trap for the unwary reader snaps when a highly satisfactory reading is obtained by taking the words in their modern sense. It is often vexing to learn that passages of what we think plain sense had an idiomatic twist for Wyatt which disappeared with the sixteenth century. We can find a notable instance in the last line of *What shall I say*. It is easy to think of the phrase *Farewell, unkissed!* as pathetically touching. I felt a slight shock of disappointment when I first discovered that this phrase was a regular formula for a disgusted rupture of friendship. It was a proverb before Chaucer used it in *Troilus*:

> Unknowe, unkist, and lost that is unsought.

The full flavour of the phrase can be tasted in a miniature play scene in Heywood's *Dialogue of Proverbs*, where a 'niece Alice', who has married imprudently, appeals in vain for financial help from her aunt, and reports her parting from her as follows:

> She and I haue shaken handes, farewell vnkyst,
> And thus with a becke as good as a dieu gard
> She flang from me, and I from her hitherward.

But once the idiom is digested, the closing bitterness of the phrase does wonders for Wyatt's poem.

The most insidious mistakes are those committed by the commentator himself. A striking instance in our day is to be found where modern editors have tried to reproduce the words Wyatt put into the mouth of the poor mouse as she contrasts her poverty with her 'sister's' wealth. Their texts have this or something like it:

> Richly she feedeth, and at the rich man's cost,
> And for her meat she needs not crave nor cry.
> By sea, by land, of delicates the most
> Her cater seeks, and spareth for no peril.
> She feedeth on boiled bacon, meat and roast,
> And hath thereof neither charge nor travail.
> And when she list, the liquor of the grape
> Doth glad her heart till that her belly swell.

But very little knowledge would have informed these editors that *boiled bacon* was not a delicacy, the distinctive food of the rich, but, on the contrary, the hard lot of the very poor. When the old peasant woman in Ovid's fable of Philemon and Baucis entertained the two gods, she

>   with a Forke tooke downe a flitch
> Of restie Bacon from the Balke made black with smoke,
>   [and cut
> A peece thereof, and in the pan to boyling did it put.

When Chaucer wished to give us a *poure wydow* who had to be content with *ful many a slender meel*, he allowed her

> Seynd bacoun, and somtyme an ey or tweye.

On the other hand, when the skill of Chaucer's professional cook is described, we learn that

> He coude roste sethe broylle and frye
> Make mortrewys and wel bake a pye.

The poor mouse clearly thought of her 'sister' as having all the culinary art lavished on her, meat prepared in three ways, boiling, baking (whence bake meats or pasties), and roasting. We should therefore read:

. . . boiled, baken meat, and roast.

Oldham introduces into one of his satires Aesop's fable of the pampered dog, who is made to speak as follows:

> Troth Sir (*reply'd the Dog*) 'thas been my Fate,
> I thank the friendly Stars, to hap of late
> On a kind Master, to whose care I owe
> All this good Flesh, wherewith you see me now:
> From his rich Voider[1] every day I'm fed
> With Bones of Fowls, and Crusts of finest Bread:
> With *Frigasee, Ragoust*, and whatsoe'er
> Of costly Kickshaws[2] now in fashion are:
> And more variety of Boil'd and Rost,
> Than a *Lord Mayor*'s Waiter e'er could boast.

It is also useful to know who and what a 'cater' was in a large household in Early Tudor times. We have an excellent authority in the Cavendish who has left us a Life of Wolsey. He was *ex officio* interested in elaborate meals, and in fact tells how a royal banquet was prepared at Hampton Court:

> ayenst the day appoynted/my lord called for his
> pryncypall officers of hys howsse as his steward/
> Controller And the Clarkes of his kytchen whome
> he commaundyd to prepare for this bankett at
> hampton Court And nother to spare for expences
> or trauell to make them suche tryhumphant chere
> . . . they sent forthe all ther Cators/purveyours
> & other persons to prepare of the fynnest vyandes
> that they cowld gett other for mony or frend-
> shyppe among my lordes frendes . . .

This suggests that the Cater of Wyatt's poem may have spared for no expense rather than for no danger: and that the word Wyatt wrote was not *peril* but *parayle*, which would rhyme with *travail*, both these words pronounced *parell, trauell*, to rhyme with

---

1 A voider was the name for the basket into which servants put fragments of uneaten food when clearing the table.

2 *que'ques choses*, elegant French dishes.

swell. Parayle I take to be an aphetic form of *apparayle*, meaning 'expensive preparation of all kinds and especially meals'.
There is a good instance of this use of the word in Lydgate's
Isopes Fabules, as may be seen in its proper place in the Commentary.[1] Finally, all these matters are summed up in a single
incident in Shakespeare's *Romeo and Juliet*, where hasty prepar-
ations are being made for a wedding feast. While the women are
supplying the pantry with spices, dates and quinces, old Capulet
decides to take a hand himself and calls out:

> Look to the bakte meates, good *Angelica*,
> Spare not for cost.

One of the main ways in which a commentary can serve to
increase a reader's pleasure is by supplying (where relevant) the
contemporary touches capable of bringing the passage to life. In
this spirit I have gone into detail to make clear what Wyatt and his
contemporaries understood by 'check' and 'lure'. Such meanings
are lost because the practices of hawking are no longer so common.
There is a similar need for help with unfamiliar religious practices,
as in Wyatt's version of Psalm 6, where he wrote:

> Temper, O Lord, the harm of my excess
> With mending will that I for recompense
> Prepare again . . .

It might have been sufficient to gloss *mending* as an aphetic form
of *amending*, but I found the phrase first acquiring life when I
came across a formula recommended for use by priests visiting
the dying:

> Brother, art thou glad that thou shalt die in
> Christin faith? *Resp.* Ye.
> Knowleche that thou hast nougt wel liued as
> thou shuldest? *Resp.* Ye.
> Art thou sori therfor? *Resp.* Ye.

---

1 Cavendish continued:
   Also they sent for all the expertest Cookes . . . The purvyours brought and sent
   In suche plenty of Costly provysion as ye wold wonder at the same/The Cookes
   wrought bothe nyght & day in dyuers subtiltes [elaborately wrought dishes
   usually containing sugar in some form] and many crafty devisis/ where lakked
   nother gold, Syluer ne any other costly thyng meate for ther purpose . . .

Hast thou wil to amend the, yif thou haddist
space of lif? *Resp*. Ye.

My aim in general has been to make it unnecessary for a
reader to turn to any other books for contemporary light on the
chosen poems. But in the fields of religion and history nothing
can be done with short notes. The references to Catholic and
Protestant 'sources' are invitations to range in two fascinating
fields. The two most helpful tips I could offer are, for Wyatt's
religious outlook, the *Enchiridion* of Erasmus. This was once the
best-loved book in Christendom, as popular among the simple as
with the learned. For life at court, I have found most enlightenment from staring at the drawings of Wyatt's contemporaries
made by Holbein. The records of the times do not help much, and
the snippets of anecdote I have reproduced need to be taken with
a generous pinch of salt.

If one of the pleasures of reading Wyatt's better poems is
to savour the distinctive 'tang' or special mark Wyatt imprinted
on his successes, it becomes important to distinguish his original
creations from successful borrowings. It therefore seemed of
interest to note, where possible, striking phrases that Wyatt could
have found in the work of his predecessors. For instance, in these
lines:

Then if I die, and go whereas I fear
To think thereon, how shall thy great mercy
Sound in my mouth unto the world's ear?

it is worth placing on record that this phrase *the world's ear* is
to be found in Gower's *Confessio Amantis*:

Forthi[1] good is that we also . . .
Do wryte of newe some matiere . . .
So that it myhte . . .
Whan we ben dede . . .
Beleue[2] to the worldes eere
In tyme comende after this.

In this very passage it is also interesting to watch Wyatt making
something new out of given materials. If we extend the passage
for two more lines:

1 therefore
2 remain

For there is none that can thee laud and love
For that thou nilt[1] no love among them there . . .

we can see that the germ of these lines is visible in the Vulgate:

Quoniam non est in morte qui memor sit tui. In inferno quis confitebitur tibi?

which Wyatt may have taken to mean:

Since there is nobody in death who might speak of thee. Who will acknowledge thee in hell?

But Wyatt also had Aretino's development before him:

. . . *& morendo in cotale stato l'anima andrà doue a pensarlo tremo . . . come potrò io Signore porre innanzi alle genti per eterno essempio i benefici riceuuti da te . . . et andandoci, non essendo lecito che iui niuno ti ami, perche non uuoi da tali essere amato . . .*

For the present argument a literal version will serve to make the point:

. . . and dying in such a state the soul will go where I tremble to think of . . . Lord, how shall I be able to put before people as an eternal example the benefits received from thee . . . and if I go there, it not being permitted that any may love thee there, since thou wishest not to be loved by any such . . .

Wyatt has turned these external phrases inwards and found the lines of power. On the way he caught up the corresponding passage in the meditation by John Fisher:

. . . how shall we do yf we be in hell, truely in that terryble place no creature shall neyther loue god, neyther laude hym.

Whereas I have been principally concerned in this commentary to gather up all the relevant information garnered by my predecessors, there is one area where new ground has been broken. This is in revealing the extent of Wyatt's debts to Erasmus. An

1 will not allow

example may be seen in the commentary on a poem hitherto passed over by editors in silence:

> In court to serve, deckéd with fresh array,
>   Of sugared meats feeling the sweet repast,
> The life in banquets and sundry kinds of play
>   Amid the press of lordly looks to waste
>   Hath with it joined oft times such bitter taste
> That whoso joys such kind of life to hold
> In prison joys, fettered with chains of gold.

More needed than to note that Wyatt was speaking of banquets where he wrote (as did all his contemporaries) *banketts*,[1] was to explain that the second line of the epigram means 'savouring the highly-spiced food'. Once again, we need first to bring to mind the 'Burgundian' extravagance of Tudor 'conspicuous consumption'. But the bitter point comes from Erasmus' sarcasm on the 'life in banquets and sundry kinds of play' in his *Praise of Folly*:

> . . . After that to the dyse, to tables, to cardes, or to boules, nowe with iesters, nowe with fooles, now with courtisanes, daunces, and dalliaunces to trifle out the tyme, not without one, or two collacions afore supper, and after supper theyr bankettes one vpon an other.

The actual bitter taste may have come from a famous passage in Lucretius:

> *eximia ueste et uictu conuiuia, ludi,*
> *pocula crebra, unguenta, coronae, serta, parantur,*
> *nequiquam, quoniam medio de fonte leporum*
> *surgit amari aliquid quod in ipsis floribus angat*

which Dryden rendered:

> French fashions, costly treats are their delight;
> The Park by day, and Plays and Balls by night.
> In vain: — —
> For in the Fountain where their Sweets are sought,
> Some bitter bubbles up, and poisons all the draught.

---

1 and that by *bankett* Wyatt was probably thinking of a spiced drink, as in *Romeo and Juliet*, I v 121: We have a trifling foolish banquet towards . . .

The clinching couplet owes something to an Adage by Erasmus, and the fact that chains of gold were worn by all prominent public servants, as we may see from a well-known picture of Sir Thomas More, which exemplifies the whole point of the poem.

There is one debt to Erasmus which deserves particular mention in a commentary on Wyatt's poems: it is the introduction to Plutarch's *Moralia*. It has long been known that Wyatt used a Latin translation by Budé of one of Plutarch's moral essays. He also turned to the translations of Plutarch made by Erasmus and published for the first time in 1514. Some of the most characteristic lines of poetry Wyatt ever wrote come from that source:

> Like lice away from dead bodies they crawl . . .
> . . . this wound shall heal again,
>   But yet, alas, the scar shall still remain . . .
>   . . .
> . . . Wouldst thou I should for any loss or gain
>   Change that for gold that I have ta'en for best
>   Next godly things, to have an honest name?

No apologies are needed for pointing out that, as Wyatt matured, so he was able to take over more from Chaucer. Although Chaucer has too many sides for one example to stand for all, Wyatt's appreciation of Chaucer's humour may be given special place. Many other commentators in fact have seen what looks like an obvious 'allusion' in Wyatt's account of the shock to the country mouse when she spies the cat:

> In France
> Was never mouse so feared, for though the unwise
>   Had not yseen such a beast before,
>   Yet had nature taught her after her guise
> To know her foe and dread him evermore . . .

for there is a similar episode in the *Nun's Priest's Tale*, where the cock is confronted with the fox:

> For naturally a best desireth to fle
> Fro his contrary yf he may it see
> Though he neuer had seen it erst wyth his eye . . .

This encourages me to suppose that Wyatt was doing something similar in his other epistle to Poyntz, where he is openly referring to Chaucer. The conjecture *y-told* for the *told* of the manuscripts in these lines:

> And praise Sir Thopas for a noble tale
> And scorn the story that the Knight y-told . . .

is based on the supposition that Wyatt was deliberately recalling Chaucer's remarks at the end of the *Knight's Tale*:

> Whan that the Knight had thus his tale ytolde
> In al the company nas ther yong ne olde
> That he ne sayd/ it was a noble story . . .

Although it appears from the commentary that Wyatt drew on the complete works of Chaucer, including many poems we now know were written by others, he had a special love for *Troilus* and the *Knight's Tale*. This comes to the reader's rescue when he is attempting to decide among the extant versions of Wyatt's poems which words were really his. A trifling, but nevertheless significant, example occurs in the first epistle to Poyntz, where the better manuscripts read:

> I am not he that can allow the state
> Of him Caesar, and damn Cato to die . . .

Yet I must confess that at first I went along with most others, including some of Wyatt's contemporaries, who preferred *high* to *him*. Yet in the *Knight's Tale* we twice find this phrase, *e.g.*

> Thys was the forarde[1] playnly to endyte
> Betwyx duke Theseus ande hym arcyte . . .
> . . .
> For jalousye ande feer of hym arcyte . . .

In keeping with the spirit of this commentary, I have quoted in full every passage of Chaucer which seemed to me 'behind' Wyatt's poems. For Wyatt is an important moment in the after-life of Chaucer's poetry. But the commentary has a further ambition which, as far as Chaucer is concerned, is served by quoting the text of Chaucer, not from modern editions, but, for the *Canterbury Tales*, from Caxton's edition, and for the other poems from Thynne's edition of 1532.

The ambition is at last to break with a long-standing 'taboo'. Some such word as *taboo* is needed, since I do not believe that

---

1 agreement

anybody would come out *openly* and say that poetry can be written without reading. Yet because we know so much about Wyatt's other activities, and so very little of his literary studies, there has been a silent conspiracy to suppose that he had no time for books. (It is no compensation to go to the other extreme and posit immense reading in Spanish, Italian and French without naming any works and showing the evidence for names.) I am in no position to say even in outline what books were in fact lining the shelves[1] of any study or library Wyatt maintained at Allington Castle, in Kent, where the family resided. But it did seem worth quoting, when illustrating the language of the poems, from books that might have been on his shelves. (I have assumed that Wyatt's library had room for such light fiction as *Huon of Bordeaux*.) But whereas some names, such as Chaucer and Erasmus, can be regarded as certain, and Seneca's Epistles and a host of 'forbidden' Protestant pamphlets are highly probable, it is only by patient accumulation of scraps of evidence that a portrait can be drawn of Wyatt, the reader of books, ancient and modern, English and foreign. But the possibility must be kept open that Wyatt's powers as a poet consisted largely in his ability to select from, refine and re-combine materials which came to him from books.

I can hardly characterise my efforts even as a first step towards a sketch of such a man. But I hope that those who would care to pioneer and prospect in this area will be glad to have the following table of the commoner references which might serve to increase a reader's pleasure in this selection of Wyatt's poems.

---

1 or in the presses.

LIST A

A DESCRIPTIVE LIST OF FURTHER
CORROBORATIVE READING

Alamanni, Luigi
(1495–1556)

Opere Toscane, two volumes, published in Florence in 1532 and in Lyons, 1532–1533.

Wyatt seems to have enjoyed his poems in *terza rima*, particularly the 'Juvenalian' satires, and above all, the tenth, which he translated and transformed into a verse letter to his friend, John Poyntz. Wyatt may also have taken a hint from Alamanni's Seven Penitential Psalms, based on each of the Seven Deadly Sins. The chief interest for the reader of Wyatt lies in the contrast in culture of two men whose outlook, education, and career were so similar. Humanism in the years 1520–1540 was a different thing north and south of the Alps.

Barclay, Alexander
(1475?–1552)

The shyp of folys, 1509, ed. T.H. Jamieson, 1874.
The Eclogues, ed. B. White, 1928.

Both books will interest a reader who found the 'satire on the court' side of Wyatt's work attractive. *The shyp*, along with Brant's *Narrenschiff*, makes a useful foil to Erasmus' *Praise of Folly*. *The Eclogues* offer versions of Latin court satires in pastoral form by Pope Pius II and Mantuan.

Bourchier, John,
Lord Berners,
(1469–1533)
[Uncle of Sir Francis Brian]

The Boke of Duke Huon of Burdeux, 1534?, ed. S.L. Lee, 1888.

The survival of this book, which blends the incredible, the impossible, fairyland and folk lore, will serve as a specimen of the 'light reading' indulged in by all people whose main reading was 'serious'. I must record my surprise at finding this wistful attempt to cling on to all that once was taken seriously in chivalry and romance far more agreeable than the genuine romances of the Middle

107

108   A DESCRIPTIVE LIST

Ages. [The Oberon who figures largely in *Huon* has only the name in common with Shakespeare's figure.]

[Beryn]

The Tale of Beryn, ed. Furnivall and Stone, 1909. The scope of this literary portrait of Sir Thomas Wyatt has not allowed me to dwell sufficiently on the great popularity in Wyatt's circle of tales then attributed to Chaucer but now seen not to be his. Several are still readable. *The Second Merchant's Tale* might repay a glance.

Brian, Sir Francis,
(1498?–1550)

A Dispraise of the Life of a Courtier, 1548. It would be extremely illuminating for any reader interested in the court of Henry VIII to have all the surviving notices collected, for Brian (or Bryan) was more deeply involved in all the goings-on there at all levels than Wyatt himself. The chief interest of his translation through the French of the *Menosprecio de corte* by Antonio de Guevara lies in the little additions Brian made as a result of his own experiences at court and of Wyatt's poems.

Castiglione, Baldesar
(1478–1529)

Il Libro del Cortegiano, ed. V. Cian, Florence, 1947. Thanks to the translation made by Sir Thomas Hoby in 1561, this Renaissance classic, written substantially by 1516 but not published until 1528, has become widely known in England. I believe Wyatt had come to know it well by the time he was writing in *terza rima*. The reader who uses the original will find Cian an admirable guide. The reader of Hoby has an excellent introduction to it in *Some Authors,* by Sir Walter Raleigh, from whom I take these lines:

> No single book can serve as a guide to the Renaissance, or as an index to all that is embraced by 'the comprehensive energy of that significant appellation'. But if one, rather than another, is to be taken for an abstract or epitome of the chief moral and social ideas of the age, that one must be The Courtier (p. 42).

Cavendish, George,
(1499?–1561?)

The Life and Death of Cardinal Wolsey, ed. R.S. Sylvester, 1959.

A faithful servant's reminiscences (c.1537) of his life in Wolsey's household. The editor says:

> There can scarcely be any doubt that the major portion of his book is the product of his own direct experience.

As such, it is an invaluable source for the historian. But for the reader of Wyatt, the most interesting parts are the descriptions of banquets and other public occasions at court at which Wyatt may have been present as a boy and a young man. I heartily concur with the verdict given by R. Fiddes in his own *Life of Wolsey* (1724):

> His Stile is clear and, for the Time wherein he lived, significant and polite enough. He writes with the free and negligent Air of a Gentleman, which much becomes him, and he is sometimes happy, without appearing to have any such Design, in addressing himself to the Imagination and Passions. There are some Passages in him, whereby a Reader who has any true Taste, will find himself agreeably moved.

Caxton, William,   *The recuyell of the historyes of Troy*, ed. H.O.
(1422?–1491)   Sommer, 1884.
The metamorphoses of Ouid, tr. 1480, 1968.
Chronicles of England, 1480, 1482.
Godefrey of Boloyne, 1481, ed. M.N. Colvin, 1893.
The mirror of the world, 1481, ed. O.H. Prior, 1913.
Reynard the Fox, 1481, ed. N.F. Blake, 1970.
The Golden Legend, 1483, ed. F.S. Ellis, 1892.
Fables of Aesop, 1484, ed. R.T. Lenaghan, 1967.
Eneydos, 1490, ed. M.T. Culley and F.J. Furnivall, 1890.

The list is long, but could very well be made longer, for in a book which lays so much stress on the advent of Humanism it is important to recall how eager all classes, from the highest to those who would have to have the printed books read *to* them, were to have translations from the French of popular mediaeval works. I suspect that almost all the learned were more impressed by the stories about Troy which Caxton translated than by the stumbling *versiones* of the *Iliad* which were beginning to come out of Italy. I think Wyatt

had a special interest in the *Chronicles* (see the
Commentary on *Tagus, farewell*) and the *Fables
of Aesop*. But the work I most heartily recommend is the *Legenda Aurea* of Jacobus de Vora-
gine. I have made a substantial quotation from it
when telling the story of David and Bathsheba,
in order thereby to tempt the reader to explore
further.

Chaucer, Geoffrey, *The Canterbury Tales*, Caxton, 1484, facs. 1972.
(c.1340–c.1400) *The Workes*, 1532, repr. 1969.
To obtain a quick general impression of the effect
on Wyatt and his contemporaries of the works
of Chaucer, I can think of nothing better than the
edition of the works brought out in 1532, for the
reader will there find what the student now knows
to be genuine poems by Chaucer mixed with
anonymous work and poems by known authors,
such as Henryson, Lydgate, Sir Richard Ros,
Thomas Usk, Thomas Hoccleve, and John Gower.
It is possible that Wyatt had access to pieces by
Chaucer not then in print. His own interest seems
to have lain chiefly in *Troilus* and *The Knight's
Tale*, but his 'borrowings' prove that his knowledge
of the *Canterbury Tales* was detailed and extensive.

Cooper, Thomas, *Thesaurus Linguae Romanae & Britannicae*, 1565.
(1517–1594) An indispensable work for the dictionary-maker.
The OED is notoriously inadequate for the period
1450–1550, and many necessary words which
puzzle the reader of Wyatt or, if we only had the
OED, would be thought peculiar to Wyatt, may be
discovered as the normal translations of Latin
words: *e.g.* Wyatt's *deep thy self in travail* is
found under *immergo* as *to diepe*. Conversely,
when Wyatt was translating from a Latin original,
we can find out whether his version was original.
See the Commentary for Wyatt's use of dictionaries when translating Seneca in *Stand who so list*.

Dyboski, Roman, Editor of *Songs, Carols, and other Miscellaneous
Poems*, 1908.
I described this commonplace book, put together
in the first thirty years of the sixteenth century
by a London merchant named Richard Hill, and
I quoted extensively from it in a chapter on

Wyatt's 'Devonshire' poems in *Humanism and Poetry etc.* The whole collection would be worth reprinting intact from the manuscript in Balliol college. Dyboski offered only a selection. Quite apart from being the perfect introduction to Wyatt's 'lyrics', every page of this commonplace book has some entertainment, grave or gay, and there are a few exquisite poems.

Elyot, Sir Thomas, (1490?–1546)

The Bankette of Sapience, 1534
Bibliotheca Eliotae, 1548
The Dictionary, 1538
The Doctrinal of Princes (Isocrates), 1534
The education or bringing vp of children [?before 1530] (Plutarch)
The boke named the Gouernour, 1531
The image of gouernance, 1541 (Alexander Severus)
Pasquil the playne, 1533

It would not be unfair to regard this list as a list of the works of a prose Wyatt, for both authors came equally under the influence of Erasmus and consequently read and admired the same books. Elyot was also a disciple of Thomas More even if only *usque ad aras*.[1] His whole work is essentially translation. Of *The boke named the Gouernour* it was rightly said by Berdan:

> Upon a basis taken from *De Regno et Regis Institutione* of Francesco Patrizi he grafted what he thought appropriate from Erasmus and Pontanus.

Pasquil deals with one of Wyatt's topics, 'teachynge ... maisters howe to be cyrcumspecte in espying of flatterers'. *The Bankette* 'sheweth out of holie scrypture many wyse sentences'. The utility of the two dictionaries is explained in the remark on Cooper, who incorporated them both in his own much larger Latin–English dictionary. The reader who is relying on my description ought to be warned that although Elyot is a good specimen of an educated man of Wyatt's day, he is a prosaic Wyatt, never sparkling or piquant, never odd or original.

1 This is Elyot's quotation from Erasmus' *Adagia* to indicate that he would go to the limit for More but not so far as to imperil his soul.

Erasmus, Desiderius,
(1469?–1536)

Adagiorum Opus, Basel, 1528
Proverbes or Adagies, tr. Richarde Tauerner, 1539
Apophthegmatum Opus, Paris, 1532
tr. Nicolas Udall, *Apophthegmes*, 1542
Flores Aliquot, Tauerner, 1540
Catonis Praecepta, 1514
De Contemptu Mundi, 1521
tr. Thomas Paynell, Gainesville, Florida, 1967
De Immensa Dei Misericordia, 1524
tr. Gentian Heruet, 1533
Enchiridion Militis Christiani, Strassburg, 1524
tr. William Tyndale, 1533
Epicureus (from *Colloquia*), 1533
tr. Philip Gerrard, 1545
Ex Plutarcho, Basel, 1529
Stulticiae Laus, Basel, 1515
tr. Sir Thomas Chaloner as *The praise of Folie*, 1549.
Although Wyatt probably read all the works of Erasmus he could lay hands on, he read them all in the original Latin. I have listed contemporary translations to suggest how the Latin may have passed into Wyatt's English. The beginner is recommended to ignore this list, and try, first, *The Praise of Folly*, next, *The Colloquies*, and third, if he cares for an expression of decent piety and humanity, the *Enchiridion*, in Tyndale's lively version entitled 'the manuell of the Christen knyght'. The *Opus Epistolarum* now becoming available in an English translation is a treasure for anyone who wishes to see what made Europe a literate *community*. Many of the works which made a deep impression on Wyatt, such as the translation into Latin of the Greek New Testament, have been absorbed into the work of Erasmus' successors.

Foxe, John,
(1517–1587)

Actes and monuments, 1565
The best edition for the student of this account of the Reformation in England, often called the Book of the Martyrs, is that edited in eight volumes by J. Pratt in 1877. I have included, on page 47, one illustration showing the execution of Tyndale to tempt readers to hunt for copies of the book containing the 'horror scenes' which remind one that the Reformation was a time of *burning*.

There is a whiff of reality in some of the narratives which gives life to Wyatt's lines:

> For death him grippeth right hard by the crop
> that known of all but to himself, alas,
> doth die unknown, dazed with dreadful face.

Foxe, of course, is a *partisan* author but not a professional liar. C.S. Lewis once wrote of him:

> In 1940 ... Mr J.F. Mozley ... defended Foxe's integrity, as it seems to me, with complete success. From his examination Foxe emerges, not indeed as a great historian, but as an honest man.

[Gesta Romanorum] *The Early English Versions*, ed. S.J.H. Herrtage, 1879.
A fifteenth-century compilation, made from a thirteenth-century compilation of stories with a moral. If a beginner tries one story he may well find himself sampling others.

Gower, John, *The English Works*, ed. G.C. Macaulay, 1900.
(1330?—1408?) The only piece which might deserve to be called 'corroborative' is *Confessio Amantis*. I was surprised to see how useful a light on Wyatt's moral poems was thrown by some of the stories in this poem when they touched on the same virtues and vices. The moral world of the fourteenth century seemed remarkably like that of the sixteenth.

Hall, Edward, *The Triumphant Reigne of Kyng Henry The VIII*,
(1499?—1547) ed. Charles Whibley, 1904.
For some of the reasons which make this work indispensable for a student of court culture, see *Humanism and Poetry, etc.* Hall was a naive admirer of all the pomp and ceremony of the reign. But so were many others who lived in the court. He makes an effective foil to More and Wyatt, who saw the folly of such 'Burgundian' extravagance.

Hamy, A., *Entrevue de François Premier avec Henry VIII*,
Paris, 1898.
A wonderful opportunity to learn in detail what Wyatt witnessed and suffered when he had to cross to France for this interview.

Hawes, Stephen,
(1475?–1523)

Minor Poems, ed. F.W. Gluck and A.B. Morgan, 1974.

The Pastime of Pleasure, ed. W.E. Mead, 1928.

More than any other poet Hawes illustrates the depths to which poetry had sunk in the first ten years of the sixteenth century; and the persistence of re-editions in the following forty years proves that the reading public preferred mediaeval moralising styles to modern.

Hervieux, Léopold,

Les fabulistes latins, Paris, 1884–1899.

A labour of love and of immense erudition. The vitality of the fable tradition is abundantly illustrated in fascinating detail. Wyatt's apparent 'borrowings' suggest that he had access to much now lost material.

Heywood, John
(1497?–1580?)

A dialogue of proverbes concernyng two maner of mariages, 1546.

An hundred epigrammes, 1550

Woorkes, 1562

'Merry *Iohn Heywood*', as he continued to be called long after his death, has in our day been pronounced unreadable. But if he is opened as one might seat oneself at a bar and offer a series of drinks to a local wag, he can provide in the incidental background to his pointed stories (as in his interludes) a moral picture of his age much nearer the knuckle (especially on marital relations) than the impression we derive from 'straight' moralists. He commands a lively flow of English more pungent and racy than that of the run of loud-mouthed satirists, and he is not always straining to be 'funny'.

Langland, William,
(1332?–1400?)

Piers Plowman, A-Version, ed. G. Kane, 1960, C-Text, ed. W. Skeat, 1873.

Chiefly of interest here for the treatment of those moral truths which would have modern applications for Wyatt.

Leland, John,
(1506–1552)

Naeniae in mortem Thomae Viati, 1542.

Some valuable snippets of information from a contemporary who was more interested in topography than in literary criticism can be extracted from these funeral epigrams. Leland unfortunately was not on oath in commending Wyatt, and felt that the occasion licensed much looseness and empty rhetoric. The Latin text is available in Miss Foxwell's edition of Wyatt. A verse translation by Kenneth Muir will be found in his *Life and Letters.*

Molins, El Marqués de, Editor of *Crónica del Rey Enrico Otavo de Ingalaterra,* Madrid, 1874. Translated by M.A.S. Hume, 1889.

Historians who have been quick to point out obvious inaccuracies and pure romance in this chronicle of the reign of Henry VIII have never been able to account for certain pieces of knowledge about events such as Cromwell's last words to Wyatt, which the author could not have made up.

More, Sir Thomas, *The workes,* 1557.
(1478—1535) There is no line of More's that would not be found worth reading by a genuine student of Wyatt. But for undiluted pleasure I can recommend only the Latin work, *Utopia,* 1516 (translated by R. Robinson 1551). In his unpleasant handlings of his religious opponents he points out acutely their real shortcomings. The spirit of a beautiful Christianity breathes in his latest writings. His letters should be sampled by everybody. A true portrait of More will not be drawn until he can become, as it were, uncanonised. A newcomer to More might with profit start from a sketch made by Erasmus in the course of a letter sent on July 23, 1519. (*Ep.* 999 in Allen's edition of the *Opus Epistolarum.*)

Orléans, Charles, duc d', *The English Poems,* ed. R. Steele, 1941.
(1394—1465) I have tried to indicate the utility of these poems to the student of Wyatt's 'Devonshire' poems in *Humanism and Poetry in the Early Tudor Period,* pp. 164-165.

Palsgrave, John, *Lesclarcissement de la langue Francoyse,* 1530.
d.1554 Indispensable for the dictionary-maker, e.g. where Wyatt wrote:
For swine so groanes . . .
it is helpful to learn that Palsgrave records:
A hogge groneth: *vng porceau grongne.*

Petrarca, Francesco, *Il Canzoniere*, ed. Ettore Modigliani, Rome, 1904.
(1304–1374) I have cited this edition since it is instructive to learn how Petrarch actually spelt his poems. It would, however, be better if we could decide which edition(s) Wyatt himself used. Although in the first place the collection is useful for poems actually translated by Wyatt, many turns were borrowed by him from sonnets he did not translate. In reading Petrarch for this purpose it should be remembered that Wyatt saw Petrarch as a modern, and read him as those Italians did who had watered down and systematised his poems, as explained by Professor L.W. Forster in *The Icy Fire.*

[*Pilgrimage of* *A deuoute treatyse in Englysshe, called the Pyl-*
***Perfection*]** *grimage of perfection*, 1526, 1531.
Although I have found this work of great value for getting acquainted with the devotional language of monkish piety, I have never been able to read it right through.

Plutarch, Moral Essays, translated into Latin by Erasmus:
(43–120)   *De curiositate*, 1525
         De discrimine adulatoris et amici, 1514
         De non irascendo, 1525
         De tuenda bona valetudine precepta, 1513
         De utilitate capienda ex inimicis, 1514
         De vitiosa verecundia, 1526
Moral Essays translated into Latin by G. Budé: (1510)
         De fortuna Romanorum
         De fortuna uel uirtute Alexandri
         De tranquillitate & securitate animi
         translated by Wyatt as *the Quyete of mynde,* 1527, ed. C.R. Baskerville, Cambridge, (Mass.), 1931.
Although Wyatt would have read the *Lives* in Latin, the only parts of Plutarch which emerge in his poems are these essays, which Wyatt no doubt found apt for his own case.

Serafino Ciminelli *Opere*, Florence, 1516
dall'Aquila *Die Strambotti*, ed. Barbara Bauer-Formiconi,
(1466–1500) Münich, 1967.
It is an accident of the choice of poems to make

up this portrait of Wyatt that it has resulted in leaving Serafino to one side. Patricia Thomson has an excellent chapter on him in her *Sir Thomas Wyatt and his Background*, 1964, in which she wrote:

> He is . . . Wyatt's biggest creditor after Petrarch, and provides, besides some general inspiration, the sources of five [six] of his translations and four of his imitations.

She reminds those who are shocked to find Wyatt so entranced with this model that during Wyatt's life-time Serafino had a great reputation in France. Sergio Baldi in *La Poesia di Sir Thomas Wyatt*, 1953, went so far as to write:

> *Coll'Aquilano, però, il Wyatt ha maggiori affinità di temperamento; ed egli lo coglie soppratutto nei suoi aspetti più lontani dal Petrarca, nei suoi toni arguti, satirici ed anche sprezzanti che trovano la loro maggiore espressione negli Strambotti* (p. 191).[1]

Skelton, John, (1460?–1529)

The Poetical Works, ed. A. Dyce, 1843.

The great advantage of turning to Skelton after Wyatt is to see the difference between being in the court and being of it, succinctly presented in the contrast between Skelton's *The auncient acquaintance* and Wyatt's *Ye olde moyle*. For the present study the most useful poems of Skelton are those on Wolsey and the Court, *The Bowge of Courte*, *Colyn Cloute*, and *Why come ye nat to courte?*

---

1 'Wyatt certainly has greater temperamental affinity with Serafino than with Petrarch; and he follows him most often when he is furthest away from Petrarch, in his use of wit and satire and his mocking familiar tone, which are to be found most clearly in the *strambotti* (i.e. short eight-line poems).' *Sir Thomas Wyatt*, by Sergio Baldi, translated by F.T. Prince, 1961.

COMMENTARY ON THE POEMS

An Excellent Epitaph

Surrey's poem can be dated approximately by recalling that Wyatt was buried on October 11, 1542, and that the poem is referred to in a dedicatory poem to a collection of funeral poems on Wyatt entitled *Naeniae* by Leland, a friend of both Wyatt's and Surrey's. This collection was published in 1542. The relevant lines are as follows:

> *Tu modo non viuum coluisti candidus illum*
> *Verum etiam vita defunctum carmine tali*
> *Collaudasti quale suum Chaucerus auitae*
> *Dulce decus linguae vel iuste agnosceret esse.*
>
> You, a man of incorruptible judgement, not only worshipped him in his life-time, but when he passed away, you sang his praises in a splendid poem which Chaucer, the Old Master of our tongue and himself a sweet singer, might well have acknowledged as equal to the best he himself could write.

Another reference to the poem may be found in 'The Epistle of the Translatour' of *The preceptes of warre*, 1543 by Peter Betham:

> Wyate was a worthye floure of our tounge, as appereth by the mornefulle ballet made of hys death in Englysshe, whyche is mooste wyttye fyne and eloquent.

quick]	'Alive'.
quick . . . rest]	The conceit may have come to Surrey from the epigram on the tomb of Jacopo Trivulzio (d. 1518) as recorded by Camden in his *Remaines* (1605) p. 39: HIC MORTVVS REQVIESCIT SEMEL, QVI VIVVS REQVIEVIT NVNQVAM. Here rests in death one who never once rested in life.

disdain]   It is remarkable that, although when Wyatt died he
he was enjoying royal favour, Surrey in this poem
and two other poems written after Wyatt's death
stresses the attacks of envious and malicious
enemies. The logic of the whole stanza forces us
to take *disdain* as the contempt felt for Wyatt
by his enemies.

hammers]   Surrey may be recalling these lines from Wyatt's
Since you will needs:
> Such hammers work within my head
> That sound nought else unto my ears
> But fast at board and wake abed . . .

beat still]   'Were continuously beating'.

stithy]   'Anvil'.

Visage]   Surrey's portrait of Wyatt is confirmed both by
Holbein's drawings and Leland's pen-portrait:
> *Prosopographis*
> *Corpore procerum finxit natura Viatum*
> *Eius & inuictis neruos dedit illa lacertis.*
> *Addidit hinc faciem qua non formosior altra.*
> *Laeta serenatae subfixit lumina fronti*
> *Lumina fulgenteis radijs imitantia stellas.*
> *Caesariem iuueni subflauam contulit: inde*
> *Defluxit sensim crinis, caluumque reliquit*
> *Sylua sed excreuit promissae densula barbae.*
> (Nature fashioned for Wyatt a tall body and
> gave vigour to the arms she joined to it.
> Then she set upon it a face unmatched in
> beauty. Beneath his clear brow she fixed
> happy eyes which shone as bright as stars.
> Nature also gave him while young a head of
> light-blonde hair. This hair gradually dis-
> appeared and left him bald. But a thick bush
> grew from his chin into a long beard.)

mark]   'The centre of a white, an archery target'.

unparfited]   'Unporfocted'.
His untimely death cut short the full development
of his poetical genius.

served . . . King]   Wyatt served abroad in a subordinate diplomatic
capacity in 1526 and 1527. His ambassadorial
career began in 1537.

courteous . . . heart] The action of such an ideal courtier as was described by Castiglione in *Il Libro del Cortegiano*. When Wyatt in 1539 listed the things he missed through absence from his mistress, he wrote:
> The wise and pleasant talk, so rare or else alone,
> > that did me give the courteous gift that such had never none . . .

travail] 'Hard literary labour'.

affect] 'Strong feeling inducing partiality'.

allure] The verb was used to mean attracting friends to one's side without using improper means, as in Tyndale's translation of Erasmus' *Enchiridion* sig. a 5 *recto*:
> to alure very many to a christen mans lyfe.

impressed] 'Pressed in'.

lift] 'Lifted up', especially with pride. The thought is found in the 'sayings of Cleobolus' in Erasmus' *Apophthegmata:*
> *Rebus secundis ne efferaris, aduersis ne dejiciaris*
> Wyth prosperitie be thou not lyfted vp, and wyth aduersitie be not caste downe

(Richard Taverner in *Flores Aliquot*, 1540 *sig.* A iiij. *recto*) and in Erasmus' *Enchiridion* p. 65 *verso*; [how many]
> *Qui neque prosperis rebus insolescere, neque aduersis frangi potuerunt?*

which Tyndale translated as:
> whom neyther prosperyte coulde make proude/wilde & wanton/ neyther aduersite coulde ouercome and make heauy herted . . .

and in Cardinal Fisher (see List B) on Psalm 51 p. 114:
> shall neyther be lyfte vp by presumpcyon nor caste downe by dyspayre.

swell] 'Become puffed up with pride'.

wealth] 'Prosperity'.

Happy . . . Nature set] Surrey was recalling the last words of Dido in Book Four of Virgil's *Aeneid*, perhaps in his own version:

> Swete spoiles, whiles God and destenies it
>   wold,
> Receve this sprite, and rid me of these cares.
> I lived and ranne the course fortune did
>   graunt,
> And under earth my great gost now shall
>   wende.
> A goodly town I built, and saw my walles,
> Happy, alas to happy, if these costes
> The Troyan shippes had never touched aye.*
> (871–877)

* at all

Nature . . . mould]
Nature is being thought of as a mass manufacturer of similar products. Further creation becomes impossible once the mould is lost or broken. Nobody has been able to find this conceit in English before Surrey. He used it in the poem beginning *Give place*:

> I could rehearse, if that I would,
> The whole effect of Nature's plaint,
> When she had lost the perfect mould
> The like to whom she could not paint.

But in a poem about Pygmalion in Tottel's *Miscellany*, once attributed to Wyatt, we find these lines:

> My dear, alas, since I you love,
>   what wonder is it then
> In whom hath Nature set
>   the glory of her name
> And brake her mould in great despair
>   your like she could not frame.
> (*In Grece somtime*)

simple]
'Free from guile'.

covet . . . know]
'To desire eagerly but purely to know Christ'. *The Pilgrimage of Perfection* (1531/Fo. cclxxxvii. recto.

> a couetyng desyre to fulfyll the commaunde-
> mentes of god . . .

Witness]
For the argument that Surrey was a crypto-Protestant and completely converted to the *doctrine* at the heart of Wyatt's *Psalms*, see *Humanism and Poetry* &c. pp. 240–248.

Surrey is clearly regarding as a precious legacy the translation of the Seven Psalms about which he had expressed himself in the poem beginning *The great Macedon* as follows:

* deeds

> In the rich ark if Homer's rhymes he placed,
> Who feigned gests* of heathen Princes sang,
> What holy grave, what worthy sepulture
> To Wyatt's Psalms should Christians then
>   purchase?

wealth] 'Spiritual salvation'.

The earth . . . ghost] A traditional close:
Ecclesiastes The XII. Chapter:

> Or dust be turned againe vnto earth from whence it came, and or the sprete returne vnto God, which gaue it.

This noble poem inspired Raleigh to compose a fine *Epitaph vpon the right Honorable sir Philip Sidney knight . . .*

They flee from me

flee] Run like a deer, fly away like a falcon, go away rapidly like a human being.
Charles d'Orléans *English Poems* ed. Steele p. 45/ 1347:

*once

> They flee fro me they dar not onys* abide

sometime] 'Formerly, at some time in the past, once', as in the line:

> Some tyme I stode so in her grace

in the poem beginning *If euer man*, which resembles

> Ons in your grace I knowe I was . . .

(see page 130)

stalking] 'Approaching stealthily' not necessarily like an animal. Chaucer uses the verb for human movement particularly at night, as in *The Knight's Tale*/ 1479, where Palamon 'fleeth' in the night to a grove, where:

*full of dread

> Wyth dredful* foot than stalketh [he] . . .

and in *The Legend of Good Women*/1781, of Tarquin:

*like a thief

> And in the night ful thefely* gan he stalke

Whan euery wight was to his reste brought . . .
cf; Shakespeare in *The Rape of Lucrece*:
Into the chamber wickedlie he stalkes . . .

gentle, tame and meek] The three epithets define and confine each other: they all have the effect of increasing the antithesis. As Palsgrave put it in *Lesclarcissement de la langue Francoyse*, 1530:
Meke nat wylde.
All are applicable to wild creatures that have become submissive to man. But this would not extinguish the noble suggestions of *falcon-gentle*, the female of the peregrine falcon, as in Skelton, *To maystres Margaret Hussey*:
Ientill as fawcoun
Or hawke of the towre
where it is not clear whether Margaret is being praised for her aristocratic manners or for her excellent breed or spirit.
Gentle and tame was a set phrase in Wyatt's day, as we may see from Tyndale's translation of Erasmus' *Enchiridion*, sig.a.vij.*verso*
kyndnesse/wherwith euen very wylde beestes be woxen gentle and tame . . .

wild] Once they return to the state of nature, they are hard to hold. (See *Whoso list to hunt*.) The chief suggestions are, 'not subjected to man's will', 'given to wanton sexual behaviour'.

in danger] 'In my power'. The phrase has sinister or evil overtones. There is a good example in Chaucer's Prologue to his *Canterbury Tales*, where he is describing how his Somonour had the young people at his mercy:

in his usual way   In daunger hadde he at hys owen gyse*
                          Alle the yonge gyrlis of the dyocyse
their   And knew of hyr* counseyl . . .
The phrase also meant 'in captivity'. cf. *Pilg. Perf.* Fo: vi.*verso* (see list A):
Jerusalem . . . is fie from all captiuite & daunger
Fo: xxiiii. *recto*:
man is delyuered from Egipt/ and from the daunger of Pharao: that is to say/ from

synne & from the tyranny and power
of . . . the dyuell.

George Joye in his translation of Bucer's Psalms
(see list B) (1530) has:

> The argument into the .60. psal.
> In this psal. David remembreth howe God
> some tymes in his wrathe leveth his people
> in the daunger of theyr enymes.

Sir T. Elyot *Bankette of Sapience* p. 35 *recto*:

> whan thou perceyuest him [thyn ennemy]
> to be in thy danger, thynke that to be
> vengeance sufficient . . .

Tyndale in his translation of Erasmus' *Enchiridion*
sig.E.iij.*recto* has:

> [Jacob . . . hath euer Esau suspected] neyther
> dare come within his daunger.

None of these quotations could dismiss the thought
that girls and animals were running what T.S.
Eliot once called 'a terrible risk'.

take bread]

In the commonplace-book kept by a London
merchant, Richard Hill (last entry *circa* 1536),
there is a poem about women with this phrase:

> Sum be tame, I vnderstond

* man's

> Sum will take bred at a mannus* hand

range]

The verb is normally used of wild animals moving
about freely in search of food. A close parallel
showing its use for fickle women is to be found
in *The Paradyse of daynty deuises* 1576 p. 63:
a poem by M. Edwards:

> A. Why then there is no choice, but all
>   women will chaunge.
> B. As men doe vse so, some women doe
>   loue to raunge . . .

Another suggestive parallel to Wyatt's use of this
language to describe court behaviour can be found
in Spenser's *Mother Hubberds Tale*:

> But tell vs (said the Ape) we doo you pray,
> Who now in Court doth beare the greatest
>   sway . . .
> Marie (said he) the highest now in grace,
> Be the wilde beasts, that swiftest are in
>   chace . . .
> So wilde a beast so tame ytaught to bee,

* obedient

And buxome* to his bands, is ioy to see . . .
But his late chayne his Liege vnmeete
   esteemeth;
For so braue beasts she loueth best to see,
In the wilde forrest raunging fresh and free.

Thanked be fortune]

The phrase occurs at the opening of Book Four of
Chaucer's *Troilus and Criseyde*:
   But al to lytel/ welaway the whyle
   Lasteth such ioye/ ythonked be fortune
   That semeth trewest/ whan she wol begyle . . .
Wyatt used the phrase in *Since love is such*, where
he was rejoicing that for him love was over and
done with:
   And few there is but first or last
   A time in love once shall they have,
   And glad I am my time is past,
   Henceforth my freedom to withsave.
   Now in my heart there shall I grave
   The grounded grace that now I taste:
   Thanked be fortune, that me gave
   So fair a gift, so sure and fast.

In especial]

This was the common form in Wyatt's day; sometimes written as one word.

after . . . guise]

'In a pleasing fashion'. This might refer to fashion
in clothes, as in Skelton's *Elynour Rummyng*:
   With clothes vpon her hed . . .

* coiled

   Wrythen* in wonder wyse
   After the Sarasyns gyse . . .

loose gown]

Wyatt's contemporaries may have had an exact
picture of this garment and the moral and social
significance of wearing it in this situation. Some
resemblance may be found in Marlowe's translation of Ovid's *Amores* I,v. *Corinnae concubitus*:
      . . . uppon a bedde I lay, . . .
   Then came *Corinna* in a long loose gowne . . .
   I snatcht her gowne: being thin, the harme
      was small . . .
   What armes and shoulders did I touch and
      see . . .
      . . . all likt me passing well . . .,
But there the resemblance stops.

long and small]

'Agreeably slender in shape'. Charles d'Orléans has a roundel beginning: [4137]

> The smyling mouth and laughyng eyen gray
> The brestis rounde and long smal armys
>   twayne . . .

Caxton said that Dido's hands were 'soupple and thynne, with long fyngers and smalle . . .'

This meaning is brought out in Book Three of Chaucer's *Troilus and Criseyde*, where he is describing the hero's caresses:

> Her armes small/ her streyght backe & softe
> Her sydes longe/ flesshly/ smothe/ and white

*called blessings down on?

> He gan to stroke/ & good thrifte bade* ful
>   ofte
> Her snowysse throte/ her brestes rounde &
>   lyte . . .

But all is turned . . . fashion]

Sir T. Elyot *Pasquil the Playne* (1533) p. 13 *recto*:

> But now all this is tourned into an other
>   fascion . . .

thorough]

'Through'.

gentleness]

The word on which the whole poem turns, for it determines the level on the human scale of these affairs of the heart, at least as concerns the male speaker. For he is claiming that he has treated each woman with the loyalty and courtesy of a true knight. The precise meaning of *gentleness* is determined in a stanza from an adaptation of Petrarch (*Mine old dear Enemy*) where the schooling of Love, which turns *l'homme moyen sensuel* into a worthy lover is outlined:

> Ever more thus to content his mistress
> That was his only frame of honesty.

* continuously

> I steered him still* toward gentleness
> And caused him to regard fidelity,
> Patience I taught him in adversity.
> Such virtues he learned in my great school . . .

strange fashion]

One meaning would be 'newfangled'.

forsaking]

The pathos in the word can be gathered from Wyatt's various uses, as when addressing God in the Psalms, when referring to his friends, as in

Luck, my fair, and, above all, in *Disdain me not*, particularly in these lines:

> Forsake me not till I deserve

and

> Forsake me not now for no new.

leave to go] The whole line treats the lady as *royalty*. It is well illustrated in Chaucer's *Legend of Good Women* (2279):

> This olde Pandion, this kyng, gan wepe
> For tendernesse of herte, for to leue
> His doughter gon, and for to yeue* her leue;
> Of al this world he loued nothyng so;
> But at the last leue hath she to go . . .

* give

goodness] The OED has a quotation of 1548:

> The kynge of hys goodnes remitted their offence . . .

newfangleness] A word that was extensively used from Chaucer's time to express all the forms of conservative dislike of change and instability. It had a particular application to mutability in love relations. In *The Squire's Tale* Chaucer expounds the thought that love itself is by nature changeable, fickle and unreliable:

> Men loue of propyr kynde* newefangylnesse
> As bryddis* doon that men in cagis fede
> For theyh* thou nyght & day take of hem hede
> Ande straw her* cage feyre & softe as silk
> Ande yeue* hem suger hony brede ande mylk
> Yet ryght anone as that hys dore is vp
> He wyth hys feet spurneth doun hys cup
> Ande to the woode he wol ande wormes ete
> So newfangyl ben they of her* mete
> Ande loue noueltres of proper kynde
> No gentylnesse of bloode may hym bynde.

* by nature
* birds
* though
* their
* give

* their

Some darker thoughts on our nature can be found in the opening of *The Manciple's Tale*:

> Flessh is so newfangyl wyth myschaunce
> That we ne konne in no thyng haue plesaunce
> That sownyth* vnto vertu ony whyle*

* is consonant with
* at any time

kindly]
Pronounced 'kindily'. At least two meanings are to be entertained. 'According to female nature', as in the poem beginning *Divers doth use*, which ends:

> I will not wail, lament, nor yet be sad,
> Nor call her false that falsely did me feed,
> But let it pass, and think it is of kind
> That often change doth please a woman's
>   mind . . .

and 'considerately'.

served]
Quite simply, 'treated'.

deserved]
The deliberate ambiguity of the poem is preserved in this word, which refers as much to praise as to blame.

WYATT'S USE OF SET PHRASES IN *AND WILT THOU*

The commentator cannot *explain* the magical beauty of this poem, but some expression of wonder and amazement is in place once it is recognized that there are many set phrases in this poem, phrases which must have been portable properties, passed round and passed down from one poet to another. At any rate Wyatt himself has used them in other poems without raising their quality above the mediocre. How they come to be magically transformed here is to me a mystery. While it does not explain anything to recall the facts, it may serve to remind the reader of the paradox of original creation in this field of writing.

1) The first example is the use of *thus* in the refrain line:
> And wilt thou leave me thus?

The implications, 'in such a brutal manner' and 'in such a desperate state', are brought out in two other poems, *Farewell, all my welfare*, where we find:
> To leave me thus all comfortless

and *Disdain me not*, which has these lines:
> Forsake me not now for no new
> Thus leave me not.

2) *Say nay*] In *What should I say*
          Can ye say nay . . .?

3) *for shame*] A similar appeal (also rhyming with *blame*)
     can be found in the poem *Heaven and earth*:
          Why do I die? Alas, for shame, for shame!

4) *long*] A traditional element in the lover's complaint,
     as in *Forget not yet*:
          Forget not yet thine own approved,
          The which so long hath thee so loved.

5) *wealth and woe*] 'In good and bad fortune' as in *How
     should I*:
          I never meant
          For to repent
        In wealth ne yet in woe.
     Also in *I have sought*:
          All shall be one in wealth or woe.
     The phrase seems to have run parallel with: *weal and
     woe*.

6) *pain nor smart*]   In *Absence absenting* we find
          Farewell, all pleasure! Welcome, pain and smart!
     And in *If with complaint*:
          This restless pain and smart.

7) *have . . . pity*] In *Madame, withouten* we have
          And if of one that burneth alway
          Ye have any pity at all . . .

And wilt thou

blame]   'My complaint, making you responsible for, and
                            accusing you of causing, my pain.' As a verb it is
                            used in a similar sense in *If it be so*:
                                Then may I well blame thy cruelty . . .

grame]   'Trouble' The word is rare in Wyatt's poetry, and
                            he may in fact have been the last reputable poet to
                            use the phrase: grief and grame. But it was a
                            common set phrase before his day. In *Cursor
                            Mundi/* 8405 we find: *grefe ne grame*. There is a

good illustration in a Bodley manuscript, Rawl. poet. 36, printed in *Religious Lyrics of the XVth Century*, ed. Carleton Brown, 1939, No. 172, where the rhyme words are fame, game and shame:

> Whan gladnes growyth in to grame . . .

among]   'All the while without breaking off'. Wyatt uses the word again in this sense and at the end of a line in *My hope, alas*:

> And to my self I said among . . .

so strong]   I have been unable to find another use of the phrase in this sense, which I take to be, 'So unfeeling, so stubbornly tenacious of its purpose.'

to depart]   'To be severed', as in Caxton (OED, 1483):

> That god hath ioyned man may not departe

Quondam was I

This is a wittier version of the following poem, also found only in the Trinity College, Dublin manuscript, and here modernised:

> Once in your grace I know I was,
>   Even as well as now is he,
> Though fortune so hath turned my case,
>   That I am down, and he full high,
>   Yet once I was.
>
> Once I was he that did you please
>   So well that nothing did I doubt,
> And though that now ye think it ease
>   To take him in and throw me out,
>   Yet once I was.
>
> Once I was he in times past
>   That as your own ye did retain,
> And though you have me now outcast,
>   Showing untruth in you to reign,
>   Yet once I was.
>
> Once I was he that knit the knot
>   The which ye swore not to unknit,
> And though ye feign it now forgot

In using your newfangled wit,
Yet once I was.

Once I was he to whom ye said,
'Welcome, my joy, my whole delight!'
And though ye are now well apaid,
Of me, your own, to claim ye quit,
Yet once I was.

Once I was he to whom ye spake,
'Have here my heart, it is thy own.'
And though these words ye now forsake,
Saying thereof my part is none,
Yet once I was.

Once I was he before rehearsed,
And now am he that needs must die,
And though I die, yet at the least
In your remembrance let it lie
That once I was.

Quondam] 'Once upon a time'. 'A quondam' was a regular phrase for some one who once held a post but had been ejected from it. The word itself is a self-mocking, ironic variant on the pathetic 'once I was', and corresponds to our modern wry expressions for the rejected politician, such as 'has-been'. A similar self-ironical application of the word can be found in a letter of 1554, written in an Oxford prison, 'Bocardo', 'a stinking and filthy prison for drunkards and harlots', to which Ridley had been sent on being deprived of his bishopric. He wrote:

> As yet there was never learned man, or any scholar or other, that visited us since we came into Bocardo, which now in Oxford may be called a college of quondams.

grace] 'Favour'. The OED rightly traces this sense back to the king's regard for his subjects:
1463 That he stonde welle and cler in the kyngges grace . . .
It then records the extension to the world of aristocratic courtship:
1489 And how he was in her goode grace, and she lyke wyse in his . . .

But the dictionary does not record the cynical use of the word, of which there is an excellent illustration in the religious controversy between Sir Thomas More and William Tyndale, arising from his translation of the New Testament. More objected:

> he chaungeth commonly the name of grace into this worde fauour, where as euery fauour is not grace in english: for in some fauoure there is little grace. (*Workes* p. 222 H)

To which Tyndale retorted that there was little goodness in some grace:

> And when we saye he stondeth well in my ladis grace we vnderstonde no greate godly fauoure.

trod the trace]

'Followed down the beaten track'. Since both verb and noun could also apply to dancing, we might consider the meaning 'dance the old daunce' as used by Chaucer of his Wife of Bath:

> Of remedyes of loue she coude per chaunce
> For of that arte she coude the olde daunce

which would suggest the gloss, 'when you have been through all the regular stages of a love-affair'.

dissever]

A word not found elsewhere in Wyatt. His word was *depart*, as in *And wilt thou*:

> That hath given thee my heart
> Never for to depart . . .

the more]

Wyatt wrote 'the mo', as elsewhere in his poems. It refers to the many lovers who have been rejected. The sense of being one of a large company comes out well in Nicholas Udall's translation of Erasmus' *Apophthegmata* p. 341 *verso*:

> *Demosthenes* is reported to haue sailled on a tyme to ye citee of *Corinthe*, enticed & allured with the fame of *Lais* a *Courtisan* there of greate name, to thentente that he also emong the mo mighte haue his pleasure of the paramour . . .

Similarly, on p. 237, we find:

> the said *Herode* had commaunded to bee murdreed & slain all ye young babes in Jewrie as many as wer not aboue ye age of

                         twoo yeres, & how that emong ye moo
                         Herode his owne soonne also had gon to
                         ye potte . . .

But what though]   'Even if', 'in spite of the fact that . . .'

What no, pardie

pardie]   A form of saying, 'By God!' with varying degrees
                         of emphasis, recorded as early as 1290.

make . . . lure]   The practice of hawking is at the bottom of this
                         language. Some birds are reclaimed by the falcon-
                         er's voice calling them down from the air. The
                         falcon itself was brought down by the shaking or
                         whirling of a lure, which usually consisted of a
                         bunch of feathers attached by a long cord or
                         leather thong. An attractive morsel of food, such
                         as a pullet, was presented in this apparatus, and
                         the falcon, on catching sight of it, would usually
                         pounce at once.
                             When the phrase was used of human actions,
                         as in the warning given to Chaucer's Manciple:
                             Another day he wyl perauenture
                             Recleyme the and bryng the to lure
                         [*The Manciple's Prologue*, lines 71-72] the basic
                         idea is not 'entice' but 'bring under the control
                         of a master'. A good example comes in Skelton's
                         Why come ye nat to courte, where Wolsey's
                         domination of the whole state apparatus is ex-
                         pressed in the image:
                             The red hat with his lure
* under his control   Bryngeth all thynges vnder cure.*
                             That this is true also of love relations, such as
                         those referred to in Skelton's *Phyllyp Sparowe*:
                             With wordes of pleasure
                             She wold make to the lure
                             And any man conuert
                             To gyue her his hole hert . . .
                         is made probable by a passage added to the trans-
                         lation of Erasmus' *Enchiridion*, where the task
                         was to render these words: *pendere de nutu
                         dominae, pati regnum mulierculae* – to hang on
                         his mistress' nod, to be subject to the tyranny

of a mere girl — where the translator, Tyndale,
let himself go as follows:
> Set before thyne eyen howe vngoodly it
> is/ howe altogyder a mad thing to loue/
> to waxe pale/ to be made leane/ to wepe/
> to flatter/ and shamfully to submyt thy
> selfe vnto a stynkyng harlot most fylthy
> and rotten/ to gape & synge all nyght at
> her chambre wyndowe/ to be made to the
> lure & be obedyent at a becke/ nor dare do
> any thing except she nod or wagge her
> heed . . . [sig.Q.vij. *recto*]

contraring]

'Saying one thing and looking another, your
behaviour contradicting your words', from a verb
contrair, Fr. *contrarier*, as in Sir Thomas More's
Workes p. 262H, where he is describing the un-
masking of a crypto-Lutheran:
> Setting neuerthelesse all the colours he
> coude to make it seme that though the
> wordes which they spake or wrote were
> straunge & contrarye to right beleue, yet
> the/ effect of their mening was not much dis-
> crepant from the trew fayth of chrystes
> church. Howbeit whan he was reasoned with
> all, & sawe that he could not so shifte it of,
> but that for any coloure he could finde one
> part of hys tale euer contraried another, at
> last he shewed plainly their oppinions . . .

counterweighing]   'Doling out successively equal quantities of'.

trayed]   'Betrayed'.

craft . . .ure]   'Where sexual duplicity is practised'.

cure]   'Loving attention', as in Psalm 51:
> From Thine eyes' cure cast me not in unrest

procure . . .to]   Palsgrave offered as a translation of *je procure*:
> 'I deuyse meanes to bringe a thynge to
> passe'.

pure]   'Genuine', 'uncontaminated', as in Tyndale, *Matt./*
5/8:
> Blessed are the pure in herte.

unstable . . . wavering]   All these words are defined against a desired opposite of loyalty and steadfastness.

without recure   'Without any possibility of putting things right'.
See Psalm 6:
I , Lord, am strayed, I, sick without recure

Whoso list to hunt

As Wyatt's 'source' it has become customary to name Petrarch's sonnet
No. CXC, which I here print as the author wrote it:

> *Una candida cerua sopra lerba*
> > *Verde mapparue con duo corna doro*
> > *Fra due riuiere allombra dun alloro*
> > *Leuandol sole a la stagione acerba.*
>
> *Era sua uista si dolce superba*
> > *Chi lasciai per seguirla ogni lauoro*
> > *Come lauaro chencercar tesoro*
> > *Con diletto laffanno disacerba.*
>
> *Nessun mi tocchi al bel collo dintorno*
> > *Scritto auea di diamanti & di topaçi*
> > *Libera farmi al mio cesare parue.*
>
> *Et eral sol gia uolto al meçço giorno*
> > *Gliocchi miei stanchi di mirar non saçi*
> > *Quandio caddi nelacqua & ella sparue.*

But, as the following rough translation indicates, Wyatt shows no interest
in the beautiful religious symbolism:

> As the sun was rising in the bitter season, a white hind with two
> golden horns appeared to me in the shade of a laurel on the green
> grass between two streams. So pleasant-proud was its appearance
> that I left my work, and, like a miser in whom the pleasure of
> hunting for treasure mitigates the inherent vexations, I followed the
> hind. Round its fair neck was written in diamonds and topazes:
> Let no man touch me, for Caesar's will is that I remain free. The sun
> had reached midday when, my eyes weary but not satiated with
> gazing, I fell into the water, and the hind disappeared.

and has transformed the situation to one familiar to members of an earthy
Tudor court, where the king might earmark a desirable girl and warn his non-
royal rivals to make way for him.

Great as is the difference between Wyatt's sonnet and Petrarch's, it is
plausible to suppose that it was this Italian poem which started Wyatt off.

We have the evidence of much closer translations to support the view that Wyatt frequently turned to the *Canzoniere* for starting-points. One small difference, the treatment of the motto on the diamond collar, has caused some editors to propose another Italian sonnet as Wyatt's model. I have given the passage where the resemblance occurs in its place in the following commentary, but I do not believe that Wyatt was familiar with the work of Romanello.

Editors sometimes allow themselves to suppose that Wyatt was here alluding to Anne Boleyn. I suppose that by the time that Henry began to put his collar round her neck Wyatt had ceased to be her lover, as is explained in the commentary on *Some time I fled*. On the other hand, the 'stubborn tradition', as it has been called, evidently goes back to the time of composition, as is shown by the reference to this poem in George Wyatt's papers.

to hunt]	Wyatt may have counted these two words as one syllable.
vain travail]	'Fruitless labour'.
farthest . . . behind]	'At the back of the hunt'. But for its application to love, see Chaucer in Book Two of *Troilus and Criseyde*, where (1106) Criseyde asks Pandarus:
	Howe ferforth be ye putte in loues daunce?
	and he answers:
	I hop alwaye behynde.
fleeth]	To be scanned as a monosyllable, as in the Dub spelling *flyth*.
Fainting]	'Losing strength'.
net . . . wind]	Wyatt throughout his poems shows a special fondness for 'impossibles'. Erasmus collected many such proverbs in his *Adagia*. In col. 176 we find:
	Reti uentos uenaris . . . id est Reti uentos captas. i.e. you hunt the winds with a net, you try to grasp the winds with a net.
	But Wyatt might have found the phrase in Petrarch *Rime* CCXXXIX /37:
	In rete accolgo l'aura
	I gather the wind in a net.
	It is just possible that Wyatt knew Sannazaro *Arcadia* 8/10–12:
	Nell' onde solca e nell'arene semina,
	e'l vago vento spera in rete accogliere
	chi sue speranze fonda in cor di femina.

He ploughs in the waves and sows in the sands and hopes to get the wandering wind in a net who founds his hopes on the heart of a woman.

graven]

Other contemporary forms of the participle are, *grave*, *graved*, and *y-grave*, *ygrauyn*. The manuscripts of *Marvel no more* have:

And in my hert also
Is graven with lettres diepe

which suggests that the word was scanned as a monosyllable.

diamonds]

In *The Passetyme of Pleasure* (169–172) Stephen Hawes writes of two symbolical white greyhounds that:

Theyr colers were of golde and of tyssue fyne
Wherin theyr names appered by scrypture
Of Dyamondes that clerely do shyne.
The lettres were grauen fayre and pure . . .

Noli me tangere]

We are not obliged to suppose that Wyatt knew a sonnet written in imitation of Petrarch's by Giovanni Antonio Romanello, beginning *Vna cerua gentil*, which has these lines:

Toccar non lice la mia carne intera
Caesaris enim sum

It is not allowed to touch my unsullied flesh, for I belong to Caesar

since Wyatt may have been familiar with other forms of this Latin prohibition, 'Keep off, crown property'. Nor need we find blasphemy in the use of a Biblical phrase, the very words, in the Vulgate, used to rebuke Mary when she mistook the risen Christ for a gardener, 'touche me not, for I am not yet ascended to my father', since the phrase has passed into ironic popular speech in various ways. The OED quotes Thackeray for:

The saucy little beauty . . . assumed a touch-me-not air . . . and the French have a slightly different phrase:

un petit air de sainte nitouche

for a demure look.

Caesar's I am]

George Wyatt, in his 'Defence' of the poet, reports of Anne Boleyn:

again, she had her usuall words, I am Ceasars [*sic*] all, let none ells touche mee.
(D.M. Loades, *The Papers of George Wyatt Esquire*, 1968, pp. 185, 187.)

And ... tame]   If Wyatt did not allow *wylde* the metrical force of two syllables, it is hard to scan this line as of the same length as the others. (In the Dublin MS the line begins: wyld to be caught . . .)

The bird that

(For a discussion of this poem and the grounds for its inclusion in the canon, see the Critical Introduction pp. 11-16).

there as]   'There, in that place'.

taken ... leave]   'Bid a final, solemn, ceremonial farewell to'.

mine host]   Not the landlord of an inn but 'the man who lodges and entertains another in his house: the correlative of *guest*', as at the end of the Epistle to the Romans, where Tyndale has:
> Gaius myne hoste and the hoste of all the congregacions . . .

harbour]   'Provide a lodging or lodging-place for'.

Of ... conceive]   The syntax is uncharacteristically indeterminate. If it depends on *her choice*, the meaning might be 'of one I have now come to understand as permanently fickle'.

chief]   'Principally'.

check]   The noun means, 'A false stoop, when a hawk forsakes her proper game, and pursues some baser game that crosses her flight'. 'To check at the fist' means 'to refuse to come to the falconer's fist'. But *check* itself means merely 'to make a check', as in J. Heywood *A sixt hundred of Epigrammes* (1562):
> lewre falcones when ye list
> They wyll checke oft, but neuer come to the fist.

fair]   'Gently, with no fuss'.

What should I

led]   i.e. by the nose.

my part]   An obscure expression, perhaps, 'my share in mutual love'.

You . . . take]   If a satisfactory meaning for this line could be found, it might be possible to restore the missing line in the stanza.

Is . . . mind]   As in *What needeth these*:
                                    To rob your good iwis is not my mind . . .

Your . . . kind]   No satisfactory suggestion has been made to supply the line missing here. *Kind* is merely one of the conventional words in *-ind*.

And . . . find]   As in *Ah, Robin*:
                                    Thou art happy while that doth last,
                                        But I say as I find,
                                    That women's love is but a blast
                                    And turneth like the wind.

So . . . trust]   An illustration occurs in Lydgate's poem, *Amor uincit omnia:*
                                    As thow fyndest, so make thyn owne
* surety   suerte*
                                and
                                    Lete al men trust as that they causes fynde . . .

But that]   A regular contemporary use after verbs of denying. The force is the same as the modern, 'Can you deny you said . . .?'

obeyed]   Since in all his extant love poems Wyatt never speaks of obedience, its use here raises the possibility that he had the marriage service in mind. Some of the English phrases used in contemporary marriage services are printed by William Maskell in his *Monumenta Ritualia Ecclesiae Anglicanae* (1882) Vol. I, *e.g.* a manuscript Salisbury manual is said to have these words: '*N*. take the, *N*. to myn wedded wyf, to have and to hólde from this day forward, for beter for wers, for richere for porere, for fayrere for fowlere, in seknes and in helthe, til dethe us departe'. The bride in addition promised, 'to be boner and buxum as a wyf owyd to hur husband'. The question put to the bridegroom was, 'Wil tow have this woman to thin wif, and loue here, and worschipe here, and hold hire and kepe here, in seknes and in hele, as an housbonde owyth to his wif, and alle other women to forsaken for hire, and only to drawe to hire as longe as yowre bothe lyues to gedere lasten?' The pair completed their promise with, 'and therto I plight the myn trouthe'. The bride's promise to obey, hidden in the old phraseology, 'to be bonere and buxum in bedde and at the borde', is plainly to be seen in the priest's question: '*Vis habere hunc virum in sponsum et ei obedire et seruire . . .?*' Will you have this man as your husband to serve and obey? The poem may therefore be referring to his adulterous wife.

ere that]   'Before I knew what was going on'.
In several poems in the Devonshire manuscript the word *ere* is written *ore* and *or.*

Farewell, unkissed]   Almost a polite form of 'to hell with you'. That the phrase had become proverbial by Chaucer's time we may judge from a quotation in OED of 1401:

> On old Englis it is said,
> unkissid is unknowun . . .

and from the way it is introduced by Chaucer into his *Troilus and Criseyde* Book I/809:

> Unknowe, vnkist, and lost that is vnsought . . .

Heywood *Prouerbes* /732:

> She and I haue shaken handes. Farewell vnkyst.
> And thus with a becke as good as a dieu gard,
> She flang fro me, and I from her . . .

/977:

> Vnknowne vnkyst, it is lost that is vnsought

Madame, withouten

This poem incidentally provides an opportunity to compare the Italian, French, and English national characters, since there are extant three poems on the same topic which are sufficiently alike for their differences to be significant. Although the dates of their composition cannot be precisely fixed, the Italian poet was clearly the first to produce a text, but the succeeding versions all have independent variants. The Frenchman took as many liberties as Wyatt did with this common 'source'. Wyatt may have had the French before him as well as the Italian while composing his own poem.* For these reasons we may be glad to have the foreign versions before us while considering Wyatt's poem. The Italian poem is the work of Dragonetto Bonifacio and the French is by Mellin de Saint-Gelais:

> *Madonna, non so dir tante parole.*
> *o uoi uolet' o no. Se uoi uolete,*
> *oprat' al gran bisogn' il uostro senno*
> *che uoi saret' intesa per un cenno*
> *& se d'un che sempr' arde al fin ui dole,*
> *un bel si un bel no gli respondete;*
> *se'l sar' un si, un si scriuero'n rima,*
> *se'l sar' un no, amici come prima;*
> *uoi trouaret' un'altr'amante & io*
> *non potend' esser uostro, saro mio.*

Lady, I cannot use so many words. You either are willing or you aren't. If you are, apply your good sense to the wonderful opportunity, for you will be understood at a wink. And if you in the end feel sorry for one who is constantly on fire, answer with a fair 'yes' or 'no'. If your answer is 'yes', I'll write my consent to rhyme with yours. If it is 'no' — friends as at first. You will find another lover, and I, not being able to be yours, shall be my own.

> *S'amour vous a donné mon coeur en gage,*
> *De quoy vous sert user tant de langage?*
> *Ou vous voulez, ou vous ne voulez point;*
> *Quand vous voudriez deux mille ans deviser,*
> *Si faudroit-il à la fin s'aviser*
> *Qu'on s'en ennuye et venir à un point;*
> *Si vous voulez, ne faites que branler,*
> *Car j'entendray le moindre signe en l'air,*
> *Et vous seray ami non decevant.*
> *S'il ne vous plaist? amis comme devant!*
> *Un autre aurez, et moy, ne pouvant estre*
> *Servant de vous, de moy je seray maistre.*

* The Dublin manuscript version opens with these words: *Mestris what nedis many words.* There is nothing like this in the Italian, but the French has: *De quoy vous sert user tant de langage?* And the Egerton manuscript has: *Ye shall another man obtain,* which is close to the French: *Un autre aurez.* Wyatt has also converted a *dizain* into a *douzain.*

Since Love has pawned my heart to you, what is the point of so much verbiage? You are either willing or you aren't. Even if you took two thousand years to discuss the matter, you would have in the end to recognize that boredom ensues, and so make up your mind. If you are willing, all I need is a wink. The slightest hint will be picked up by me, and I shall be your loyal lover. Perhaps you do not care? Friends as before! You shall have another man, and I, not being able to be your servant, will become my own master.

many words]	*Of many words* means 'wordy', the opposite of *of few words*, as in the Answer to this poem. The idiom seems to be similar to the one we find in Chaucer's *Prologue* to the Canterbury Tales/ 808-809:

> Tel me anone, withouten wordes mo,
> Ande I wyl erly shape me therfore.

(The variant in the Dublin manuscript is also Chaucerian: *what nedeth wordes mo?*)

Once]	'Eventually', 'the day must come when'.
bourds]	'Jokes', 'mockery'. The general sense is, 'stop playing about and giving evasive, un-serious answers'. Wyatt was in a more pathetic mood in *Where shall I have*:

> Nought moveth you my deadly moan,
> But all you turn it into bourds.

use your wit]	This is close to the Italian '*oprat*'. . . *il uostro senno*'.
beck]	'A silent signal indicating assent or notifying a command'. 'To be at the beck and call' of a woman was thought to be a matter of reproach by some divines. A good instance may be found in a note in the Commentary on *What no, pardie*. Erasmus gave this advice to a young wife:

> Be your selfe alwayes redy at a becke, berynge continuali in minde what reuerence the wife oweth vnto her husband (*A merry dialogue*, 1557, sig. cii. *recto*).

fair]	'Truly', 'courteously'.
fain]	'Well-pleased'.

The epigram seems to call for an answer. (There were many coarse replies to the Italian version.) An English reply was supplied in both manuscripts, but not in Tottel. The general rule was for the 'answer' to be in the same metre and to answer the original point by point. It was usually the work of the author of the original. Although in this case I do not suppose that this 'Answer' was written by Wyatt, I do think that the poem could help us to understand the import of *Madame, withouten*, and that any comments will have the same effect.

Answer

Of few words, sir, ye seem to be,
    And where I doubted what I would do,
Your quick request hath caused me
    Quickly to tell what ye shall trust to.

He that will be called with a beck
    Makes hasty suit on light desire,
Is ever ready to the check,
    And burneth in no wasting fire.

But whether ye be lief or loath,
    Or whether it grieve ye light or sore,
I am at a point. I have made an oath.
    Content ye with nay, ye get no more.

Of few words]	A man of few words is sparing of speech.
quick]	'Lively', 'prompt', 'witty'.
hasty suit]	'Eager chase'.
ready . . . check]	'Quick to follow any inferior game that crosses the hawk's flight'.
wasting fire]	The classical description of the effects of love occurs in Horace's *Odes* Book I/13, where he describes how he was burning inwardly with a slow, wasting fire: *lentis penitus macerer ignibus* I am wasted deeply within with slow-burning fires.
lief or loath]	'Willing or unwilling'. The phrase occurs in Chaucer's *Knight's Tale*/1837: al be hym loth or leef and in the *Merchant's Tale*/1961: be she leet or loth . . . Sir Thomas More in his poem 'to them that seke fortune' has: but be you liefe or lothe, Holde you content . . .

grieve . . . sore]   A common phrase in the Chaucerian corpus, as
                              in the *Romaunt of the Rose*/4530:
                                   doth me soore greue

I . . . point]   'My mind is made up'. The same use is found in
                          Sir Thomas More's *The historie of king Richard
                          the thirde*:
                                   And albeit he would gladly that she shold
                                   take it wel, yet was at a pointe in his owne
                                   mynde, toke she it wel or otherwise.

                          There is a variant of this poem in the Dublin
                          Manuscript which ends:

                                   The yea desired, the nay not.
                                        No grief so great, nor desire so sore
                                   But that I may forbear to dote.
                                        If yea, forever; if nay, no more

                                   To trouble ye thus: speke on, therefore.
                                        If that ye will, say yea; if not,
                                   We shall be friends even as before,
                                        And I mine own that yours may not.

WYATT AND ANNE BOLEYN

The commentary is virtually treating as an established fact what is
merely highly probable, that every statement in *Sometime I fled*
has an autobiographical reference, and that it passes in review all
the stages of a love-affair with Anne Boleyn. To begin with the
least controversial remark:

> And now I follow . . .
> From Dover to Calais against my mind . . .

I take it that this refers to a notable moment in Anne Boleyn's
progress to her exalted position as King Henry's wife. From
September 1, 1532, when she was created a Marchioness, it
became obvious to all court observers that she was both the reign-
ing mistress and the future Queen. Henry was anxious to show her
off to Francis I, and on October 11 a magnificent party of English

nobility accompanied the pair from Dover to Calais.

This state occasion was recorded in detail by contemporaries in France and England. Wynkyn de Worde brought out a pamphlet entitled, 'The maner of the tryumphe at Caleys and Bulleyn'. Most of the evidence was collected in a monograph by A. Hamy in 1898. One item omitted is a report by a contemporary Spanish merchant living in London. His *Crónica* is rightly ignored by historians as it contains much romance and more nonsense and a great deal of biassed prejudice. But the author had access to certain details otherwise unknown, which he derived from Cromwell's nephew, Richard, and possibly from Wyatt's son, Thomas. Consequently, the historically worthless chronicle becomes an authority on minute episodes in which these two men were concerned. It has the best account of Cromwell's last words on the scaffold. The following extract contains no new facts, but gives the flavour of contemporary gossip:

Chapter XVI.
How the King went over to Calais with his queen, Anne.

The King was so madly in love with his new Queen that he made up his mind to cross over to Calais and to take her with him to show her to the King of France, and he made plans to go in triumph to hold talks with the King of France. So he left England and stayed in Calais. The King of France, who was at Boulogne, came to Calais, and there were magnificent receptions and many banquets. Queen Anne paid great respect to the French King. She had been at his court when she was a girl. Some even said she had been on the best of terms with the Admiral.

And Wyatt? *Mais que diable allait-il faire dans cette galère?* The printed pamphlet does not mention him, but a paper at Longleat includes him and four servants among many of his friends, relations, and enemies (and the young Earl of Surrey) as having gone on the trip. So far as external events go, then, Wyatt has been true to the facts. May we also take him at his word about his own state of mind both at the time of the crossing and in the years preceding?

No doubt his social position at court required his presence at Calais, and the obligation may have been irksome for many reasons. But if we press the question, what exactly did he feel for Anne at the time, much turns on the interpretation of 'quenched coals'. If we accept the definition given in the commentary, we may still suppose that he had a residue of kindly feeling left in 1532, even if the phrase will not square with the implied feeling of *Whoso list to hunt*. And if we ask what went before, the emphasis on coals that once were burning, on the flight, presumably abroad, even if only as far as Calais, and above all, the complex image in the last line of the poem, force a biographer to research into a true, passionate and *mouvementé* story.

But research is fruitless if there are no records. Since there are no hard facts, we have to squeeze what we can out of fictions. The Spanish chronicler, who is so knowledgeable about what happened to Wyatt in 1536, when he was arrested and put into the Tower to await trial and execution, claims to know the contents of a letter Wyatt was induced to write to the King about his relations with Anne Boleyn. It is possible that 'evidence' was required in case the faked trial of the Queen did not go the way Henry wanted, and there may have been an original letter by Wyatt, which has not survived. But between such an original and what the Spaniard wrote there is much folk fancy and malice against the dead Queen. Perhaps nevertheless a drop of reality is mixed up in the tale, and if taken sceptically can assist us to cross over to the times in which Wyatt lived and loved.

Chapter XXXI.
How Master Wyatt wrote a letter to the King, and how he was pardoned.

The night before they were to take out the Duke and the others to cut off their heads, our good Wyatt was given assurance that he would not be joining them. So he took paper and ink and wrote the following letter to the King:

Your Majesty knows that you said to me before you married the Queen, "Wyatt, I am thinking of marrying Anne Boleyn. What have you to say?" I told your Majesty that you should not do it, and when you asked me why, I said she was a bad woman, whereupon your Majesty flew into a rage and forbade me to appear at court for the next two years. Since you did not then wish to hear my reasons, what I could not say after that, I shall now put down in writing.

One day when the Lady Anne's mother and father were in attendance at Court eight miles from Greenwich, where, as everybody knows, the court was then established, that very evening I took horse and arrived there just when Anne Boleyn had gone to bed. I entered her chamber, and when she caught sight of me she cried out, "Jesus, Wyatt, what are you doing here at this time of night?" "Mistress", I replied, "my tormented heart which has been yours so long has drawn me here into your presence in hope of some comfort and that you may rue upon my grievous pain." Then I went up to her bed and kissed her. She submitted without a murmur. I put my hands round her breasts and still she said nothing, and when I allowed my hands to stray lower down, still she stayed mute and mum. I was just going to take off my clothes when there came a terrible banging overhead. The lady rose from her bed and put on her petticoat and went out by a staircase behind her bed-head. I waited for more than an hour, and when she returned she would not let me come to her.

I think I suffered the same fate as an Italian gentleman who, like me, was head over heels in love with a lady, and had brought his good fortune to the very same point. He also heard a terrible banging and his lady left him to go upstairs. But the Italian was more of a man of the world than I was, for as soon as his lady left him he followed close after and caught her sporting with a stable lad. I think I should have made a similar discovery if I had had the wit to creep after her and find what she had been up to.

Your Majesty must be told that less than a week after that night I had her at my will, and

if your Grace had permitted me to speak when
you banished me, I should have told you all that
I have here written.

Some time I fled

Some . . . land]

No biographer has been able to establish beyond
doubt when or where Wyatt went. 'Sometime'
would suggest 'on one occasion'.

fire]

Wyatt scanned this as a word of two syllables.

coals . . . quent]

'Quenched', 'dead'. It could, however, refer to
cinders, 'small pieces of coal from which the
gaseous or volatile constituents have been burnt,
but which retain much of the carbon, so that they
are capable of further combustion without flame.'
Chaucer uses the phrase in two very different con-
texts to mark the opposition between hot and
cold love, e.g. in his *Knight's Tale*/2319:
    That al hyr hote loue and al hyr desyre
    Ande al hyr besy turment ande al hyr fyre
    Be queynt . . .
and in *The Miller's Tale*/3754:
    Hys hoot loue was colde ande al queynt . . .
Wyatt may have counted *coles* as two syllables. In
which case, *folow* would count as one, as in this
line from *Such vain thought*:
    In following her whom Reason bid me flee.

Calais]

Pronounced *Caliss* with the accent on the second
syllable. This pronunciation may be reflected in
Cavendish's *Life of Wolsey*/14/13:
    [The kyng] passed the sees bytwen Douer
    and Calice . . .

against . . . mind]

'Without my inner consent.' The OED gives as of
1512: ayenst the will and mynde of . . .

sprung . . . spent]

'Sprung' could apply to birds driven from covert.
'Spent' could refer to exhaustion of energy.

whilom]

'Formerly'. This is the only place in the poems
where Wyatt used the word.

And all . . . scorn]   Wyatt often complains in his poems of losing his labour, as for example in *Like as the wind*:

As labour lost so is my suit

and in *My lute, awake*:

this is the last

Labour that thou and I shall waste . . .

The mood of the line and much of the poem finds a parallel in *Tangled I was*:

The woeful days so full of pain,

The weary night all spent in vain,

The labour lost for so small gain,

To write them all it will not be.

But ha, ha, ha, full well is me,

For I am now at liberty.

I take *he laugh* to be the equivalent of *he may laugh*. The Tottel editors favoured *he laughs*.

Coverdale Psalm XXII/7:

All they that see me, laugh me to scorne.

Cooper *Derideo*: To laugh to scorne.

Meshed in the briers]   'Entangled, trapped in the thorns'.

Surrey has a line:

How smal a net may take and mesh a hart of gentle kinde.

The use of *briers* for 'difficulties, dangers, and entanglements' is noted before and after Wyatt's day. George Wyatt, for instance, in his 'Defence' of the poet against the libels of Nicholas Sanders, wrote:

whereas he had by the malice of his adversarie, twice bene brought in to the Briers . . .

(D.M. Loades *The Papers of George Wyatt Esquire* 1968 p. 184.)

But there is no recorded instance in all these proverbial expressions of *meshed* or *mashed*.

erst]   'Once upon a time'.

all-to torn]   'Torn to pieces'.

Many readers have taken the lines to be marking a distinction between being meshed at the time of writing and being torn to pieces in the throes of the earlier love-affair. Others suppose that the whole line refers to the earlier period, when the lover was like an animal killed in the attempt to escape the hunters. It is torn to pieces as it struggles in the briers. Therefore the alternatives would in effect read:

> Now, finding himself entangled in briers in which formerly he had been torn to pieces

or:

> He laughs who formerly was entangled in the briers and torn to pieces by them.

Now farewell

As a glance at the Note on the text of this poem will indicate, what is printed here does not correspond to any of the versions which have come down to us. The conclusion I have come to is that we do not have the poem as a whole in a final text, and that we are therefore compelled to go in for a certain amount of reconstruction. What complicates matters is a further conclusion that Wyatt virtually wrote two poems, one resembling that we find in D, the other close to what is extant in E. Both I take to be making autobiographical points by taking up a conventional theme — the lover's farewell to love — and giving it a personal twist. I used the word 'virtually', since it might seem perverse to speak of two poems where the only difference is to be found in the third and fourth lines. But each version is thereby given a different point, for there is a world of difference in giving up love because it has proved painful:

> Too sore a proof hath called me from thy lore
> To surer wealth my wits to endeavour

and in abandoning love altogether for moral philosophers:

> Senec and Plato call me from thy lore
> To perfect wealth my wit for to endeavour.

My third conclusion is that Wyatt made no other change, and that a more plausible text can be obtained by correcting D from E.

There is, however, one further problem, how to read aloud the words *ever, endeavour, persever, liefer*. The Tottel editors assumed that the accent in all was on the last syllable. I think Wyatt followed common practice in treating the last two syllables as one with a sound like *-effr*. An example where Chaucer rhymes two of these words comes in the *Monk's Tale*, where Ugolino's son is speaking:

> I am so hungry that I may nat slepe.
> Now wolde God that I myghte slepen evere!

Thanne sholde nat hunger in my wombe crepe;
Ther is no thyng, save breed, that me were levere.

farewell . . . ever]

A traditional opening. It occurs in a religious context in a fifteenth-century poem beginning:
Ffarewell this world! I take my leue for euer,
I am arrestyt to appere at godis face.
Mercyfull god, thow knowest I had leuer
Then al this worldis good . . .

laws]

In the Devonshire manuscript there is a poem, possibly by Wyatt, with a similar theme, *Since love is such*, containing these lines:
For in my years of reckless youth
Methought the power of love so great
That to her laws I bound my truth . . .

baited hooks]

Although fishing is the head reference, the phrase is probably to be thought of figuratively, as 'enticements'. When Aretino was describing the temptations of the flesh in his paraphrase of Psalm 6, he spoke of
gli hami . . . l'esche de i loro inganni
the hooks . . . the baits of their deceits
which Wyatt rendered as
To these mermaids and their baits of error
I stop mine ears . . .
Udall translating Erasmus in 1548 wrote:
his hooke bayted with ye enticement of vayne glory

tangle]

'Catch in a net or snare', as in the poem beginning *Tangled I was in Love's snare.*

Senec]

Wyatt's interest in this Latin author of plays and moral essays can be detected in a letter to his son, in which, after recommending 'sayings of the philosophers', he added:
And it is no small help to them the good opinion of moral philosophers, among whom I would Seneca were your study . . .

perfect wealth]

'Full spiritual well-being', 'the ideal health of the soul'.

my wit . . .endeavour]   'Direct my thoughts toward'.

blind error]   In one of his sonnets, beginning *S'una fede*, describing subjection to love, Petrarch wrote of:

        Un lungo error in cieco laberinto,

which Wyatt translated as

        If long error in a blind maze chained . . .

persever]   This old spelling has been retained to mark the pronunciation *perséver*, which was 'the usual Eng. pronunciation down to the middle of the 17th c. or later'. (OED).

aye]   'All the time'.

liefer]   'More desirable'.

idle]   'Foolish, reckless'.

property]   'Distinctive character and quality', as in his version of *De Profundis*:

        Let Israel trust unto the Lord alway,

          for grace and favour are his property.

cf. *Gesta Romanorum* p. 133:

        hit is the propirte of mercy to have pite

spend]   'Use up all your stock of'. Petrarch in *S'i'l dissi mai*/10 has

        Amore l'aurate sue quadrella/Spenda in me tutte . . .

        If I ever said it, may Love use up on me all her golden shafts.

lost . . . time]   A similar train of thought occurs in the *Romaunt of the Rose*:

        As thou perauenture knowen shall,

        Whanne thou hast lost thy tyme all,

        And spent thy youthe in ydilnesse,

        In waste, and wofull lustynesse.

        If thou maist lyue the tyme to se

        Of loue for to delyuered be,

        Thy tyme thou shalt biwepe sore,

        The whiche neuer thou maist restore;

        For tyme lost, as men may se,

        For nothyng may recouered be.

rotten boughs to climb]   A proverbial expression. The literal meaning is 'to have an unexpected fall when climbing a tree.'

The proverbial meanings covered a wide area. A
fifteenth-century poem on the theme of too ready
trust begins:

> Allas diceyte that in truste ys nowe,
>> Duble as fortune, turnyng as a balle,
> Brotylle at assay lyke the rotyn bowe,
>> Who trustith to truste ys redy for to falle.

In the Dublin manuscript there is a poem on the
executed lovers of Anne Boleyn, which has these
lines about a musician, Mark Smeaton:

> A time thou haddest above thy poor degree
>> The fall whereof thy friends may well
>> bemoan.
> A rotten twig upon so high a tree
>> Hath slipped thy hold and thou art dead
>> and gone.

Wyatt himself in *Tangled I was* wrote:

> Was never bird tangled in lime
> That brake away in better time
> Than I that rotten boughs did climb . . .

WYATT AND THE PSALMS

(i) *'The Seven Psalms'*

'The Seven Psalms' is not a phrase that is everywhere instantly
understood. Even if we add 'of Penitence', comparatively few
readers would be able to identify the seven in the Authorised
Version as Nos. 6, 32, 38, 51, 102, 130, 143. But if we murmured
the beginning of the fiftieth psalm in the Vulgate, *Miserere mei*,
almost everybody would have some knowledge to contribute.
Dante, for example, could take for granted that his readers did not
need to be given David's name when he wrote in his *Paradiso*:

> . . . *al cantor che per doglia*
> *del fallo disse 'Miserere mei'* . . .
> . . . of the singer who in grief for
> his sin said, 'Lord, have mercy on me' . . .

The old fiftieth has always been the psalm of psalms for the
penitent Christian, for here the worst of sinners could learn that

his illustrious fellow-sinner had made a successful confession, and had been forgiven, as may be seen from these words of Erasmus (*De immensa dei misericordia*, tr. G. Heruet p. 77):

> Euen for the same pourpose oure lorde by all meanes myndynge our saluation/ suffered mooste excellente and mooste approued men to fall in greuous synnes, that by theyr example he myghte encorage & confort vs to hope to be forgyuen. What thynge in holye scripture is more laudable than kyng Dauid? He was a kynge, he was a prophet, he was a man to goddes owne mynde/ of his linage Christe was promised to come. But into howe foule/ in to howe manyfolde a synne dyd so great a man fall? He herethe of Nathan the rebuke and cruell thretnynges of our lorde. But Dauid with two wordes turneth all this angre of god in to mercy. He sayde thus: I haue offended agayne my lorde: And forthe with Nathan sayde to hym: Our lorde also hath transported thy syn, thou shalt nat dye.

The modern sinner had only to repeat the words of David's psalm to find the expressions he needed to open his heart directly to God.

(ii) *Dramatic Interest*

The popularity of this psalm outdid that of all other portions of scripture. That it had a further, dramatic, interest for Wyatt's contemporaries may be seen by looking at one of Caxton's additions to the *Golden Legend*:

> And on a tyme whan Joab was out with his men of warre lyenge at a syege to fore a cyte, dauyd was at home and walkid in his chambre, and as he looked oute at a windowe he sawe a fayre woman wasshe her and bayne her in her chambre, whyche stode ayenst his hows, and demaunded of his seruauntes who she was, and they sayd she was vries wyf. He sente for her, and laye by her, and gate her with chylde. And whan dauyd vnderstode that she was with chylde, he sente lettres to Joab and bad hym to sende home to hym Urye, and

> Joab sente Urie to Dauyd, and Dauyd demaunded howe the hoost was rewlid, and after bad hym goo home to his hows and wasshe his feet . . .

But Uriah did not fall into the trap:

> Urye abode there that daye and the next, and Dauyd made hym ete to fore hym and made hym dronke, yet for alle that he wolde not goo home but laye wyth the seruauntes of Dauyd. Thenne on the morne Dauyd wrote a lettre vnto Joab that he sholde sette Urye in the weykest place of the batayle and where most jeopardye was, and that he sholde be lefte there that he myght be slayne. And Urye bare this lettre to Joab, and it was so done as Dauyd had wreten, and Urye was so slayne in the batayll . . . Thenne our lorde sente Nathan the prophete vnto Dauyd whyche whan he came said to hym . . . Thou hast slayne Urye with a swerde and his wyf hast thou taken vnto thy wif, and thou hast slayne hym with the swerde of the sones of Ammon. Therfor the swerde shal not goo fro thy hows . . . And thenne said Dauyd to Nathan, *Peccaui*, I haue synned ayenst our lorde . . . And for thys synne Dauyd made this psalme *Miserere mei deus*, whiche is a psalme of mercy, for Dauyd dide grete penaunce for thyse synnes of aduoultrye and also of homycyde.

The choice of six more to make up a set of seven goes back a long way in the early history of the Christian Church. Long before Wyatt's day the Seven Psalms were prescribed to penitents as an act of penance, particularly for a penitent on his death bed. As Sir Thomas More wrote in his *Cumfort* (The First Booke, p. 45):

> some that lye a dying, say ful deuoutly the .vij. Psalmes and other praiers with the Priest at their aneiling.*

(iii) *English Versions*

Wyatt's first contact with the psalms may have begun when he was

---

* extreme unction

no older than the young hero of Chaucer's *Prioress's Tale*, for portions of the Psalter were often used down to Wyatt's day as a first reader or 'Babees Book'. In the Canterbury Tale we hear of

> This litel child, his litel book lernynge,
> As he sat in the scole at his prymer . . .

Whether Wyatt's book was all in Latin or in both Latin and English, it is likely that he would hear the English expressions which had been found acceptable down the centuries for rendering the traditional Latin version of the Psalms, known as the Vulgate. A number of these manuscript Primers of the fourteenth century have survived, though none is specifically composed for children. In 1891 Henry Littlehales edited one of these Primers, or English books 'intended specially for the laity, to guide the devout layman in his private daily devotions or to help him bear his part in the services of the Church', which had a special section, 'Here begynneth the seuene psalmes'. If we compare all these surviving mediaeval texts of English versions of the whole psalter or of portions of it with the text of the psalms in the 'Lollards' Bible', we may very loosely use the word 'Wyclifite' to designate a fairly homogeneous tradition. It is clear that much of Wyatt's language in his psalm versions is identical with one or other of these surviving traditional versions. Even if Wyatt had not acquired this vocabulary by reading in the Primers, he must have heard it all round him when people referred in English to this highly popular section of the Bible.

(iv) *Wyatt's Involvement*

None of this, however, brings us a step nearer to solving the first problem that would occur naturally to a reader who had come to regard the characteristic Wyatt as a composer of love poems or poems reflecting on life at court. What could have induced Wyatt to take up a verse paraphrase of the Seven Psalms? Bound up with this question is a technical puzzle; granted that Wyatt was moved as a poet, why did he not try one of the metres he had already mastered instead of this, perhaps the most difficult of European verse forms? It seems to me significant that we still refer to it as *terza rima*, for all the successes in the form are Italian, where it is comparatively easy to meet the obligation to rhyme three times on every line-end word. So far as I know, there is no successful long poem in English with the rhyme scheme Wyatt adopted for his Psalms.

The metrical puzzle yields one answer. It must have been from *Italian* poems that Wyatt derived his confidence that, like other Italian forms, notably the sonnet and the *strambotto*, this *terza rima* could be successfully adapted to suit English conditions. We could then take the solution a step further, provided we knew in what year Wyatt turned his first psalm into *terza rima*. For we might give a very different answer if we knew that Wyatt had convinced himself that he could manage this metre *before* he had occasion to write religious poems. The justification for this apparently odd reply to a query rests on our one certain fact, that at some time after 1532 Wyatt employed this metre to translate (and translate with unusual literal and formal fidelity) a satire in *terza rima*, 'Mine Own J.P.' which he had found in the *Opere Toscane* of Luigi Alamanni (see list A).

Now it might be argued that the degree of dependence of Wyatt's translation on this Italian *terza rima* original being so very much greater than anything at all similar in the Seven Psalms, it is likely that this translation of a satire was a 'first go' in this difficult metre, and that the psalm versions show Wyatt's later development in making the whole thing more subject to his natural manner. Yet no impartial observer would agree that this 'satire', beginning 'Mine own J.P.', is, as a poem, an apprentice piece when compared with any of Wyatt's Psalms.

We come to a similar dead end if we adopt a further argument, 'since we know that Wyatt translated a secular poem in *terza rima* from the *Opere Toscane*, it is probable that the impulse to write psalm paraphrases in this metre came from reading in the same volume'. It is true that Wyatt could have read there that Alamanni, thinking himself about to die, wrote seven penitential poems in *terza rima*, each devoted to one of the deadly sins. But there is nothing in the content of Alamanni's poems that reappears in Wyatt. (The same is true of the Seven Psalms in *terza rima* attributed in Wyatt's day to Dante.) Alamanni, therefore, may have contributed the form, but he has nothing to do with the substance of Wyatt's Psalms.

(v) *Aretino's Prose Paraphrase*

This present selection of Wyatt's poems does not bring out the overwhelming evidence showing that Wyatt began his own version by turning into verse a prose paraphrase by Pietro Aretino, *I Sette Salmi*. This Italian developed and exploited both main interests, the penitential and the dramatic, in the Seven Psalms by giving David a prologue before each psalm, and so keeping up the continuity of a story. His David is more the lover than the homicide, but even more the sixteenth-century rhetorician, expanding, inflating and working up the language of the Bible into a book of a hundred pages. Yet Wyatt must have found this tasteless production congenial, for, although, after translating the whole of Aretino's first prologue, Wyatt gave up the attempt to be as wordy as the Italian, he has translated many phrases from the whole book almost literally, as I have tried to bring out in the commentary.

(vi) *John Fisher's Meditation*

Strong and all-prevailing as Wyatt's interest in this David story (or romance), composed in 1534, was, it is just as clear that Wyatt had a religious attachment to the Psalms. We can become sure of this by noting how closely and how often he has drawn on a meditation in a series of sermons on the Seven Psalms by the then Bishop of Rochester, later Cardinal, John Fisher. This book survived into this century as annual Lent reading. It has many beautiful passages of traditional piety. But it is untouched by the rising tide of Renaissance humanism (it was first published in 1508) and has no trace of unorthodoxy. It is one of the most fascinating tasks of the commentary to illustrate the extraordinary blend made by Wyatt of Fisher's fifteenth-century piety and Aretino's sixteenth-century rhetoric.

(vii) *Campensis' Translation from the Hebrew*

So far it might be said that we have seen Wyatt as predominantly a man of feeling. That his head came into play in these translations may be seen in his care for what was known in his day as *Hebraica veritas*. The introduction of the study of Hebrew into universities brought home to students in Western Europe just how far from the original Hebrew the accepted Latin translation of the psalms really was. One of the new professors of Hebrew published a paraphrase of all the psalms to provide the general public with an accurate literal prose version of the complex poetic original. Joannes Campensis, to give him his Humanist name, brought out his *Enchiridion Psalmorum* in 1532. This permits the hypothesis that Wyatt may have been thinking of translating some psalms before (in 1534 or later) he came upon Aretino's dramatised story of a King's adultery with one of the ladies of his court. The commentary shows that Wyatt paid attention to the phrasing of this Hebrew scholar's paraphrase for all the seven psalms, and particularly for the last three. It is virtually certain that Wyatt used a 1533 edition of the *Enchiridion Psalmorum* which had bound up with it a shorter version in Latin prose left behind by the Swiss Reformer, Ulrich Zwingli.

(viii) *Wyatt's Protestant Interest*

The same method — noting resemblances of language where these three texts differ from the Vulgate or a literal translation — which assures us that Wyatt was using Aretino, Campensis and Fisher would suggest that Wyatt employed no other books *constantly* throughout his translating of the Seven Psalms. But there seems to be good evidence of occasional but not frequent use by him of other contemporary translations and commentaries on the psalms. This is a field for future research. So far, unfortunately, no help has been forthcoming from this line of enquiry to enable us to answer the principal question posed by these poems: what crisis are they a response to? What outer and inner circumstances were pressing on Wyatt? And are we compelled to posit a personal crisis as their necessary occasion? For although I have begun by stressing the element of borrowing and blending of phrases given externally by the authors I have mentioned, the poems Wyatt wrote are very striking original creations. We have only to place any of Wyatt's paraphrases alongside rival efforts, such as those of Milton, to see that they are much more like personal confessions than instruments of public devotion. We are therefore bound to consider whether Wyatt was more interested in making peace with God than in rehearsing David's penitence. And we must speculate whether it was in the face of imminent death that Wyatt was driven to such passionate expression.

It is perhaps more than a speculation that Wyatt found himself considering the nature of penitence itself, for this was one of the central debates in the contemporary contest between the Catholics and Protestants (of all shades). The historian of religion and the theologian are to be called in here to determine whether the words Wyatt omits, such as *attrition, contrition,* together with the predominance of *penitence* over *penance*, and a phrase such as:

And outward deed the sign or fruit alone

indicate that Wyatt had abandoned an orthodox position for a Lutheran view. No doubt if Wyatt were so inclined, we ought more properly to name William Tyndale, Luther's English disciple, as the main 'Protestant' influence on Wyatt. But if there is anything in this speculation, the facts force us to admit that passages from Tyndale's theological writings are at best merely lurking in Wyatt's first three psalms, and do not come into prominence until the last three psalms. The first psalm – the sixth in the Authorised Version – in Wyatt's hands strikes me as wholly *Catholic* or as not breaking obviously with what contemporary Catholic commentators and translators were writing. It is also possible to take Wyatt's version of *Miserere mei* as orthodox, at least if Savonarola, too, is orthodox. But since Luther was equally fond of Savonarola's meditation on this psalm, we may properly regard Wyatt's religious position here as looking both ways. I have therefore chosen the Prologue and the Psalm *De Profundis* to show Wyatt in what looks more like a Lutheran position. Wyatt's version of this psalm – the hundred and thirtieth in the Authorised Version – is also the one which has been found most palatable by those who find the whole set hard to swallow.

If we may not call Wyatt in the fullest sense a Lutheran (he was only called a sympathiser by those who wished him dead) there is one respect in which we may claim that he fell wholly under Luther's influence. The passage of Luther's I have in mind occurs in the preliminary remarks to his *Enarratio Psalmi LI* of 1538, where he insists that knowledge in theology must be *feeling*, the direct response of the experiencing heart. Religious knowledge, he says there, begins when a man truly feels he is a sinner:

> . . . *haec cognitio peccati non est speculatio aliqua seu cogitatio, quam animus sibi fingit, sed est uerus sensus, uera experientia et grauissimum certamen cordis, sicut testatur, cum dicit: 'Iniquitatem meam cognosco', hoc est, sentio, experior.* W 326/34–37.
> . . . this knowledge of sin is not speculative or the kind of thing the mind makes up a fanciful picture

of. It is real feeling, lived experience of a deeply
serious conflict in the heart. When we read in
Psalm 51, 'I acknowledge my transgressions', we
must understand David to be saying, 'I feel them,
I am experiencing them in my own person'.

I begin to understand what Luther was saying in this passage,
where he was claiming that the business of theology was to bring
home to men that their nature is 'filed with offence' (*peccatis
corruptam, contaminatam*), when I find Wyatt writing these lines,
near the end of his version of Psalm 32:

O, divers are the chastisings of sin,
In meat, in drink, in breath that man doth blow,
In sleep, in watch, in fretting still within,
    That never suffer rest unto the mind,
    Filed with offence, that new and new begin
With thousand fears the heart to strain and bind.

Here I am reminded of the Luther who wrote (364/14–16):

*Peccatum meum me urget, non admittet quietem
ullam, non pacem, non uino, non pane, non somno
sensus irae et mortis excutitur.*
My sin presses heavily on me, it will not leave me
any rest or peace. The feeling of God's wrath and
the fear of everlasting death cannot be shaken off
by drinking, eating or sleep.

Yet this is not an *exclusively* Lutheran passage. Aretino had
written:

*Si come il numero delle stelle, delle arene, e delle
frondi è senza numero, cosi sono innumerabili
i flagelli, che soprastanno al peccatore. Nel per-
cuoter di un piede, nel mouer di una mano, nello
spurgarsi, nel sonno, nel cibo, nello andare, e
nello stare, è il pericolo pronto a far inciampare
che erra nella sua punitione, e la afflittione del
corpo, & il languire del core, e le occupationi della
mente presaga del suo male, non restano mai di
molestar chi uiue in peccato.* (p. 16)
Just as you cannot count up the number of the

stars in the sky, the grains of the sands, or the
leaves on the trees, so innumerable are the whips
which stand over the sinner. At every step of the
foot, every movement of the hand, every clearing
of the throat, in sleeping, in eating, in walking and
standing still, danger is ready to trip up and punish
the man who goes astray. His body is afflicted, his
heart languishes, his mind, which foresees its
punishment, is full of troubles which never cease
to vex the man who lives in sin.

This is too rhetorically structured to sound sincere. Fisher,
however, has several moving passages on the theme:

Many dyuers and greuous punysshementes be for
the obstynate & harde herted synner that neuer
wyll be penytent . . . (41/33)
these enemyes laye awayte bothe daye and nyght,
they spare vs neyther slepynge nor wakynge,
etynge, or drynkynge, in labour, or ony other
study, but alwaye besy themselfe to catche our
soules in theyr snares . . . (83/15–19)
*Cor impii quasi mare feruens quod quescere non
potest.* The herte of a synfull persone is lyke vnto
the troublouse see whiche neuer hathe rest . . . Saynt
Ambrose asketh this questyon as thus, what payne
is more greuouse than is the wounde of a mannes
conscyence inwardly, it troubleth, it vexeth, it
prycketh, it tereth . . . (12/8–17)

The moment of dejection brought by the knowledge of sin is
for Luther only one moment in the Christian's knowledge. The
next part of knowledge is learning and hearing what grace is, and,
above all, what is justification. Then, says Luther, the sinner's
spirits are raised, and he ejaculates:

*sum iustus et iustificatus per iustum et iustificantem
Christum* . . . (W 327/33)
I am just and justified by a just and justifying
Jesus . . .

Nobody but Luther ever wrote like this. Therefore we must regard
Wyatt as Luther's disciple when he wrote in his version of Psalm 51:

> because that when
> I pardoned am, then forthwith justly able,
> Just I am judged by justice of Thy grace . . .

(This certain dependence on Luther raises an awkward question for those who would date Wyatt's psalms before 1538.)

(ix) *Relation to English Versions*

Wyatt was not the only Englishman in the early years of the sixteenth century to turn the psalms into English, but whether he made use of any of his English predecessors among those who translated his Latin paraphrases is far from clear. I have made abundant use of them in order to help readers to see what Wyatt, too, might have been saying to himself as he read through his 'sources'. It is natural to consider among these Englishmen those who included the psalms in their translations of the Old Testament or of the whole Bible. (Yet it is striking to note that in some places where Wyatt is plainly referring to the Bible he just as plainly is *not* using any of the English versions available to him. Further research will be needed to turn possibilities into probabilities.) The most interesting translator still to be named is George Joye, who is known to have brought out two English prose translations of the Psalms, and may be the translator of pieces at present anonymous.

(x) *A Personal Poem?*

The great drawback of the commentary lies in the danger that the means may come to seem more important than the end. It is undoubtedly interesting to be able to follow so clearly Wyatt's tracks as he moved from one version to another, but the poetic interest lies in the result. The question we put to these poems is, do they meet the particular claim that they are among the *characteristic* performances which reveal the valued poet? The comments will have failed if they do not serve to give these poems the best chance with an unprejudiced reader to emerge from general obloquy or neglect to (I consider) their proper place among the poems which bear Wyatt's characteristic stamp.

List B: Abbreviations used in the commentary on Wyatt's Psalms

Aretino	Pietro Aretino	*I Sette Salmi*, Venice, 1534
Becon	Thomas Becon	*A newe pathway vnto praier*, 1542
Bucer	Martin Bucer	*Sacrorum Psalmorum Libri Quinque*, Strassburg, 1529, 1532
Bugenhagen	J. Bugenhagen	*In Librum Psalmorum Interpretatio*, Basle, 1524
Campensis	J. Campensis	*Enchiridion Psalmorum*, Lyons, 1533
Coverdale	Miles Coverdale	*Biblia, The Bible*, 1535
Erasmus *Misericordia*	Desiderius Erasmus	*De Immensa Dei Misericordia* tr. Gentian Heruet, 1533
Fisher	John Fisher	*This treatyse* ... 1508, ed. J. E. B. Mayor (1876)
Joye	George Joye	*Dauids Psalter*, Antwerp, 1534 (tr. of Zwingli)
Joye (B)		*The Psalter of Dauid*, Antwerp, 1530 (tr. of Bucer)
Jerome	Sanctus Hieronymus	*Psalterium iuxta Hebraeos*, ed. H. de Sainte-Marie, Rome, 1954
Luther	Martin Luther	*Enarratio Psalmorum LI Miserere mei, Deus & CXXX. De profundis ... clamaui ... Adjecta est etiam Savonarolae Meditatio in Psalmum LI*, Strassburg, 1538 (quoted from the *Kritische Gesamtausgabe*, Weimar)
More (Confutacyon)	Sir Thomas More	*The confutacyon of Tyndales answere*, 1532, 1533
More (Cumfort)		*A Dialogue of Cumfort*, 1573
More (Dialogue)		*A Dyalogue*, 1529
More (Works)		*The Workes*, 1557
Olivetan	Pierre-Robert Olivétan	*La Bible* ..., Neufchastel, 1535
Paris, 1523		*Sancta admodum ac religiosa pietate refertissima expositio in quinquagesimum psalmum, cuius principium, Miserere mei deus, secundum magnam misericordiam tuam. Parisiis, Apud Simonem Colinaeum*, 1523
Pellican	Conradus Pellicanus	*Psalterium* ... 1527

Pilg. Perf.

A deuoute treatyse in Englysshe called the Pilgrymage of perfeccyon, 1526, 1531

Rolle   Richard Rolle of Hampole

The Psalter or Psalms of David and Certain Canticles, With a Translation and Exposition in English, Edited from manuscripts by the Rev. H.R. Bramley, Oxford, 1884
Prick of Conscience, ed. R. Morris, Berlin, 1863

Sadoleto   J. Sadoletus

Interpretatio in Psalmum Miserere mei, Roma, 1525

Savonarola   G. Savonarola

Expositio in psalmum Miserere mei Deus (1498) a cura di Mario Ferrara, Roma, 1976, tr. William Marshall as *An exposition after the maner of a contemplacyon vpon ye .li. pslalme*, 1534

Tyndale   William Tyndale

An answere vnto Sir T. Mores dialoge [1530?]

(Enchiridion)

A booke called in Latyn Enchiridion and in Englysshe the Manuell of the Christian knyght, 1533

(Expos. John)

The exposition of the fyrste epistle of Seynt Jhon, 1531

(Expos. Matthew)

An exposicion vppon the v.vi.vii. chapters of Mathew [1533?]

(Mammon)

The parable of the wicked mammon, 1528

(New Testament)

The Newe Testament, 1534 (Cambridge, 1938)

(Obedience)

The obedience of a Christen man, 1528

Vulgate

Biblia Sacra Vulgatae Editionis

Wyclif   John Wyclif

The Books of Job, Psalms, Proverbs, Ecclesiastes, and the Song of Solomon, according to the Wycliffite Version made by Nicholas de Hereford and revised by John Purvey, ed. The Rev. Josiah Forshall and Sir Frederic Madden, Oxford, 1881
The Prymer (about 1400 ed. H. Littlehales, 1891

		The Prymer, ca. 1420–1430, ed. H. Littlehales, 1895
		The Holy Bible, ed. J. Forshall and Sir F. Madden, 1850
Zwingli	Huldrich Zwingli	*Enchiridion Psalmorum*, Lyons 1533

O Lord, since

O Lord . . . call]

Aretino:
> *Signore poi ch'il tuo nome si lascia proferire dalla mia lingua & da che tu le concedi ch'ella possa anchor chiamare il Signor suo. . .*

Quotations from Aretino are placed at the head of a note wherever, as here, Wyatt's translation owes nothing to Biblical translations but is a fairly close rendering of sentences taken from *I Sette Salmi*, as may be seen from the following rough translation:
> Lord, since your name allows itself to be uttered by my tongue, and that you grant that it may still call on its Lord . . .

mighty name]

Wyatt's addition, as also in line 61:
> ne yet no mention
> Of Thy great name . . .

Sufferth itself]

Si lascia, Allows itself to be.

Here]

In the first working of grace God has opened his lips and allowed him to beg for mercy.

hope . . . all]

Aretino:
> *. . . il core, che prende felice augurio perciò, fauorisce la speranza che il suo pentirsi ha preso in quella clemenza, con cui consoli coloro che si contristano per hauerti offeso . . .*

> my heart, which takes that for a good omen, nurses the hope that its repenting has taken in that mercy with which you comfort those who are sorry for having offended you . . .

and shall]

'And shall have'. Chaucer, *Troilus and Criseyde* II/827:
> O Love, to whom I haue and shal [ben]

at . . . hand . . . mercy]	Something similar may be found where Wyatt deviates from Aretino's Prologue to Psalm 38: The soul . . . that "Mercy!" so did cry, And found mercy at Mercy's [plenteous?] hand . . . The same language was used in *The Boke of the common praier* in 1549 for the Minister examining the dying Christian: I require you to examine yourself and your state, both toward God and man, so that accusing and condemning yourself for your own faults, you may find mercy at our heavenly Father's hand . . . (Parker Soc. p. 137) Philip Gerrard, *The Epicure*, 1545, *sig.* B3 *recto*: in that fearful day, all they (as writeth S. Augustine) shal fynde mercie at the handes of god . . .
the thing]	'The important thing', as in Shakespeare's *Hamlet*: The Play's the thing, Wherein Ile catch the Conscience of the King. Because he is beginning to be repentant, David is fulfilling the first condition for asking God's mercy. After 'thing', supply 'which is . . .'.
wretched]	The word itself meant 'miserably sinful', especially when the sinner was confronted with the dreadful consequences of falling into the devil's hands; a meaning admirably summed up in *Gude and Godlie Ballatis* (S.T.S. p. 24): We wratchet sinnaris pure, Our sin hes vs forlorne . . . This became the consecrated language of the Church, as we may see from Fisher/173/25: [blyssed lorde] here vs wretched synners for the loue of [the many ryghtwyse people in thy chyrche mylytaunt], be mercyful vnto Syon . . .
Whereby]	'As a result of which'.
I dare . . . require]	Aretino: . . . *onde io ardisco con la uoce & co'l pianto di scongiurarti per la tua bontà* . . .

wherefore I dare with voice and complaint
beg you not to be . . .

Chastise . . . ire]   Here begins the translation of the Psalm. The
whole phrase is in the Wiclifite tradition:
nether chastise thou me in thin Ire . . .

According . . . just]   Aretino:
. . . *degnati* . . . *di non mi castigare* . . .*secondo la forza della tua giusta ira* . . .
deign not to punish me according to the
violence of your just wrath.

conceived]   This word and 'deserving' suggest that Wyatt had
Campensis before him:
*Domine ne pro ira tua, quam aduersum me,
licet meritò, concepisti, castiga me* . . .
O Lorde chasten me not after the wrath
that thou hast taken agenst me (though I
be worthy of yt) . . .

O Lord . . . to dread]   Aretino:
*O Iddio io ti temo & di non hauerti temuto
mi pento, & di uolerti temere mi delibero.* . . .
O God, I fear thee, and of not having feared
thee I repent, and I resolve to wish to fear
thee . . .

open . . . spread]   Wyatt may have been thinking of a pedlar and his
pack.

breadth]   Here Wyatt wrote *bred*, the usual form, as in
Fisher 95/34:
Stretes and hygh wayes be called grete for
theyr brede and wyddenesse . . .

Punish . . .furor]   'Rage', but not 'fury'. Olivétan:
& ne me chastie point en ta fureur.
asketh]   'Requires', 'calls for'.

provoked . . . offence]   'Stirred up', 'called forth'. A literal translation of
Aretino:
prouocata da nostri falli
provoked by our offences.
Wyatt in his Psalm 102 has:
Because I knew the wrath of Thy furor
Provoked by right . . .

Temper . . . again]

Aretino:

> *Tempra Signore gli sdegni, che in te hanno accesi i mali, ch'io feci, co beni, che io m'apparecchio à fare . . .*

Moderate the indignation, Lord, kindled in you by the evil things I have done by considering the good things I am getting ready to do . . .

The root idea of 'temper' is 'dilute', 'moderate your anger by considering along with my sin my desire to repent'.

harm]

Similar language may be found in Wyatt's version of Psalm 102:

> provoke the harm of my disease

where 'harm' means 'evil', as in the *Babees Bk.*/72:

> agaynst them say no harme

excess]

The OED considers the meaning to be 'outrage', but in Wyatt's day the word means merely 'wrong-doing', 'trespass', as in *Pilg. Perf.* (1531) Fo: cxl. *verso*:

> Be sory for your fall, and do due penaunce after the qualite and quantite of your excesse . . .

mending will]

'The desire to repent'. Surrey in his *Ecclesiastes* Chapter V, lines 1-2, has:

> When that repentant teares hath clensyd
> clere from ill
> the charged brest/ and grace hathe wrought
> therin a mending will . . .

The force of the expression is well brought out in a document printed by William Maskell in the third volume of the second edition of his *Monumenta Ritualia* p. 417, *De visitatione infirmorum*, where the priest is urged to conduct the following dialogue with the dying man:

> Brother, art thou glad that thou shalt die in Christin feith? *Resp.* Ye.
> Knowleche that thou hast nought wel liued as thou shuldest? *Resp.* Ye.
> Art thou sori therfor? *Resp.* Ye.
> Hast thou wil to amend the, if thou haddist space of lif? *Resp.* Ye.

recompense]

'Equivalent atonement for misdeed'. For a fuller explanation, see the commentary on the Prologue and Psalm 130. Fisher 216/22:

> It is requyred bothe of ryght and equyte a recompence to be made for a trespasse or vnkyndnes shewed to ony persone or euer the offence be vtterly forgyuen . . .

again]

'In response'.

and rather . . . weak]

'Instead of punishing me'.
Campensis:

> *Quin potius misereat te mei Domine, aeger enim sum . . .*
> But rather haue mercy vpon me/ O lorde/ for I am sicke

Vulgate:

> *quoniam infirmus sum*: for I am weak

clean]

'Altogether'.

More . . . remedy]

Campensis:

> *& te medico magis opus habeo*
> and haue more nede of the to be my phisycian . . .

whole . . . cure]

'Whole' means 'healthy', and 'leech', 'doctor'.
Wyclif *Matt*. 9/12:

> A leche is not nedeful to men that faren wel. .

Fisher 14/17:

> It is wryten in the gospel. *Non hijs qui sani sunt opus est medico sed qui male se habent.*
> They that be hole nedeth no physycyen. . .

taketh no cure]

'Pays no attention to'. *Behold love*/3:

> The holy oath whereof she taketh no cure. . .

The sheep . . . stray'th]

Tyndale *The Gospell of S. Mathew* The .xv. Chapter/24:

> I am not sent, but vnto the loost shepe of the housse of Israel . . .

The .xviii. Chapter/12:

> Yf a man have an hondred shepe, and one of them be gone astray, dothe he not leve nynty and nyne in the mountains, and go and seke that one which is gone astray?

I . . . am strayed]   Joye (B) Ps. 119 (Fo.226 *recto*):
    I am strayed like a loste shepe

without recure]   'With no possibility of recovery, past healing'.
See *What no, pardie*/24.

rebelled]   Savonarola:
    For I fynde another lawe in my membres;
    rebellynge agaynst the lawe of my mynde,
    and subduing me vnto the lawe of synne
    & dethe.

Tyndale *The epistle of S. Paul vnto the Romayns*
The .vij. Chapter 22:
    I delite in the lawe of God, concerninge the
    inner man. But I se another lawe in my
    membres rebellinge agaynste the lawe of
    my mynde . . .

despair]   Zwingli:
    quoniam totus despero
    for I am utterly desperate

flesh . . . troubled]   Wyclif:
    alle my bonys ben troblid

Spear]   'Sharp point'. Wyatt may have been thinking of
the impressive close of the fifteenth chapter of the
first epistle to the Corinthians, and in particular,
of the phrase: *Stimulus autem mortis peccatum
est*, which Wyclif rendered:
    Forsoth the pricke of death is synne.

dread of death]   Chaucer in his *Parson's Tale* has:
    grysly drede that euer shal laste
and
    drede of deth that cometh oft tyme so
    sodenly

of right]   'Justly', as Wyatt uses it in *And if an eye*/16:
    That I do claim of right to have . . .

draweth near and near]   Common for 'nearer and nearer', as in Hawes
Passetyme of Pleasure/1730: (see list A under
Hawes)
    To which we rode and drewe nere and nere

Much more . . . troubled]   'My soul fears defeat more than my body fears
death.'

Wyclif:
> And my soule is troblid

Aretino:
> *l'anima mia è oltra modo turbata*
> my soul is beyond measure troubled

Campensis:
> *Et animus meus conturbatus est multo magis*
> And my mynde is moche more vexed . . .

assaults]   Aretino:
> *e certo io mi rendero all'impeto de suoi*
> *assalti . . . se tu non mi difendi,*
> and I shall surely surrender to the violence
> of its attacks unless thou protect me . . .

Tyndale *Obedience* Fo:cl *verso*:
> there only shalt thou be sure from all stormes
> and tempestes and from all wyly assaltes of
> oure weked spirites which stody with all
> falsheed to vndermyne vs.

thick as hail]   A set phrase, as in Chaucer's *Legend of Good
Women*/655:
> For strokes which that went as thicke as
> hayle.

weak . . . frail]   Aretino:
> *tante & tali sono le tentationi, che lassal-*
> *gono, ella si stá rinchiusa dentro alle m*
> *della carne inferma . . .*
> so many and so great are the temptations
> which attack it that it remains shut up
> within the walls of the weak flesh . . .

More (*Cumfort*) p. 69:
> . . . the Diuel . . . tempteth vs by the world,
> he tempteth vs by our owne flesh, he temp-
> teth vs by pleasure, he tempteth vs by paine,
> he tempteth vs by our foes, he tempteth vs
> by our owne frindes . . .

bulwark]   Literally, 'the defences of a walled town or fortress'.

Wherein]   In the body.

Feeleth . . . vanity] 'Feels the senses conspiring with the attacks of
worldly vanities to corrupt'.

Conspire]

Aretino:

> *e le armi delle uanità mondane gli hanno congiurato contra*
>
> and the arms of worldly vanities have conspired against . . .

corrupt]

'Corrupted'. Aretino:

> *et i sensi che si risanano alle lusinghe loro, corrott. dal uedere . . .*
>
> and the senses which get their health back by their flatteries, corrupted by seeing . . .

Pilg. Perf. The seconde boke Fo: L *verso*:

> in moche worse state had we wretches ben whose body & senses be all corrupte & reason & wyll all derked . . .

Sir. T. Elyot *The Image of Governance* p. 78 *recto*:

> persons, corrupted with detestable vices . . .

A. Barclay *the fourth Egloge*/636:

> And manly vertue corrupted is with vice

Tyndale tr. *Enchiridion* sig. D.iij. *verso* − D.iv. *recto*:

> corrupte with the contagyousnes of them of the lowest sortes sholde with them also conspyre agaynst hym.

[N.B. This is a description of conflict in the soul against Reason.]

vice and vanity]

Maskell *Monumenta Ritualia* (2nd. ed.) Vol. III p. 302 has a priest's form of confession taken from Cotton Ms. Nero A3 with these words:

> And my mynd and hart ofte tymes withdrawyn tharfro [service] by ymaginacyons of vice and vanyte . . .

The OED has failed to record this set phrase, in which the two terms are virtually synonymous, but gives some suggestive quotations for *vanity*, e.g. *Prick. Consc.*

> 1619: Eful of vanyte and of syn
>
> 7228: lyfyng In-tylle vanyte and flesschly lykyng

which would support the meaning *sensual vice*, as in Lydg. *Min. Poems*:

> Lat reson brydle thy sensualite . . .
>
> Ageyn al worldly disordinat vanyte . . .
>
> (Percy Soc. p. 219)

Whereby . . . thee]   Aretino:

> . . . *onde la misera si ricoura sotto la ombra della speranza che ella ha in te . . .*
> wherefore the wretch flies for rescue under the shade of the hope it has in thee . . .

But . . . misery]   Wyclif:

> but thou lord how long

Aretino:

> *Infino à quanto indugierai à uolgere in me quegli occhi . . .*
> How long will you delay to turn on me those eyes . . .

Zwingli:

> *Tu uero Domine quousque cessas?*
> But thou, O Lord, how long do you hesitate?

after this sort]   'In this manner'.

Forbearest]   'Do you refrain from . . .?'

see . . . misery]   Aretino:

> *Deh Signore, risguarda la miseria*
> Alas, Lord, look on my misery

Campensis:

> *tu interim Domine quando tandem respicies miseriam meam?*
> but in the meane season (O Lorde) when wylt thou at the last consydere my wrechydnes?

Suffer . . . forgettest me]   Aretino:

> *Permettimi Signore che io imagini & non ueggia che tu ti scordi di me . . .*
> Allow me, Lord, to imagine and not see that thou forgettest me . . .

Return . . . benignity]   Campensis:

> *Redi quaeso Domine ad solitam clementiam*
> O Lorde I beseche the returne to the kyndnesse that thou wast wont to haue . . .

benignity]   Sir T. Elyot in the *Governour* 1531 fol. 129 *verso* defines the word as follows:

> And all thoughe there be many of the said vertues/ yet be there thre principall: by whome humanitie is chiefly compact/ beneuolence/ beneficence/ & liberalitie/

which maketh vp the said principall vertue
called benignitie or gentilnes.

Reduce]

'Restore to a previous good condition', as is shown
by the following quotations:

Cavendish *Life of Wolsey* 58/14ff.

> So that his stowte Countenaunce and bold
> wordes made them all in dowght howe to
> pacyefie hys displeasure ... And there was
> great submyssion made to hyme to reduce
> hyme to his former frendly commyny-
> cacion ...

Pilg. Perf. fol.50 *verso*:

> he shulde reduce/ bryng & helpe other to
> the seruice and fauour of god ...

leech]

'Doctor'

reconcile. . . strife]

Aretino:

> ... *hora Signore metti in concordia l'anima,*
> *la qual mira il corpo con occhio inimico* ...
> now, Lord, reconcile the soul which gazes
> on the body with hostile eye ...

Wyatt appears to have before him part of the fifth
chapter of the *Epistle to the Galatians*, perhaps
in Tyndale's translation:

> I saye walke in the sprete, and fulfill not the
> lustes of the flesshe. For the flesshe lusteth
> contrary to the sprete, and the sprete con-
> trary to the flesshe. These are contrary one
> to the other, so that ye cannot do that
> which ye wolde. But and yf ye be ledde of
> the sprete, then are ye not vnder the lawe.
> The dedes of the flesshe are manyfest,
> whiche are these, advoutrie, fornicacion,
> vnclennes, wantannes, ydolatrye, witche-
> craft, hatred, variaunce, zele, wrath, stryfe,
> ...

filthy]

By Wyatt's day this word and the noun *filth* had
acquired a specifically sexual reference as in
Pilg. Perf. (1531) Fo. .xviii.recto:

> the fylthy and stynkynge lust of the body

and in *York. Myst.* xx.80:

> All filthes of flesschely synne.

fret . . . bones]

Three meanings are conflated here. The first is

the gnawing bite of conscience. Secondly, the
consuming of passion. Thirdly, with *inward,
within*, etc., it refers to pox, as in Tyndale *Obedience* Fo: .clix. *verso*:

> it is lyke a pocke that freateth inwarde
> and consumeth the very mary of the bones. . .

fret it]   'Fret itself'.

Inward remorse]   Fisher 12/15-16:

> what payne is more greuouse than is the
> wounde of a mannes conscyence inwardly. . .

Aretino:

> . . . & *il corpo mio, che dì & notte è morso
> dalla sua conscientia* . . .
> and my body which night and day is bitten
> by its conscience . . .

sharp'th]   'Pricks painfully'.

That , but . . . dust]   The meaning may best be gathered from Aretino:

> . . . *caderà tosto & tosto si farà cenere se
> tu no'l sostieni* . . .
> unless you help it it will soon fall and turn
> to dust . . .

caitiff]   'A wretched miserable person'.
The religious use of this word is illustrated in the
OED: c.1325 *Metr. Hom.* 31:

> Hou sal* it far* of us kaytefes
> That in sin and foli lyes

* shall * fare

and 1480: Caxton *Chron. Eng.* v. (1520) 56/1:

> to vs wretches and catyves is sorowe for our
> greate synnes . . .

matter]   'A good opportunity for action', to, as Fisher put
it, 'exercyse his mercy in dede'.
Erasmus in one of his *Colloquia, Cyclops*, has:

> *Exspecto Christi manum.*
> *Vide ut tu manui ceream praebeas materiam.*
> *Poly*: I hope Christ will give me his helping
> Hand.
> *Cann.* But do you see that you render your
> · self fit Matter to work upon.

for the nonce]   'Suiting this occasion'. (But see the remarks on
this phrase in the commentary on *A spending hand*.)

For . . . operation]

   * unless

The argument is in Fisher 15/16:
> It sholde seme that he was create of god but in vayne and for nothynge, without* he myght come to the ende that he was made for. He was brought forth in to this worlde by his creacyon, to thentent he sholde knowe god . . . But these thynges can not be done in purgatorye, and moche lesse in hell, for . . .

subject matter]

'Material subjected to Him on which to work His mercy'.

operation]

'Creative activity'. See note on this word in *Miserere*.

For . . . is no]

Vulgate:
> *Quoniam non est in morte*
> For there is not in death

memory]

Bucer: (see list B under Joye B) (1529)
> *Etenim . . . non est tui memoria*
> For there is no memory of Thee

Aretino:
> *Ma se io muoio Signore, non sendo fra i morti, chi si possa ricordare di te, come potrò io far memoria del tuo nome?*
> But if I die, Lord, there not being among the dead anybody who could bring Thee to mind, how shall I be able to bring Thy name to remembrance?

Among the damned]

Zwingli:
> *Inter damnatos enim non est qui tui meminerit*
> For among the damned there is none who could remember Thee . . .

Then if . . . thereon]

Aretino:
> *. . . & morendo in cotale stato l'anima andrà doue a pensarlo tremo . . .*
> and dying in such a condition the soul will go where I tremble to think on . . .

how . . . ear]

Aretino:
> *come potrò io Signore porre innanzi alle genti per eterno essempio i benefici riceuuti*

da te . . . ?
how shall I be able, Lord, to place before
the world as an everlasting example the
benefits received from Thee?

the world's ear]

   * Therefore

   * remain

The phrase occurs in Gower's *Confessio Amantis*:
Prologue:
    Forthi* good is that we also . . .
    Do wryte of newe som matiere . . .
    So that it myhte . . .
    Whan we ben dede . . .
    Beleue* to the worldes eere
    In tyme comende after this.
Wyatt scanned *worldes* or *worldis* as two syl-
lables.

laud and love]

Fisher: 16/4:
    Than syth it is so that in purgatorye we
    can not laude and prayse god how shall we
    do yf we be in hell, truely in that terryble
    place no creature shall neyther loue god,
    neyther laude hym.

thou nilt]

'You are not willing to allow'.
Aretino:
    et andandoci [allo inferno], non essendo
    lecito che iui niuno ti ami, perche non uuoi
    da tali essere amato . . .
    and going there [to hell], it not being per-
    mitted that anybody may love Thee there,
    because Thou dost not wish to be loved by
    such people . . .

Suffer . . . remove]

Aretino:
    la tua misericordia, la quale . . . sofferisce
    non pur di solleuare ma di sublimare . . .
    your mercy which . . . permits not only to
    lift from the ground but to raise on high. . .

an hundred]

If Wyatt had wanted to stress the point of *one*
hundred, he would have written *on*, as in *When
Dido*/36:
    on hunderd yere . . . on degre

In a moment]

Aretino:
    chi l'ha ingiuriata cento anni co'l pentimento
    di un'attimo . . .

one who had wronged him a hundred years
merely by the repentance of a single moment ...

R. Burrant, *Preceptes of Cato* 1560 *sig.*
C.i *verso*:

in one little momente of an houre
Tyndale translated *In momento* (I Cor. xv. 52)
'in a moment'.

How oft ... cold]   Aretino:

*Egli consentiua per gli miei prieghi a mezzo
il uerno di uscir delle piume su'l far del dì
per confessarti le colpe sue con l'oratione:
ne prima haueua fuor degli agi il piede, che
si ritornaua a couare il caldo temprato dalla
sua pigritia ...*

[My body] would at my earnest request
consent in the depth of winter to get out of
bed at the break of day to pray to God and
confess its sins, but the moment it put a foot
outside the feather bed, it would go back
again to huddle in the warmth it owed to
its laziness ...

his]   *i.e.* of the flesh.

fault and negligence]   A set phrase, as in Tyndale's *Prologue to the Book
of Numbers* (Parker Soc.) 1/435. Wyatt used it
again in *Miserere*:

And I beknow my fault, my negligence ...

down]   Wyatt's word for a feather bed, as in *My Mother's
maids*/20–21:

In cold and storm she lieth warm and dry
In bed of down ...

shroud]   A mixture of 'clothe' and 'protect'.

I wash]   Wyclif:

... waschche my bed euery nyght: with my
teres y schal wete my beddynge ...

To dull]   Campensis:

hebetata est acies eius
Myne eye is darkened (*literally* dulled).

such a fall]   David might be thinking of his own particular sins.

dry I up] Zwingli:
    emarcui inter tot hostes meos
    I have withered away among the host of my
    enemies.

my foes] They are more likely to be *inward* enemies. David
is represented more frequently by Wyatt as exclusively concerned with his 'heart's inward
restraints'. There is a striking passage in the version of Psalm 38 (A.V.) which is unambiguous:
    And when mine enemies did me most assail,
        My friends most sure, wherein I set most
          trust,
        Mine own virtues, soonest then did fail
    And stand apart. Reason and wit unjust,
        As kin unkind, were farthest gone at need.
        So had they place their venom out to
          thrust
    That sought my death by naughty word and
        deed.
        Their tongues reproach, their wits did
          fraud apply.
        And I like deaf and dumb forth my way
          yede
    Like one that hears not nor hath to reply
        One word again.
Equally unambiguous are the rare references to
David's *public* enemies. But occasionally, as a few
lines later in this version of Psalm 38, we find
David, and by implication Wyatt himself, concerned with enemies we cannot unequivocally
consider one or the other:
    In the mean while mine enemies safe increase
        And my provokers hereby do augment
        That without cause to hurt me do not
          cease.
It seems reasonable to conjecture that Wyatt
would have cleared up the ambiguity if he had
returned to the poem.

rise and grow] 'They have flourished as a consequence of my
downfall.'

beset] 'Assail on all sides', 'trap in', as in *Pilg. Perf.*
1526 fol. xxxii *recto*:

al beset about with ennemyes

secret traps]

Aretino:

i miei nimici... tendendo nuoui lacciuoli alla mia penitentia...

my enemies laying new snares for my penitence ...

Some... beauty]

Aretino:

Alcuno mi appresenta a gliocchi la imagine di colei, le cui maniere & la cui bellezze han...

Some lay before my eyes the image of her whose manners and beauty have ...

look... blind]

The same antithesis is found in *Tangled I was*/27:

Her wily looks my wits did blind ...

Some other... mind]

Aretino:

altri mi fa udire la dolcezza di quelle sue parole che hora cosi amaramente mi suonano nell' anima...

others make me hear the sweetness of those words of hers which now sound so bitterly in my soul ...

pleasant words]

Reference to the Italian makes clear that we must supply 'of hers'. Wyatt's thought is well illustrated in the first lines of *When first*:

When first mine eyes did view and mark
Thy fair beauty to behold,
And when mine eyes listened to hark
The pleasant words that thou me told,
I would as then I had been free
From ears to hear and eyes to see.

And some show]

Aretino:

altri mi mostra i trophei, & le spoglie che debbeno conquistare l'arme mie: chi promette al capo mio doppio diadema...

others show me the trophies and the spoils destined to be won by my arms: another promises a double diadem for my head ...

double]

Presumably the crown of a king of two kingdoms (Judah and Israel).

some show... riches]

Aretino:

alcuno mi pone inanzi... i superbi pallazzi ... le altre pompe Reali...

some place before me ... the proud palaces...
the other pomps of kings ...
Wyatt appears to have converted all these plurals
to singulars.

favour]

i.e. the advantages enjoyed by one who is highly
regarded by a fickle people.
Rolle on Psalm 24 has:
>   thai doe wickidly to get thaim the fauour ...
>   of this warld ...

frail]

'Inconstant', 'unreliable'. Cicero used the word in
a similar context when he spoke in his *Republic*
2.28 of the frail fortune given by the people:
fortuna populi fragilis. The identical phrase, the
favour of people, populi fauor, may be found in
a once much admired passage in Cicero's *Pro
Sestio* 54:
>   *ei uero qui pendet rebus leuissimis, qui*
>   *rumore et, ut ipsi loquuntur, fauore populi*
>   *tenetur et ducitur, plausum immortalitatem,*
>   *sibilum mortem uideri necesse est.*
>   When a man lets his fate depend on utterly
>   trifling matters, and under the fascination of
>   winning popular favour follows wherever it
>   leads him, he cannot help regarding public
>   acclaim as life everlasting and the popular
>   hiss as instant death.

pomp and riches]

Coverdale *Wisdom* 5/8:
>   what profit hath the pompe of riches
>   brought vs?
I have assumed that *riches* was a form of *richesse*,
with the accent on the second syllable, but when
used to translate the Latin *diuitige* it may be a
plural, i.e. all the allurements just listed.

mermaids]

Wyatt wrote *Marmaydes*, and may have scanned
the word with three syllables. The English term for
the creatures who in the Twelfth Book of the
Odyssey almost lured Ulysses to destruction
alternated between *sirens* and *mermaids*, as we see
from *The Romaunt of the Rose*/684:
>   Songe of Meremaydens of the see
>   That for her syngyng is so clere
>   Though we mermaydens clepe hem here

In englisshe/ as is our vsaunce
Men clepe hem Sereyns in Fraunce.
1481 Caxton:
They be called seraynes or mermaydens.
The Homeric legend was used as a stock image for the temptations a Christian was subjected to on the stormy seas of life, as the following quotations show:
Erasmus *De Contemptu Mundi* tr. Thomas Paynell, 1533 *sig.* B 1 *verso* and *sig.* B2 *recto*:
the yll melodye & swete honygall tunes of the Syrens . . .
Wolde to god thou coudest se what snares, what disceites & what nets they lay priuily to attrapt thy youth with. Loke therfore that thou flye from the bankes or see costes where these Syrens be . . .
[Ulixes] stopped his eares with waxe . . .
N. Udall, translating his *Apophthegmes* p. 40 stated more correctly:
Ulysses . . . stopped the eares of all his compaignie with waxe . . .

baits of error]   Aretino:
gli hami . . . l'esche de i loro inganni
the hooks . . . the baits of their deceits

I stop . . . goodness]   Aretino:
Et io . . . chiudendo le orecchie alle Sirene del mondo, spero abbattergli . . . & dalle reti che hanno distese insidiosamente, spero scampare non per arte mia, ma per la cura che ha la tua bontade . . .
And I . . . stopping my ears to the sirens of the world, hope to bring them down . . . and to escape from the nets they have treacherously spread not by my own skill but thanks to the care you in your goodness have for me . . .

And for . . . access]   i.e. He has confidence to reject his inner enemies because he feels that God rather than his own efforts is keeping them away from him.

Avoid]   'Go away'.

Vulgate:
> *Discedite a me.*
> Go away from me.

Avoid and flee]

A set phrase, as in Fisher:
> to make them avoyde & flee from . . .

Joye:
> But now ye shall auoyde fro me/ o al ye sinneful

Joye (B):
> Auoyde from me ye workers of wikednes: for the lorde hath hard my complaints

The argument is set out well in Fisher 20/19-25:
> Take hede & beholde the sodayne chaunge of this prophete caused by the goodnes of god, where but late he was vexed and troubled with fere and drede, neuertheles now beynge conforted by the grace of almyghty god, he hath audacyte to despyse his enemyes and commaunde them to go away fro hym . . .

The Lord . . . complaint]

Wyclif:
> For the Lord hath herd the vois of my wepyng

Aretino:
> *la voce del mio pianto*
> the voice of my complaint

engines]

'Plots', 'snares'

Campensis:
> *Discedite   a   me   quotquot   machinamini malum mihi*
> Go fro me al ye that intende me euel.

do make]

'Cause'.

senses . . . Obey]

Aretino:
> *et il senso uinto da quella ragione . . . il Signor lo farà seruo della penitentia mia.*
> and my senses overcome by that reason . . . the Lord shall make them the slaves of my penitence

rule . . . reason]

This is one of the grand European commonplaces of the inner dynamic relations of the troubled soul. It is striking to note that Wyatt is here using ex-

pressions that were found appropriate and powerful down the centuries. An almost identical
passage occurs in Book IX of *Paradise Lost* after
the account of the Fall:

> They sate them down to weep, nor onely
> Teares
> Raind at thir Eyes, but high Winds worse
> within
> Began to rise, high Passions, Anger, Hate,
> Mistrust, Suspicion, Discord, and shook sore
> Thir inward State of Mind, calm Region once
> And full of Peace, now lost and turbulent:
> For Understanding rul'd not, and the Will
> Heard not her lore, both in subjection now
> To sensual Appetite, who from beneathe
> Usurping over sovran Reason claimd
> Superior sway . . .

The phrase *reason's rule* is Latin in origin, as may
be seen from a sentence in Cicero's speech *Pro
Murena* 2/3:

> *uitam ad certam rationis normam dirigere*
> to govern one's life by a fixed rule of reason

glozing]   'Deceiving by flattery'.
A. Barclay The fifth Egloge/660:
> By glosed wordes to take vs in a trap

shamed be they]   Wyatt wrote 'shamid' scanned as two syllables.
Wyclif:
> Schamed . . . be all myn enemys

compass| 'Encircle with hostile intent'.
Coverdale Psalm xxvi [i]/6:
> myne enemies . . . compassed me rounde
> aboute . . .

missing . . . prey]   Fisher 22/11–12:
> [the devils] be sore vexed . . . seynge theyr
> praye . . . to be taken awaye fro them

rebuke| 'Shame', 'disgrace'. Shame and rebuke were often
linked, as in Tyndale's translation of Erasmus'
Enchiridion:
> It is a great shame and rebuke bothe for
> lawyers and phisycions that . . .

redound to]	'Turn to the disgrace of'.

sudden confusion]	Jerome:
	    confundantur subito
	    let them suddenly be confounded
	Campensis:
	    vehementer conturbentur
	    let them be ... sodenly brought to confusyon.

deface]	'Defeat'. This meaning is found at the end of John Bale's *Preface to the Examinations of Anne Askewe* (Parker Soc. p. 144): Thus chooseth the Lord the foolish of this world to confound the wise, and the weak to deface the mighty
crafty]	'Devilish temptation'.
suggestion]	*Pilg. Perf.* 1526 fol. 52 *recto*: the subtell and crafty suggestions of the ennemy [the Devil].
health]	Wyatt's word for 'salvation' throughout the Psalms.
essay]	'Attempt'.

WYATT AND SAVONAROLA

If Caxton's version of II *Sam.* Chapters XI and XII gives us a fair picture of how the 'common man' externally saw David, there is a more inward picture to be obtained from a document which was taken to heart by learned and lay alike, by extreme Catholic and extreme Protestant, from the time of its composition in 1498. It was in that year that Savonarola, while in prison and just before he died, completed his *Meditatio Pia* on this psalm. The number of editions in Latin in the following years tells its own tale. More significant is the number of translations into the European vernaculars, for this assures us that the work spoke to the lay man and the lay woman as much as to the learned.

Although Savonarola himself may have been in danger of a

charge of heresy, his last work was never challenged or put on the Index. Yet it was specially welcomed by Luther, who treasured it for its inwardness, although he regretted occasional traces of what he called *humanae Theologiae lutum* — traces of mud of merely human theology as distinct from that promulgated by Luther himself. Here, then, in an age where toleration was virtually unknown, and people were being tortured to death for differences in their interpretation of Christianity, we may believe that we come upon a quiet centre of true inwardness, the voice in fact of the quiet practising Christian unheard in the loud professionals' war of words. This, we may imagine, was what Europe as a whole understood by the voice of true penitence. In this meditation Savonarola became a kindred spirit of all Christians, not merely those who opposed the Papacy and condemned its works. This was well expressed by Marcel Bataillon in his *Erasme en Espagne*:

> *Confession de l'humaine misère, appel à la miséricorde divine, besoin de sentir naître en soi un coeur pur, qui est l'oeuvre de Dieu et le seul présent digne d'un Dieu indifférent aux offrandes cérémonielles, tout ce qui sera l'âme de la vie religieuse en Europe de 1510 à 1560 trouve dans ce petit livre une de ses expressions les plus émouvantes.*
> (All that in the years 1510 to 1560 is going to constitute the finer side of religious life in Europe finds one of its most moving expressions in this little book: a confession of the wretched state of sinners, an appeal to God's mercy, a need to feel the birth within of a pure heart created by God's work in man and the only worthy offering to be made to a God unmoved by ceremonial acts of devotion.)

Whereas I have not been able to convince myself that Wyatt read any English translations of the various versions of the Latin psalms (Zwingli, Campensis, Bucer, etc.), I think it is very likely that he came under Savonarola's influence as a result of reading the *Meditation* in one or other of the printed *English* Primers, devotional manuals for the use of the laity, which began to appear from 1534. The English translation of Savonarola's piece is so lively that it would deserve a place in any anthology of Early Tudor prose immediately after the inspired — no lesser word will do — Biblical versions by Tyndale and Coverdale. Although the spirit behind some of these Primers may have been pro-Lutheran —

this translation of the *Meditatio* is followed in some Primers by a section on *Faith and Good Works* which presupposes Lutheran sympathies — Wyatt himself does not in his version of *Miserere mei* incline at all heavily in Luther's direction. If Wyatt is Lutheran here, it is when he comes close to those passages of Luther's own exposition of this psalm which resemble reflections made by Savonarola and other Catholic Christians. (What chiefly brings all these men together is the conviction that in this psalm David was being granted more than human insight. They followed Peter's remarks in the *Acts of the Apostles* that David had been inspired by the Holy Ghost directly or had been given a prophetic vision of the resurrection of Christ.)

Inspection of the details of the Commentary will show that, while Wyatt continued to draw on his main 'sources', notably Fisher, they are less prominent here than in his version of Psalm 6. Although I cannot expect to have traced all Wyatt's reading in contemporary works on this popular psalm that has left a mark on his own version, I have been able to show how close Wyatt comes at various points to what we can find in some of the most prominent contemporary writings available to him. I have included Luther's book of 1538 because of the resemblances of thought and expression, but if it can be shown that Wyatt had completed his versions before this date, Luther cannot strictly be included among Wyatt's 'sources'.

Further evidence supporting the view that Wyatt's versions of the Seven Psalms are thoroughly *eclectic*, in the sense of having been drawn from many interpretations put forward by extremists both on the Roman Catholic and on the Protestant sides, as well as by traditional and middle-of-the-road theologians, comes from the presence in the translations of borrowings from a little treatise by Jacopo Sadoleto, *Interpretatio in psalmum Miserere mei Deus*. When this reached Erasmus in 1525, he expressed pleasure,[1] and may have been instrumental in having an edition brought out north of the Alps. (Wyatt may have acquired his copy in the 1533 edition of the *Enchiridion Psalmorum*,[2] Wyatt's main source of *Hebraica veritas*.) Sadoleto was admired for his Latin style but was not a professed theologian. Luther scorned the pretensions of the Italian humanist to have religious insight into the psalm.[3]

1 Erasmus, *Ep*. 1586 (Allen, *Opus Epistolarum*, Tom. VI, p. 115.)
2 Brought out by Gryphius of Lyons.
3 Luther WA Tischreden Vol. IV, No. 4341, p. 235.

Miserere mei

Rue on me]

If Wyatt is the only translator (except a contemporary Scots poet Alexander Scott, who begins his *The Fifty Psalm* with *Rue on my misery* — but this may be direct imitation) from the earliest efforts to the present to depart from the traditional 'have mercy upon us', he must have had a strong motive for the change. It may therefore be a case of further imitation that Surrey, having to translate *miserere domus* in Virgil's *Aeneid* Book IV/ 318, wrote *Rue on this realme*. Wyatt retained the phrase in his next psalm: *Rue on Sion* (A.V. 102). It is, of course, the traditional phrase in a lover's appeal.

goodness and grace]

A set phrase, to judge by Lydgate's *Pilgrimage*, where, referring to God, he speaks
> Off his grace & his goodnesse.

And not only in English, to judge by Luther's
> *bonitas et misericordia Dei* WA/321/21
> God's goodness and mercy.

of thy nature]

Fisher p. 166/6-7:
> Of his nature also he is more redy to shewe mercy . . .

Wyatt returns to this topic at the end of *De Profundis* (A.V. 130) where Campensis had:
> *est enim natura misericordissimus & suapte natura ad succurrendum propensissimus*
> for he is most mercyful of kynde & of his owne nature most redy to helpe

bountiful]

Fisher p. 172/33-35:
> Thy mercy is & at all tymes hath ben so grete & bountefull to wretched synners.

brace]

'Hold together'.

Repugnant natures]

'Things which naturally fight against each other'. At this point Wyatt leaves the psalm (and Aretino) to insert a thought endeared to him perhaps by his reading of Boethius' *Consolation* and Chaucer. At the end of the *Knight's Tale* Theseus makes an important speech which begins:

The fyrst mouer of the cause aboue
Whan he fyrst made the fayre cheyne of loue
Greet was the effect & hygh was hys entent
Wel wyste he why & what ther of he ment
For wyth that fayr cheyne of loue he bonde
The fyre the eyr the water and the londe
In certeyn bondis that may not fle . . .

Chaucer was here drawing on the *De Consolatione Philosophiae* Book II Metrum VIII, where we may find a line corresponding to Wyatt's *repugnant natures*:

quod pugnantia semina
foedus perpetuum tenent . . .

It is Love that governs earth, sea and heaven, which sees to it that seeds which would otherwise fight against each other observe a perpetual treaty of amity . . .

On the other hand, both Sadoleto (See List B) and Luther saw a contradiction in the very phrase *miserere mei*, for David the sinner was asking help from the enemy of sins. Sadoleto wrote (*sig.* B iv *recto*):

Nihil autem inimicius est, nec magis infestum inter se quam peccatum & Deus, ut nullo pacto possint in unum conuenire . . .

What things could be more repugnant and more mutually at war with each other than Sin and God? They could never possibly be brought together.

In his *Enarratio* of 1538 Luther wrote (WA 332):

Hoc uero est coniungere duo incompatibilia, ut loquuntur . . .

This is indeed a case of what people call joining together two things which are incompatible.

quiet wonderful]   'Miraculous peace'.

number without end]   All the commentators have been happy to say this. Sadoleto has:

Dei misericordia infinita est . . . iniquitates & peccata, quarum multitudo nullo contineri numero uidetur, longe tamen sint plures miserationes Dei . . .

God's mercy is without end . . . sins and wickedness cannot be numbered, yet God's mercies are far more numerous.

plentiful]　　　In the Prologue to Psalm 38 we find:
And found mercy at Mercy's plentiful hand. That this was one of what were called in the Critical Introduction 'consecrated phrases' may be seen from many contemporary uses, such as this from *Gest. Rom. Add. Stories* p. 439 (See List A):
ye . . . shall fynde ye mercy of God plentefull . . .

much more . . . sin]　　　Fisher p. 97/32:
How greuous and how grete so euer our synne be, yet the mercy of god is moche more . . . And how many soo euer they be in nombre, yet the mercyes of hym be many more by the whiche he may do awaye all our trespasses . . .

Do way]　　　'wipe out'.
In the 'Wyclifite' Primers we find *do away, do thou awei*, and *do way*.
Fisher p. 98/4:
Good lorde doo awaye my synne . . .

offend]　　　Aretino:
cotali iniquità che offendono
such wrongs as offend . . .

Again]　　　'Again and again', translating the *etiam atque etiam* of many versions.
Joye:
Nowe & yet agene washe me fro my wikednes
Joye (B):
And yet agayn wassh me more/ . . . and make me cleane . . .

clean]　　　Fisher p. 100/20–21:
make me clene fro my synne

aye]　　　'For ever', 'always'.

wont]　　　Savonarola:
. . . deale gently, as thou arte wonte to do.

no number . . . said]　　　Wyatt is following the argument of Savonarola that we should apply to the relations between man and God what was laid down in the New Testament for the behaviour of man to man.

The Gospell of S. Mathew. The .xviii. Chapter:
> Then came Peter to him, and sayde: master howe ofte shall I forgeve my brother, yf he synne agaynst me, seven tymes? Iesus sayd vnto him: I saye not vnto the seven tymes: but seventy tymes seven tymes.

Savonarola:
> Dost thou vse to spare a synfull man vntyll a certayn nombre of his synnes?

interprets Jesus' seven times to stand 'for an infinite nombre'.

prescribe]   Erasmus *Misericordia* p. 26 *recto*:
> he prescribeth no nombre of synnynge

hearts returned]   The meaning is made clear in the Prologue to *De Profundis* (A.V. 130):
> . . . rightful penitence
> Which is alone the heart returned again
> And sore contrite . . .

beknow]   'Acknowledge', as in Bucer:
> *Nam scelera mea agnosco*
> I acknowledge my crimes.

in my sight]   Fisher p. 103/6-7:
> my synne is as an objecte to my syght, it is euer in my syght

fixed]   Wyatt wrote 'fixid', scanned as two syllables.

perfect]   i.e. in order to complete all the stages of full repentance. Wyatt is giving a 'Protestant' version of the 'Catholic' phrases in these lines of Savonarola:
> *ita perfice contritionem meam, imple confessionem meam et perduc ad finem satisfactionem meam.*

In *A goodly prymer* of 1534 we find a similar 'Protestant' deviation:
> Therfore (oh lorde) as thou has gyuen this grace vnto me to know my wyckednes, and to bewayle my synne: euyn so accomplyshe thy beneuolence, gyuying me a perfecte fayth, and drawyng me vnto thy son, whiche

hath made a full satisfaction for all my synnes.

To thee . . . trespassed] Wyclif:
> To the a lone y haue synned

Fisher p. 102/36:
> onely to the I haue trespassed and offended before thy syght

measure . . . fault] Wyatt has returned to a thought in Psalm 6, where he said:
> I open here and spread
> My fault to thee, but thou for thy goodness
> Measure it not in largeness nor in breadth . . .

but thou alone] The commentators were puzzled about the sense here.

Sadoleto:
> *Solum fuisse Deum conscium Dauidici criminis, primum quia ipse solus maxime cordium inspector est . . . Deinde peccatum certe Dauidis occultum hominibus fuit . . .*
> God alone knew of David's crime, first because he alone is the true scrutineer of hearts . . . Then David's sin was certainly hidden from men . . .

For in thy sight] Vulgate:
> *malum coram te feci*
> I have done evil in thy presence

Savonarola:
> for I haue synned euyn in thy syght

aghast] Rolle:
> *non reueritus offendere faciem domini sui*
> [like a servant] not afraid to offend the countenance of his master

Campensis:
> *non reueritus conspectum tuum*
> not fearing thy presence

Savonarola:
> I was nothyng ashamed to synne before thy face.

judging . . . So that] i.e. deciding that so long as no man knew of my sin it did not matter that God knew of it.

hid . . . man]

Savonarola:
> Oh mercyfull god, howe many synnes haue
> I done in thy syght, which I wolde in no
> wyse haue done before mortall men, yea
> that I wolde not in any case that men
> shulde knowe? I feared men more than
> the [e.]

Paris 1523 (see List B):
> *feci coram te quod coram hominibus non*
> *fecissem*
> I have done in thy sight what I would not
> have done in the sight of men

majesty]

'Terrible power'.
cf. Job 37/22:
> with God is terrible majesty.

In the Prologue to the First Psalm Wyatt had
written of David:
> Forgetting eke God's majesty as fast,
> Yea, and his own . . .

Savonarola:
> I fynde no name, by the which I may
> name or expose thyn inenarrable maiestie

know . . . repent]

The emphasis on *repent* is found only in Zwingli.
Joye:
> it beruweth me and it repenteth me to haue
> had done this grevouse sinne in thy sight

Whereby . . . stable]

i.e. in doing so Thou shalt remain true to Thy
solemn promise.

pure and clean]

'Irreproachably uncorrupted'. The only translator
to make this point was Martin Bucer:
> *propterea uere iustus agnosceris in uerbis*
> *tuis & purus*

which Joye translated:
> wherfore very iuste shalt thou be knowne
> in thy wordis and pure . . .

forthwith . . . grace]

The meaning is obscure, but might run as follows:
'I am immediately made capable of being justified
by God's free gift'. [God justifies, makes me
righteous and capable of salvation, by his just
judgement.] The passage puzzled all the commentators. Wyatt's meaning and play on the

root 'just' resembles Luther's:
> *sum iustus et iustificatus per iustum et*
> *iustificantem Christum*   327/33
> I am just and justified by a just and justi-
> fying Jesus.

Luther's meaning is made clear by his gloss:
> Wherefore remember that God's justice is
> that by which we are justified or the gift of
> the remission of sins. This justice in God is
> pleasing, for it makes of God not a just judge,
> but a forgiving father who wishes to use his
> justice not to judge sinners but to justify and
> release them from their sins.   445/25-29

unstable]   Sadoleto:
> *nostram fluxam & labentem ad delinquen-*
> *dum naturam*
> our frail and unstable nature

Formed in offence]   Bucer:
> *En ego cum iniquitate fictus sum*
> Lo, I was fashoned in wikednes

conceived]   Fisher p. 106/1-2:
> Beholde I was conceyued in synne

This is likely to be a reference to the doctrine of
'original sin', as in Savonarola:
> in her am I polluted with originall synne.

nativity]   Fisher p. 225/18:
> from our natyuyte and first comynge in to
> this worlde

excuse]   Aretino:
> *Non per iscusare il mio fallo*
> Not to excuse my sin

Paris 1523 (see List B):
> *Nec haec dico deus meus, ad excusandas*
> *accusationes quibus a te de peccatis possem*
> *merito accusari . . . sed vt tu deus . . . ad*
> *miserendum mei facilius inclineris . . .*
> My God, I do not say this to excuse the
> accusations with which I might justly be
> charged by you for my sins, but in order
> that you, God, may be more readily inclined
> to take pity on me . . .

But of]

Aretino:
> *ma per dimostrare quanto bisogno io ho della tua misericordia*
> but to show what need I have of your mercy

For, lo, . . . truth]

Wyclif:
> For lo thow lovedist truthe

Fisher p. 106/29–30:
> thou arte true and louest trouth aboue all thynge

Wyatt occasionally omits the final -t of the second person singular. Here *loues* appears to be a monosyllable.

inward heart]

In stressing 'inward', which is not found in any of the English ('Wyclifite') versions based on the Vulgate, Wyatt may have been influenced by the body of Protestant commentary, represented here by quotations from Bucer and Bugenhagen (see List B).

Bucer:
> *sapientiam, quae in penetrali cordis resideret*
> wysdome which thou woldst to sitte in the secrets of my harte
> *in intimis cogitationibus & affectibus . . . in operto penetrali cordis*
> in intimate thoughts and feelings in the hidden secret places of the heart.

Bugenhagen:
> *dilexisti ueritatem in nobis, ut abiecta hypocrisi uere in intimis cordis nos agnoscamus qui simus . . .*
> You have loved truth in us that we might throw away hypocrisy and know who we really are in the intimate places of our hearts . . .

to follow the *Hebraica veritas* expounded by Campensis:
> *tu fidem tamen et candorem, qui in pebetralibus pectoris situs est maxime amare soles*
> yet wast thou wont to loue fayth & innocencie that lyeth within the harte . . .

This was one of the major points where Protestants were happy to quote from the Holy Fathers of the Church. Not that they rested their case solely on these authorities, but, as Becon put it in *The Pathwaye vnto Prayer* (The fifthe chapter):

> I haue called the holy & catholyke Doctors to witnes, bicause they teach the same thynge that the Scripture dothe . . .

Two of his quotations from St. Augustine appear to confirm this claim. The first is to be found at the beginning of *De Magistro* Liber Unus:

> *Deus autem in ipsis rationalis animae secretis, qui homo interior uocatur, & quaerendus & deprecandus est: haec enim sua templa esse uoluit . . .*

Which Becon translated as follows:

> But God is both to be soughte & to be prayed vnto, euen in the very secrete partes of a reasonable soule, which is called the inward man. For he wylleth that these be his Temples . . .

Augustine goes on to quote from the New Testament:

> *An apud Apostolum non legisti, Nescitis quia templum Dei estis, & spiritus Dei habitat in vobis & In interiore homine habitare Christum?*

> Have you not read in the Gospel: *Are ye not ware that ye are the temple of god, and how that the sprete of god dwelleth in you?* (The fyrst epistle of S. Paul to the Corinthyans. The .iii. Chapter) and *that ye may be strengthed with myght by his sprete in the inner man* (The epistle of S. Paul to the Ephesyans. The .iii. Chapter)

In the same treatise Becon quotes from a work which was reissued in 1531 in a format which could go into Wyatt's smallest pocket:

> *Sententiae aliquot . . . ex omnibus Augustini . . . libris, per PROSPERVM episcopum Rheginensem . . . selectae, Coloniae . . .*

No. CCCXXXIII:

> *Quid supplicaturus deo locum aptum & sanctum requiris? Interiora tua munda, et omni inde mala cupiditate depulsa, praepara tibi in cordis tui pace secretum. Volens in*

*templo orare, in te ora; & ita age semper,
vt dei templum sis . . .*

which Becon rendered:

> . . . make cleane thy inward partes, & all
> euell lustes expulsed from thence, prepare
> thy selfe a secrete place in the peace of thy
> herte. Thou wyllyng to pray in the temple,
> praye in thy selfe, and so behaue thy selfe
> alway, that thou mayste be the temple of God.

Becon also cites from the New Testament *Matt.*
6.6:

> *Tu autem cum oraueris, intra in cubiculum
> tuum, et clauso ostio ora Patrem tuum in
> abscondito . . .*
>
> But when thou prayest, entre into thy cham-
> ber, and shut thy dore to the, and praye to
> thy father which ys in secrete . . .

and 2 *ad Cor.* 6.16:

> *Vos enim estis templum Dei uiui . . .*
>
> Ye are the temple of the lyuynge god . . .

These passages will help the reader to answer the
questions posed in the Critical Introduction (see
pp. 19–20):

> Does Wyatt in fact embody the best that
> the age had to offer? Is he the poetic voice
> of the religious revival which can be dis-
> cerned in all shades of Christian belief?
> Has he embodied what the finest religious
> spirits cared for?

Though . . . lore]   Campensis:

> *Quanquam ego uitiatae carnis impulsu
> foedissime lapsus sum*
>
> though I haue gotten a foule fal thorow
> the motion of my corrupte flesh

frailty]   'Weakness of the flesh', as in Psalm 6: the flesh
frail. Tyndale *Obedience* Fo: xcix *verso*:

> As oft as thou fallest thorow fraylte/repente
> and come agayne

Pellican:

> *non ex malitia & contemptu, sed ex fragil-
> itate carnis . . . permotus fuerit* (see list B.)
>
> . . . was moved not by malice and contempt
> but by the frailty of the flesh

overthwart]   i.e. overcoming my true self, my fidelity

wilful malice]   'Deliberate evil will', as in *Pilg. Perf.* (see list A):
                              Mortall synnes, & carnall consentes to the
                              same, and wylfull delectacyons in synne
                    Campensis:
                              non enim tam malitia hoc scelus admisi
                              quam concupiscentia uictus
                              for I haue not done this wickednesse so
                              greatly of malice as ouercome with con-
                              cupiscence

drawn . . . apart]   'Seduced'.

Wherefore . . . lore]   'Campensis:
                              quare iterum occultis inspirationibus docere
                              me solidam sapientiam, sicut soles, non
                              dedignaberis
                              Wherfore thou shalt yet voutsafe to teach
                              me thy perfect wysdome as thou wast wont
                              to do

hidden wisdom]   Aretino:
                              le cose . . . occulte della tua sapientia
                              the hidden things of thy wisdom

faith . . . decay]   Campensis:
                              [fidem et candorem] a quo non omnino
                              sum alienus . . .
                              [Fayth & innocencie] . . . from the which I
     * swerved   am not swarued* al together

                    Pilg. Perf. (1526) fo: lii *recto* (list A):
                              [feyth] in tyme & case of necessite whan
                              it shulde seme to decay

Jews . . . leper]   Several commentators here refer the reader to
                    Leviticus Ch. 14, because the main details of
                    cleansing lepers were thought to be figuratively
                    applicable to penance.

leper sore]   Possibly 'the disease of leprosy' rather than 'the
                    diseased man'.

With hyssop . white]   Wyatt is close to the Vulgate:
                              Asperges me hyssopo, et mundabor: luuubis
                              me, et super niuem dealbabor.
                              Sprencle and make me clene lyke as with
                              ysope: thou shalte wasshe me and I shall
                              be made more whyte than snowe.

how foul]

Presumably 'however foul', although I have not found an exact parallel. The more usual idiom is represented by Fisher 97/32:

> How greuous and how grete so euer our synne be . . .

but in a letter by Tyndale to John Frith we find:

> Sir, if you may write, how short it be, forget it not.

Pellican:

> *ut . . . omnes cognoscant te poenitentium susceptorem, quamlibet grauiter peccauerint.*
> that all may know that you are the champion of the penitent however deeply they may have sinned.

gladsome tidings]

Although *glad tidings* may be traced at least as far back as the thirteenth century, the only use of *gladsome* I have found is in Charles d'Orléans Ballade 31 (p. 39) line 1135:

> O come to me sum gladsum tidyng newe

Luther explains at length what these tidings were:

> For we hear of joy in baptism when it is said, I baptise you in the name of the Father, the Son and the Holy Ghost. 'He that believeth and is baptized shall be saved.' We hear of joy in the Last Supper where it is said, 'This is my body, which is given for you', 'this is the cup of my blood which is shed for [you] for the remission of sins.' In Confession, too, or what I should better call absolution . . . we hear the sound of joy. 'Believe, your sins are forgiven through the death of Christ.'   411/24-30:

Sadoleto and others thought rather of the specific promises made to the historic David about the future prosperity of his house, as set out in II *Sam*. Ch. VII, 12-17.

When . . . dust]

'When, at the Second Coming, Christ, the Remitter of our sins, shall come down from heaven, then shall the dead arise and rejoice.'

Wyatt appears to have started from a hint in Campensis:

> *tum exultabunt ossa mea*
> then shall my bones be mery

or Erasmus *Misericordia*:
> my humble bones shall leap for joy

but the development comes from Sadoleto, who may have put *consumed to dust* into Wyatt's head, for he argued that the *ossa humiliata* of the Vulgate meant bones reduced to smithereens, bones ground to dust. More important, Wyatt followed up Sadoleto's argument (which had the support of Peter's remarks in the Second Chapter of the Acts:

> Therfore seinge he was a Prophet, and knewe that God had sworne with an othe to him, that the frute of his loynes shuld sit on his seat (in that Christ shulde ryse agayne in the flesshe) he sawe before: and spake in the resurreccion of Christ, that his soule shulde not be left in hell: nether his flesshe shuld se corrupcion).

that the Holy Ghost enabled David's confidence to extend beyond the promises made to his house and to reach the *Dies Irae* and the resurrection of our bodies at the Second Coming. But it seems to be Wyatt's own decision to make David anticipate the account of that Day which is given in *The fyrst epistle of S. Paul to the Tessalonyans*. The .iiii. Chapter:

> For the Lorde him selfe shall descende from heuen with a showte and the voyce of the archangell and trompe of God. And the deed in Christe shall aryse fyrst ...

Look ... offending] Fisher p. 116/19:
> Good lorde loke not vpon my synnes

do away] Wyclif:
> and do awei alle my

Make a clean heart] Wyclif:
> Make a clene herte in me god

in the midst of] Paris 1523:
> ... *dares nobis cor nouum, & splrltum houum poneres in medio nostri*
> give us a new heart, and put a new spirit in the midst of us ...

sprite upright]

A literal translation of the Vulgate: *spiritum rectum*. Wyatt used the phrase again in his Seventh Psalm:

> For thou, my God, thy blessed sprite upright

Savonarola:

> an vpryghte spirite make a newe within me

voided]

A stronger expression than *purged*. Cooper (see list A) used it to translate *euacuatus*.
Pilg. Perf. 1531 Fo: lxxix. *recto.*

> voyded from all . . . pryde

Maskell, Vol. III p. 7 quotes from a primer of 1545:

> That oure heartes be voyded quyte
> From phansy and fond delyght . . .

thine eyes' cure]

'Overseeing'. This may be Wyatt's invention.

cast me not]

Wyclif:

> Caste thou me not awei fro thi face

Fisher p. 120/32:

> cast me not out of thy syght

unrest]

Wyatt uses the word in the context of love, as in *The flaming sighs*:

> . . . can well declare
> The heart's unrest . . .

sprite of holiness]

'The Holy Ghost'.
Wyclif:

> and take thou not awei from me thin hooli spirit

Render to me]

Vulgate:

> *Redde mihi leticiam salutaris tui*
> Render to me joy of thy salvation

Campensis:

> *restitue mihi gaudium quod de salute mihi per te praestanda concepi*
> sende me the gladnesse ageyne which I had gotten because of the health that thou shuldest gyue me.

My will confirm]

'Strengthen'.
Vulgate:

> *spiritu principali confirma me*
> Strengthen me with a principal spirit

Wyclif:

> and conferme thou me

steadfastness]

Fisher p. 121/32:

stedfaste in all vertue without any wauerynge
. . .

p. 122/12:

Lorde make me stedfast in fayth

Sadoleto:

stabilitatem in recta uoluntate... firmitatem constantis in Deum uoluntatis . . . firmitatem ac stabilitatem rectae uoluntatis . . .

steadfastness in a right will . . . the strength of a constant will toward God . . . the strength and steadfastness of a right will. . .

And by this]

Campensis:

Hoc ubi praestiteris mihi

When thou hayst done this for me

address]

'Steer', 'direct'.

Wyclif:

dresse oure feet

Joye:

And I shal directe transgressors in to thy waye

They shall return]

Joye:

and sinners shalbe converted vnto the

Savonarola:

They shal leaue theyr owne wayes,

and come vnto thyne . . .

Zwingli:

peccatores ad te redibunt

sinners shall return to thee

My tongue shall praise]

ut celebret lingua mea

that my tongue might praise

Coverdale has these very words.

justification]

Joye:

thy rightwysmaking

Wyatt's rejection of the traditional word 'justice' and the substitution of 'justification' suggest the distinction drawn by Luther:

. . . your justice, that is to say, the grace by which you forgive sins and take pity on us. I must confess that this word 'Justice' caused me much sweat because it is commonly interpreted as the truth by which God damns according to deserts or judges those who have done wrong. They used to contrast this justice and oppose it to the mercy by which believers are saved. This interpretation is not only empty but highly dangerous, for it stirs up a latent hatred against God and his justice. For who could love a being who deals with sinners strictly according to their deserts? You must therefore remember to think of God's justice here as that by which we are justified or the gift of remission of our sins.

444/35– 445/26.

My mouth]   Campensis:
    ut os meum praedicet laudes tuas
    that my mouth maye speake of thy prayses

spread . . . glorious]   Savonarola:
    Thy chyldren haue spredde thy glory thrugh-
    out all the worlde

of thyself]   Bugenhagen:
    solius est opus dei & creatio
    it is the work and creation of God alone
  Bucer:
    Dei opus est non nostrum
    it is God's work not ours

operation]   Tyndale *A Prologe to the Romayns* p. 295:
    Suche a newe hert and lusty corage vnto the
    lawe warde, canst thou neuyr come by of
    thyn awne strength and enforcemente, but
    by the operacyon and workynge of the
    spirite.
  Luther *Enarratio Psalmi LI,* 1538/364:
    Hoc enim tuum tempus, tempus est, quod
    requirit diuinam operationem et opem, qua
    peccatorem iuues et consoleris
    For this is your time, the time which asks
    for divine working and aid to help and com-
    fort the sinner.

blood]   Presumably the vicarious murder of Uriah.

Among the just]   The passage supposes that David was looking into
the future to the time when Christ would be able
to save men, that is, free them from sin, and join
them to the blessed immortals. Only then would
they be able to praise God rightly. The passage

already quoted from the first epistle to the Thessalonians continues:

> then shall we which live and remayne, be caught vp with them also in the cloudes, to mete the Lorde in the ayer. And so shall we ever be with the Lorde.

Sadoleto took a similar line:

> We now pray that by God's own gift, a sense of grief, worthily felt to match our crimes, may open our mouths that we may ask Him for mercy, in order that, when we are eventually received back into favour, and admitted into the company of the Kingdom of Heaven, we may speak out and publish His praise. This is what David wanted to take place even then, for even then he had been instructed with foresight by the Holy Ghost, and was already beginning to understand Christian mysteries.

relation]   i.e. that I may be included among.

Erasmus *Coll*. p. 472 has:

> *in diuorum consortium relatis*
> included in the company of the gods

Becon *Pathway of prayer* The seventh chapter.

> Who woulde not have thought thys holy religious father worthy to be canonysed & related into the number of Sayntes?

Bucer:

> *uere . . . in numerum filiorum Dei cooptati*
> truly elected to join the company of the Sons of God

lauds]   'Praises'.

my lips]   Erasmus *Misericordia* p. 82 *recto*:

> O lorde thou shalte open my lyppes and my mouth shal shew thy preise

Although Wyatt wrote *lypps*, he may have intended *lyppis* and thus a line of ten syllables.

unloose]   Thomas Sternhold *Al suche psalmes as 'l'. Sternehold didde in his life time draw into metre*, 1549:

> My lips that yet fast closed be
> Do thou, O Lord, vnloose

if thou . . . esteemed]   'If Thou hadst thought it would be pleasing to Thee'.

Wyatt wrote *estemid* and would scan the word as having three syllables.

Aretino:

> *se tu hauessi uoluto altro sacrificio*
> *certamente io te lo haurei fatto*
> if thou hadst wished for any other sacrifice
> I would surely have made it for you

Wyclif:

> For if thou haddist wold sacrifice

outward deeds]   Although the phrase was a 'fighting remark' of a typical Protestant, it is found both in Aretino:

> *sono cerimonie che appaiano di fuora*
> they are ceremonies which appear outwardly

and Campensis:

> *Externis sacrificijs . . . non placaberis*
> Thou wylt not be pacifyed wyth outward sacrifyces

yet the whole passage down to 'dream and devise' must have been dictated by anti-Catholic feeling, as we may judge from Tyndale's tone here: *A Prologe to the Epistle of Paule to the Romayns*

> This word Lawe maye not be understonde as it goeth with mannes lawe where the lawe is fulfilled with oute warde workes only, though the hert be never so farre of. But God iudgeth the grounde of the herte, ye and the thoughtes and the secret mouynges of the mynde, and therefore his lawe requireth the grounde of the hert and loue from the botome there of, and is not content with the oute ward worke only: but rebuketh those workes most of all which springe not of loue from the ground and low botome of the herte, though they appere outward neuer so honest and good, as Christ in the gospell rebuketh the Pharises aboue all other that were open synners, and calleth them ypocrites, that is to say Simulars, and paynted Sepulchres. Which Pharises yet lyued no men so pure, as perteynynge to the outewarde dedes and workes of the lawe.

I would have]	Savonarola: I wolde surely haue . . .
offered]	Joye (B): or els I had offred them
delightest not]	Joye (B): thou delytest nat in them Wyatt wrote: *delyghtes.*
gloze]	'Flattering deceit', as in *the glosing bait* of Psalm 6.
dream and devise]	A sneer, as in Tyndale's *A Prologe to the Romayns*: Faith is not mans opinion and dreame, as some ymagin and fayne . . . So Luther used *somniare*, dream.
thee, Lord,]	This is how I believe Wyatt shaped the line, but the very same spelling and want of punctuation would have been used by him if he had wanted what all his editors suppose he intended, i.e. a third-person reference, *the Lord.* It must be conceded that Wyatt's first thought certainly was to follow the versions which kept close to the Vulgate: *Sacrificium Deo spiritus contribulatus,* such as Joye's: The sacrifice that god desierth is a contrite spirit, when he wrote: The sacryfice that plesithe god most is spryte contrite . . . But it is hard to see why Wyatt should then make a change which made no difference to the sense. I suppose the change was made to keep the direct second-person address to God (Thou, Thee, Thy) running through the poem from the first line to the last without the one break we find in the Vulgate (which, incidentally, does not appear in the modern Vulgate). A more obvious case of the general failure to follow Wyatt's intentions occurs when editors print the opening of his version of Psalm 102 in the A.V. as: Lord, hear my prayer, and let my cry pass Unto the Lord without impediment. Here Wyatt was literally following the Vulgate:

Domine, exaudi orationem meam:
Et clamor meus ad te veniat
or the close translation made by Aretino:
fa che il mio grido giunga a te
let my cry come to Thee.
There are several such editorial failures to recognize when Wyatt intended *Thee* by his *the*, the normal spelling of *thee* at this time, but none is so certain as this.

liketh]   This impersonal use of *liketh* is found in Coverdale's Bible:
that euery one shulde do as it lyked him.

low . . . humble]   The OED offers an excellent parallel in Gower's *Confessio Amantis* I/118:
thou most . . . with low herte humblesce suie . . .
Cooper translated *humilis* with both words, *humble and low.* For *humilis ac demissus* he gives *Humble and lowly.*

pleasant host]   'A sacrificial victim pleasing to God', as in Bucer: *Hostiae Deo gratae*, translated by Joye:
Acceptable sacrifyces to god.
Surrey reworded the passage and tacked it on to the fourth chapter of his version of Ecclesiastes:
In humble sprite is sett the temple of the
Lorde
wher yf thow enter loke thy mouth and
conscyence may accorde
whose churche is buylt of loue and decte
with hoote desyre
and symple fayth the yolden hoost his
marcy dothe requyre . . .
In booste of owtwarde workes he taketh no
delight . . .

Make Sion . . . still]   Traces of this thought can be found in Aretino. In his paraphrase of the next psalm (A.V. 102), he wrote:
il Signore ha edificato Sion nelle sincere menti de gli huomini eletti dallo Spirito santo
the Lord has built Sion in the pure minds of the men elected by the Holy Ghost.
But the full significance of *inward* is best brought

out in Paris 1523 *sig.* d.ij.*verso*:

> Sion here means the higher part of the soul.
> Just as in the citadel placed on the high
> ground of the physical Jerusalem the watch-
> man lying awake used to shout aloud when
> he caught sight of corporeal enemies, so that
> higher part of reason, called so because it is
> built in the highest ground of my soul, looks
> out and sees spiritual wickednesses attacking
> my inward Jerusalem and constantly roars
> and cries out against them . . .

A little later, glossing the reference to walls, he
went on:

> the walls, that is to say, of that inward
> Jerusalem which is my soul . . .

ghost] 'Spiritual'. Sadoleto here said that David, inspired
by the gift of prophecy, was looking forward to a
spiritual Sion.

strength the walls still] 'Continuously strengthen the walls of the Jerusalem
of the heart'.
The OED shows that the verb was commonly
used in connection with the walls of castles and
fortifications. The nearest parallel occurs in Sir
Thomas More's *A dyalogue of comforte* p. 2 *verso*:

> to stable and strength the walles of our
> hartes . . .

Then shalt thou] Wyclif:

> Thanne thou schalt take plesauntli the
> sacrifice of rightfulnesse . . .

Campensis:

> *Tum grata tibi erunt sacrificia, quae signa
> sunt iustitiae internae*
> Then shalt thou be pleased wyth sacrifyces
> (which are tokens of the inwarde ryght-
> uousnesse)

thee alone] Luther remarked that 'here, too, he attributes
everything to the kindness of God and not to his
own deserts and exertions'. I have not found such
a remark in any other contemporary commentary.
(This strengthens the case for supposing that
Wyatt's version was made after he had read Luther's
Enarratio of 1538.)

Of deep secrets

At this point in his *I Sette Salmi* Aretino put in a page in which he described how David meditated on the preceding psalm. Wyatt translated the substance in the three stanzas following these lines which, formally, constitute the first stanza of his Prologue to Psalm 102. But in this first stanza he continues the thought of the last lines of the psalm. It is in fact a piece of totally independent translation, as regards Aretino, but the thought, as the commentary shows, is similar to that of Luther and all those who supposed that David had been given unusual insight into the mysteries of the Christian religion. The lines therefore belong, not with the rest of the prologue but with the last portion of *Miserere mei.*

deep secrets]   Wyatt appears to be recalling the words of Paul in the second chapter of the first epistle to the Corinthians, where he is contrasting the wisdom of the world with the wisdom of God, which wisdom God may reveal to man through the Holy Ghost:

> The eye hath not sene, and the eare hath not hearde, nether haue entred into the herte of man, the thinges which God hath prepared for them that love him. But God hath opened them vnto vs by his sprete. For the sprete searcheth all thinges, ye the bottome of Goddes secretes.

The chapter ends with the proud boast:
> But we vnderstonde the mynde of Christ.

Of mercy . . . Justifying]   Wyatt's summary of the heads of the preceding psalm is interestingly both like and unlike Luther's 420/32:

> We have completed the chief part of this psalm in which the chief topics of our religion are handled, that is to say, what is Penitence, what Grace, what Justification, what are the causes of Justification.

astone]   'Astound'.

Who hath expressed]   Luther was one with other Christians in thinking that David had been visited by the Holy Spirit. In his introductory remarks he wrote 316/23:

> For who of men could so speak of Penitence and Remission of Sins as the Holy Spirit

speaks in this psalm?

entreat]   'Handle', 'treat of'.
                              Pilg. Perf. 1526 Fo: xl *recto*:
                                  Howe holy fathers entreated the secretes of
                                  religion.
                              Gerrard in *The Epicure* [C 3 *verso*] :
                                  Let vs intreate of other thynges . . .

WYATT AND LUTHER

If Wyatt himself in these Psalms seems to us to have anticipated
the pure eirenic spirit of the modern ecumenical movement, the
professional contestants in the tragic religious squabble seem to
have gone to the other extreme. We have to rub our eyes when we
see good men like More and Tyndale regarding each other as
desperately damned. If we follow one only, we shall never come to
understand the other. Consequently, as dialogue proved impossible,
the two rival views hardened and became irreconcilable, and
Christendom was split up. More saw it all coming, and helped it
to come by failing to see anything but *heresy* where he might have
found merely a shift of accent, and by turning his victims over
to the tender mercies of the 'secular arm'. The charge of heresy in
Tyndale's substitution, in his translation of the New Testament, of
penitence for *penance* appears to have been based solely on the
implied by-passing of the activity of the priest who heard *confession* and imposed *satisfaction.*

And on the other side, instead of seeing what was the real value
to Christian men of having priestly help, Tyndale fell back on the
words of the Bible as the sole authority:

> . . . by this word penaunce, they make the people
> vnderstonde holy dedes of their enioynynge, with
> which they must make satisfaccion vnto godwarde
> for their synnes. When al the scripture preacheth
> that christ hath made full satisfaccyon for oure
> synnes to godwarde, and we must now be thanke-
> full to god agayne and kyll the lustes of oure flesh
> wyth holy workes of gods enioynynge and to

> take pacientlye all that god layeth on my back.
> And if I haue hurte my neyboure, I am bounde to
> shriue my selfe vnto hym and to make hym a
> mendes, yf I haue where with, or if not then to axe
> him forgeuenesse, and he is bounde to forgeue me.
> And as for their penaunce the scripture knoweth
> not of. The greke hath Metanoia and metanoite,
> repentaunce and repente.

Similarly, More exaggerated the Lutheran contrast between 'faith' and 'works', and cried out:

> ... what can be a worse bylyefe, then to byleue
> that mennis good wurkes be they neuer so well
> done, be yet nothyng worthe, nor the man neuer
> the better for them, nor no rewarde for them
> commyng towarde man in heuen?

Wyatt nailed his colours to the mast in the prologue he composed, following Aretino, to go before his version of Psalm 130, *De Profundis* in the Vulgate. He made his position unmistakable in these lines:

> But our David judgeth in his intent
>   Himself by penance clean out of this case,
>   Whereby he hath remission of offence
> * praise   And ginneth to allow* his pain and penitence.

> But when he weighs the fault and recompense
>   He damns his deed and findeth plain
> Atween them two no whit equivalence
>   Whereby he takes all outward deed in vain
> To bear the name of rightful penitence
>   Which is alone the heart returned again
>   And sore contrite, that doth his fault bemoan,
>   And outward deed the sign or fruit alone.

> *fight With this he doth defend* the sly assault
> off   Of vain allowance of his void desert,
> And all the glory of his forgiven fault
>   To God alone he doth it whole convert.
> His own merit he findeth in default.

It is this explicit statement that enables us to proclaim that the
last lines of *Miserere mei* and the opening lines of the succeeding
poem form the doctrinal core of the poem. If we had any doubt
that these lines placed before *De Profundis* mark the point of
Wyatt's conversion to the views of Luther and Tyndale on the
topic of faith and works and the nature of true penitence, we have
only to look at the religious poems of Surrey to confirm the
impression that this Prologue made on him. I have discussed the
details in a former work.

Unfortunately, we come here to an instance where Wyatt has
not turned his argument into triumphant poetry. Indeed he moves
us less than Tyndale setting out what he called 'the order of
Justifying':

> Note now the ordyr/ first God geueth me light to
> se the goodnesse and ryghtwysnesse off the lawe
> and mine awne synne and vnryghtwesnesse. Out of
> whych knowlege springeth repentaunce. Now
> repentaunce teacheth me not that the law ys good/
> and I euell/ but a lyght that ye spyryte off God
> hath geuen me/ out of whych lyght repentaunce
> springeth.
>
> Then the same spirite worketh in myne herte trust
> and confidence to beleue the mercye of God and
> hys trueth/ that he wyll doo as he hath promised.
> whych beleffe saueth me. And immediatly out of
> that trust springeth loue towarde the lawe of god
> agayne. And whatsoeuer a man werketh of any
> other loue then thys it pleaseth not God/ ner is
> that loue Godly. Now loue doeth not receaue thys
> mercy but fayth only/ out of which fayth loue
> springeth/ by which loue I power out agayne
> vppon my neyboure that goodnesse wych I haue
> receaued of God by fayth. Here of ye se that I
> can not be iustified wyth out repentaunce and yet
> repentaunce iustyfieth me not. And here of ye se
> that I can not haue a faith to be iustified and
> saued/ excepte loue springe therof immediatly/
> and yet loue iustifieth me not before God.
>
> *(An Answere* Fo: C.xxi *verso)*

Wyatt's most explicitly 'Protestant' remark comes in these
lines:

> rightful penitence
> Which is alone the heart returned again
> And sore contrite that doth his fault bemoan,
> And outward deed the sign or fruit alone.

For this is the language of Luther, almost literally translated by Tyndale in his Prologue to the Epistle of Paul to the Romans:

> but as Abrahams circumcision was an outeward
> signe whereby he declared his righteousnes whiche
> he had by faith, and his obedience and redynes
> vnto the will of god, euen so are all other good
> workes outewarde signes and outeward frutes of
> fayth and of the sprite, which iustifie not a man,
> but that a man is iustified all redy before God in-
> wardly in the hert . . .

To this extent we may say that Wyatt was here siding against Sir Thomas More in the spirit of Tyndale, who wrote in his controversy with More:

> And when he [More] sayth/ yf fayth certyfye
> oure hertes that we be in the fauoure off God and
> oure synnes forgeuen and become good yer we doo
> good werkes/ as the tre must first be good yer it
> bringe forth good frute/ by christes doctrine/ then
> we make good workes but a shadowe where with a
> man is neuer ye better. Naie Sir we make good
> werkes/ frutes where by oure neyboure is the
> better and wherby God is honoured and oure flesh
> tamed. And we make of them sure tokens where
> by we know that our faith is no fayned imaginaciom
> and deed opinion made with captiuynge oure
> wyttes after the popis tradicions/ but a lyuely
> thinge wrought by the holygoste.
>
>   (*An Answere* Fol: C.xxii *verso*)

De Profundis

depth]   The usual word was *depenes*. The first to use
                            depth in this context was Savonarola's translator
                            in the *Primer* of 1534:
                            Lyfte vp me, whiche am so myserable;

*Abyssus abyssum
inuocat
Ps. 41(42)/8

shewe thy worke in me, & exercise thy power vpon me. One depthe requireth another,* the depthe of myserye requireth the depth of mercy. The depth of synne axeth the depth of grace and fauour. Greater is the depthe of mercy than the depthe of mysery. Let therfore the one depthe swalowe vp the other. Let the botomlesse depthe of mercy swalowe vp the profounde depthe of mysery.

heart's sorrow|

Wyatt may have pronounced something like *hartis sorw*, and certainly scanned the former word as two and the latter as one syllable.
Fisher p. 210/13–15:
    a grete inwarde sorowe comynge from the very depnes of the herte . . .
    . . . an inwarde sorowe of the mynde set in the preuy place of the herte . . .

repair]

'Haunt, habitual dwelling-place'.

Thee have I called]

Campensis:
    tuum auxilium imploraui o Domine
    I called for thy helpe o lorde

borrow]

'Pledge, surety'.
The old spellings, *borh, borw,* and the frequency of the rhyme with *sorw*, suggest the pronunciation, and indicate the scansion.
Rolle: *Psalter*
    Answere for me, that is, be borgh of myn amendynge
The religious use of the word is well brought out in Spenser's *Shepheardes Calender*, where in the poem on May, the remark: (lines 150–151)
    by my deare borrowe,
    If I may rest, I nill liue in sorrowe . . .
is glossed: 'that is our sauiour, the commen pledge of all mens debts to death'.

In my voice]

Bucer:
    Audi in uoce mea
    Hear in my voice

plaint]

Campensis:
    ad lamentabiles precationes meas

vnto my dolorous peticyons
Zwingli:
ad uocem querimoniarum mearum
vnto the voice of my complaynt (Joye)

overthrow]   'Defeat and discomfiture'.

grant]   'Promise'.
Wyclif:
      thei hadden graunt of Christ that he
      wolde algatis haue mercy . . .

entend]   'Listen sympathetically'.
Wyclif:
      Lord, here thou mi vois. Thin eeris he maad
      ententif in to the vois of my biseching . . .
      takynge entente to the voys of my preyere . . .

No place . . . Thine ear   Aretino:
thereto]
      perche non è niuno centro si profondo che
      ti uieti lo ascoltare . . . anzi le odi si come
      chi le fa ti fosse presente . . . adunque
      ascolta me . . .
      for there is no depth so deep that it prevents
      your hearing [the sinner's plaints] . . . rather
      you hear them as if the man making them
      were present to you . . . therefore hear me . . .

observe]   Vulgate:
      Si iniquitates obseruaberis, domine
      Lord, if you observe the wickednesses
Shakespeare put a similar thought into the mouth
of Angelo in *Measure for Measure*:
      Oh, my dread Lord,
      I should be guiltier then my guiltinesse,
      To thinke I can be vndiscerneable,
      When I perceiue your grace, like powre
                  diuine,
      Hath look'd vpon my passes . . .
but he may have had the Vulgate's Psalm 138
in mind:
      Imperfectum meum uiderunt oculi tui . . .
      Thine eyes did see my substance, yet being
      unperfect

And put]   'And if thou put?'

native]

Campensis:
> *quod geniunum est tibi*
> which is natural for the[e]

recompense]

'Equivalent punishment or reward'.

endure]

Given by Cooper as a translation of *sustinere* along with 'abide or withstand'. 'To undergo without succumbing'.
Campensis:
> *subsistere quis poterit?*
> who maye be able to abyde?

faint]

'Lose heart'.

Who . . . account?]

Wyatt was probably thinking of the Last Judgement.
Rolle *Pr. Consc.*/5612:
> All that sal com byfor Crist that day
> Sal strayt* account yhelde

*strict

Knight de la Tour/59:
> God will axsc hem acompte at the dredfulle day

Fisher. 241/17–20:
> Alas what shall we do, how shall we behaue our selfe whan our fader and lorde shall aske accompte at the dredefull daye of his strayte Iugement how we haue ordred our porcyon of substaunce . . .

Dread, and not reverence]

The words Wyatt here distinguished were usually joined. For example, in a form of confession for a monk, we find:
> And specyally at masse, not treytinge that holy sacrament with so gret dewoycyon, dred and reuerence . . . as I aught to do.
> (Cotton Mss. Nero A 3 p. 136b)

Campensis:
> *Sicque ad synceram uenerationem tui inuites*
> And so to induce them to the right worshippinge of the[e]

Zwingli:
> *ut te reuereamur*
> that we might reuerence and fear thee (Joye)

Pellican:
> *ut nisi talis esset ut peccata condonare uelit, nemo ex animo ipsum uenerari posset,*

sed omnes ut tyrannum tantum metuerent...
unless he was such as to be willing to pardon
sins, nobody could reverence him sincerely,
but all might fear him as a tyrant ...

large]   'Without restriction or restraint'.

residence]   This may be a translation of *apud* (in the house,
or residence of) in the Vulgate:
> *Quia apud Dominum misericordia*
> For there is mercy with the Lord

hearts]   Wyatt wrote *hertis*, and scanned the word as having
two syllables.

My soul]   Vulgate:
> *sperauit anima mea in Domino*
> my soul hoped in the Lord

approve]   'Declare to be true'.
Campensis:
> *nunquam   dubitaui   quin   esset   staturus*
> *promisso.*
> I douted not but that he wolde abyde by
> his worde.

stay]   'Support'.
The same language is found in Wyatt's poem on
Cromwell:
> The pillar perished is whereto I leant,
>   The strongest stay of mine unquiet mind
> ...

pretence]   'Claim on God's mercy', as in the Prologue to
Psalm 143/32:
> '... Then will I crave with sured confidence'
> And thus begins the suit of his pretence

My soul ... thirst]   Campensis:
> *Anima mea ardentius expectat aduentum*
> *Domini   quam   uigiles   nocturni   tempus*
> *matutinum*
> My soule wayted more feruently for the
> Lordes commynge then the night watchers
> loke for the mornynge tyme ...
Joye (B):
> as the watche men in the morninge watche

Wyatt appears to have preferred the singular.

relief]   If the meaning is relief of a watch, then this is the first recorded instance.

thirst]   Wyatt wrote *thrust*.

Let Israel trust]   Joye:
> Let Israel truste vnto the Lorde

Luther:
> This is a truly golden verse and worthy to be studied with all possible care p. 367.

grace and favour]   The phrase was commonly applied to God's grace by every shade of religious opinion, as the following examples will illustrate:

Pilgr. Perf. fo: viij. *verso*:
> blessed lorde receyue me into thy grace and fauour

Sir T. Elyot *The bankette of sapience* p. 22 *recto*:
> The grace of Chryst . . . is called *Gratia*, (whiche dothe sygnifie fauour in englishe) . . .

Savonarola:
> iustifie me by thy grace and fauour

Luther:
> God is finally nothing else than grace and favour p. 463.
> Grace means the favour with which God embraces us, forgiving our sins and freely justifying us through Christ . . . p. 421.

Tyndale *Obedience* Fo: cxv. *recto*:
> By grace I vnderstonde ye favoure of God and also the giftes & workinge of his sprite in vs/ as love kyndnes/ pacience/ obedience/ mercyfulnes/ despisynge of worldly thinges/ peace/ concorde & soch lyke . . .

his property]   'An essential quality, part of his nature'.

Campensis:
> *est enim natura misericordissimus & suapte natura ad succurrendum propensissimus*
> for he is most mercyful of kynde & of his owne nature most redy to helpe

Wyatt in Psalm 32/54:
> So by thy great merciful property

Savonarola:

It is one of thy chefest properties to forgyue
& be mercyfull . . .
There is a prayer in the Litany: *deus cui proprium*
(Littlehales *Lay Folks* p. 50):
God! to whom it is propred to be merciful
euere, & to spare

Plenteous]　　　　This is the epithet that was traditionally found
right for redemption, as in these examples:
Wyclif:
plenteous redempcioun is at hym
Fisher 230/9–10:
our redempcyon so plenteuous

redeem]　　　　Vulgate:
Et ipse redimet Israel ex omnibus iniquit-
atibus eius.
virtually translated by Joye in 1530:
And it is he that shall redeme Israhel frome
all his wykedneses.

WYATT AND HIS KING

Tagus, Farewell is the strangest poem in the whole extant body of
Wyatt's verse. For there is a remarkable general agreement among
modern readers that a sense of plenitude and a power of conviction are created by the interlocked phrases, which make the final
release at the close the most passionate single utterance Wyatt
has left us. And yet, on the evidence of his life and work, is it
credible that it was his feelings for the King, his master, and the
country he had been serving as an ambassador abroad that were
giving speed to his horse and wind to the sails of the ship that was
to carry him back from Spain to London? Since we know that
Wyatt was not given to rhetoric or hyperbole, we must somehow
yield to the conviction in the style, hard as it may be to picture
the foundations and the structure of Wyatt's patriotic feelings,
when almost all his other reflections about life at the court of
Henry VIII express only slightly less passionate disgust and repul-
sion. For Wyatt knew his king intimately, he had seen him at too
close quarters, and he understood the crooked ways of his

tortuous royal diplomacy.

This poem is one more reminder of the double entity of Tudor kingship. Even though Wyatt may never have gone so far as Shakespeare's Richard in thinking that the divinity of the post was visible in ordinary day light, I do not doubt that in a certain light Henry would be seen by Wyatt as a divine minister. The 'certain light' of this poem is a strange creation of Gothic legend, which darkens the all-too-brand-new Tudor monarch with a colouring of ancientry, making him one with the kings of times even before the Wars of the Roses. But the most powerful current of feeling is borne by the natural power of a river that is both *alma mater* to the metropolis and a heavenly luminary come down on earth to be both protector and ornament, making the nursling wealthier than the gold-laden sands of Tagus.

If we are drawn into mysterious depths of feeling by the body of the poem, we are for once left in no mystery about its occasion. For Wyatt's heading 'in Spain' is in all probability an indication that he made the poem just before he left Spain in 1539, and travelled from Toledo to Lisbon, where he took ship for home. We happen to know from surviving letters that Wyatt had been asking to be allowed to come home for months before he obtained permission. Further evidence of his feelings may be found in a poem that Wyatt may have written just before *Tagus, farewell*. At the close of *So feeble*, a poem written in the form of a letter to his mistress, Elizabeth Darell, from whom he had been absent a whole year, he wrote:

> All this is hid from me with sharp and cragged hills,*
> At others' will my long abode my deep despair fulfils,
> But if my hope sometime rise up by some redress,
> It stumbleth straight for feeble faint, my fear hath such
> excess.
> Such is the sort of hope, the less for more desire,
> Whereby I fear and yet I trust to see that I require,
> The resting place of love, where virtue lives and grows,

---

* Presumably a reference to the physical appearance of the Sierras. In *Childe Harold's Pilgrimage*, Canto I xxxii Byron was describing the same geographical features of Portugal and Spain:
> Where Lusitania and her Sister meet . . .
> Doth Tayo interpose his mighty tide?
> Or dark Sierras rise in craggy pride?

Where I desire my weary life also may take repose.
My song, thou shalt attain to find that pleasant place
Where she doth live by whom I live, may chance thee
                                        have this grace.
When she hath read and seen the dread wherein I starve,
Between her breasts she shall thee put, there shall she thee
                                        reserve.
Then tell her that I come, she shall me shortly see.
If that for weight the body fail, this soul shall to her flee.

It is therefore possible that the love, the mighty love, of *Tagus,
farewell*, besides the tribute to his loyalty and patriotism was
also a mask for his love for his mistress.

Tagus, farewell

Tagus, farewell]

Dryden, in the notes to his Juvenal, remarked:
'Tagus a Famous River in *Spain*, which discharges
itself into the Ocean near *Lisbone* in *Portugal.*
It was held of old, to be full of Golden Sands.'
Although Wyatt may have been actually looking at
the river as he wrote, he uses words that would
occur to a man in his study thinking of the one
thing for which the river was known all over the
world by those who knew nothing else, *viz.* the
gold in its sands. This is how the river is casually
brought into *Phyllyp Sparowe* by John Skelton:
    Of Thagus, that golden flod,
    That passeth all erthly good:
        . . .
    With his golden sandes.
Wyatt would know of similar casual references in
Ovid and Boethius.

westward]

Ovid wrote in his *Metamorphoses* II/251:
    *quodque suo Tagus amne uehit fluit ignibus
    aurum.*
    and the gold that Tagus carries along becomes
    itself liquid when the flames melt it.
Wyatt may have taken from this the thought that
the grains of gold were carried down the stream
towards the sea.

Turns up]

In a similar way Erasmus referred to this gold in *De Contemptu Mundi* tr. Thomas Paynell 1533 *sig.* C 4 *recto*:

> ... all the gold that the ryuers Tagus & Pactolus reuerse & tourne in theyr red sandis ...

Wyatt may have recalled Juvenal's Third Satire/55:

> ... opaci
>
> *omnis harena Tagi quodque in mare uoluitur aurum*
>
> But let not all the Gold which *Tagus* hides,
> And pays the Sea in Tributary Tides ...
> (Dryden)

already tried]

Grains of gold were obtained by sieving the sand. Wyatt is saying that the action of the river water had already performed this operation for the gold-seekers.

With ... side]

A rough paraphrase might run, 'For I am going by horse and ship to try to reach the river Thames, which proudly displays her wealth in the face of the sun, and lends her powerful bank, curved like the crescent moon, to the town which Brutus was guided by dreams to try and find.'

spur ... sail]

Presumably travelling as fast as he could by land and sea. He may have ridden from Toledo to Lisbon and there embarked.

Gainward]

Possibly, 'over against', 'facing', 'full in the sight of' as Chaucer used *ayenst* in the *Legend of Good Women,* Prologue/48:

> To seen this flour ayenst the sonne sprede.

Brutus]

Wyatt is drawing on the traditional story that the English derive from the old inhabitants of Troy. According to Geoffrey of Monmouth in his *Historia Regum Britanniae* Brutus, a direct descendant of Priam and Aeneas, rescued the remnant of Trojans. On their wanderings they came upon a temple of Diana, at which Brutus prayed for guidance:

> And when it was the third hour of the night,
> the time of sweetest sleep,

he thought the goddess appeared to him and told him that in the far west there was an island in

which he would found a line of kings to whom the
whole world would eventually be subject. Wyatt
seems to have followed Caxton's Chronicle:

> Brute and his men wenten forth and sawe
> aboute in diuerse places wher they myght
> fynde a good place and conuenable that they
> myght make a Cite for hym and for his
> folke. So at the last they comen by a fair
> Riuer that is called the Thamys and there
> brute bigan a fair cite and let calle it newe
> Troye in mynde and remembrance of the
> grete Troye from whiche place all hir linage
> was comen . . .

But he might, like Cromwell, have owned a book
'of Brute coming into this realm'. (See *Reform and
Renewal*, G.R. Elton 1973 p. 13.)

bended] 'Bent like a bow'. Chaucer wrote of The bente
moone in his *Troilus and Criseyde* III/624

side] 'Water-side'.
Dunbar wrote in *A treatise of London*:

> Above all ryuers, thy ryuer hath renown,
water clear as beryl > Whose boryall stemes plesant & praeclare,*
*illustrious > Vnder thy lusty walles renneth down . . .

In the light of this we might be tempted to give
lusty a more overtly sexual meaning. Drayton is
explicit in *The Legend of Robert, Duke of Nor-
mandy*:

> Downe to faire *Thames* I gently tooke my way,
> With whom the Winds continually doe play.
>   Striuing to Fancie his chaste Brest to moue,
> Whereas all Pleasures plentifully flow,
> When him along, the wanton Tyde doth shoue,
> And to keep backe, they easily doe blow,
> Or else force forward, thinking him too slow,
>   Who with his Waues would check the
>   Winds imbrace,
>   Whilst they fanne Ayre vpon his crystall
>   face.
>   Still forward sallying from his bountious
>   Sourse,
> Along the Shores lasciuiously doth strayne. . .
> And looking back on *Londons* stately Tow'rs,

So *Troy*, thought I, her stately Head did
rere . . .

WYATT AND THE COURT

To relish the mastery of *In Court to serve*, which contains much in little, two kinds of balance must be kept. The first consists of a mass of court behaviour in which Wyatt had been obliged to participate from his early adolescence, which has to be balanced against the traditional theme of the evil of court life in general, as expressed in various proverbs. The second balance is embodied in the phrase 'splendid servitude', which Erasmus applied to the courtier's life in his adage, 'Golden Fetters'..

The similarities in words and sentiments in this poem and that beginning *Mine own J.P.* allow us to suppose that the revulsion against court life was felt personally. At the same time it is worth observing that the note of bitterness may have been derived from Wyatt's reading, for this in Erasmus' colloquy *Epicureus* bears a striking similarity:

> *Conuiuia, comessationes, amores, choreae, canti-*
> *lenae, caeteraque quae iuueni uidebantur suauia,*
> *seni sunt amara . . .*
> feastes, ryotous banketyng, syngyng, and daun-
> synge, with manye suche other wanton toyes and
> pastimes which he was communely yeouen[1] vnto
> and thought very plesaunt when he was young, bee
> nowe paynfull vnto hym beyng olde . . .

But an even closer similarity is borne by a famous passage in Lucretius' poem *On the Nature of Things*, which makes a profound and unforgettable reflection on the Roman equivalent of the Early Tudor court:

> *eximia ueste et uictu conuiuia, ludi,*
> *pocula crebra, unguenta, coronae, serta, parantur:*
> *nequiquam, quoniam medio de fonte leporum*
> *surgit amari aliquid quod in ipsis floribus angat.*

1 given

Dryden applied these lines to the Court as he knew it, in these words:

> French fashions, costly treats are their delight;
> The Park by day, and Plays and Balls by night.
> In vain:—
> For in the Fountain where their Sweets are sought,
> Some bitter bubbles up, and poisons all the draught.

Wyatt may have read the passage like this:

> Banquets are prepared with goodly furniture and sugared meats; there are sundry kinds of play, much drinking and ornamenting of the body. But all is for nothing, since from the very centre of this fountain of pleasures something with a bitter taste comes up that pains in the very act of pleasing.

To feel that this is profound, we must believe simultaneously that such a life is both the height of life and a pure waste of time. So, to appreciate Wyatt's epigram, we must do more than learn the darker side of a courtier's life as it is, for example, sarcastically reported by Erasmus in his *Praise of Folly*:

> . . . these be the qualitees they holde most mete for a kynde gentilman, and ruffler[1] of the courte . . . These my hoglynges slepe euery daie till midnoone, and hauyng euin yet theyr eyes full of slepe, thei sende than for some huntyng chaplaine, who whiles they are in makyng ready, or rather risyng out of theyr beddes, maie slynge them vp a post masse. In the necke whereof commes theyr breckfast, and that scantly finisshed, go they to diner. After that to the dyse, to tables, to cardes, or to boules, nowe with iesters, nowe with fooles, now with courtesanes, daunces, and daliaunces to trifle out the tyme, not without one, or two collacions afore supper, and after supper theyr bankettes one vpon an other. And thus without felyng any tediousnesse of theyr life, thei passe easily ouer, bothe houres, daies, monthes, yeres, and whole ages.

1 arrogant swaggering fellow

For the court expressed the finest consciousness of what made life worth living. These banquets were far more than heavy meals. If we follow Hall in his *Triumphant Reign*, we might think the state banquet was merely an occasion for 'conspicuous consumption', for showing off how much gold plate Henry possessed beside what was being used for the many courses of his meals. I shall therefore choose an instance from Cavendish's account of one of Wolsey's 'triumphant banquets', since it shows how many kinds of play were indulged in by all the young people who followed the King. (I shall pass over the most striking feature, the various uses of music and song because Wyatt is strangely silent on this whole topic.)

> And whan it pleased the kynges maiestie for his recreacion to repayer vnto the Cardynalles howsse (as he dyd dyuers tymes in the yere) at wiche tyme there wanted no preparacions or goodly furnyture with vyaundes of the fynnest Sort that myght be provided for mony or frendshippe. Suche pleasures ware than devysed for the kynges comfort & consolacion as myght be Invented or by mans wytt Imagyned. The bankettes ware sett forthe with Maskes and Mummerreys in so gorges a sort and Costly maner that it was an hevyn to behold. Ther wanted no dames or damselles meate or apte to daunce with the maskers or to garnysshe the place for the tyme with other goodly disportes
> . . .

Cavendish describes how the King and a select company disguised themselves and gate-crashed Wolsey's banquet as if they were a party of foreign ambassadors. A childish sport, one might think, but their disguises would have cost many acres of a nobleman's estate:

> I haue seen the kyng sodenly come in thether in a maske with a dosyn of other maskars all in garmentes lyke Shepherdes made of fynne clothe of gold and fyn Crymosyn Satten paned[1] and Cappes of the same with visors of good proporcion of

1 made of strips of coloured cloth

> visonamy,[1] ther heares & beardes other of fynne
> gold wyers or elles of syluer . . .

The 'foreigners' begged leave to salute the ladies and:

> to accompany them at Mume chaunce[2] And than
> after to daunce with them.

As if to emphasize Wyatt's point in 'fresh array', Cavendish tells how when the King had made himself known, and was invited to take the magnificent seat at the banquet:

> the kyng answered that he wold goo first & shifte
> hys apparell and so departed/ and went strayt to
> my lordes bed Chamber . . . And there newe apparel-
> led hym with riche & pryncely garmentes . . . Than
> the kyng toke his seate vnder the clothe of estate . . .

Cavendish estimates the number of dishes to have been more than two hundred:

> of wonderous costly meates & deuysys subtilly
> deuysed . . .

The elaboration of the *subtleties* surpassed that of any modern wedding cake. Even if we smile at the repetition of 'it was a heaven to behold', we can see that in the cost alone these banquets, designed to impress, were in that vulgar sense impressive. And perhaps oppressive. Here, for instance, is an instance from Hall of a temporary banqueting house erected on one side of the tilt yard at Greenwich in 1527:

> this house was richely hanged and therin was raised
> a cupbord of seven stages high and xiii. foote long,
> set with standyng cuppes, Bolles, Flaggons, and
> greate pottes all of fyne golde: some garnyshed
> with one stone and some with other stones and
> perles, on the other side was a nother cupbord of
> ix. stages high, set full of high pottes, flagons and
> bolles. All was massy plate of silver and gilte, so
> high and so brode that it was marvaile to beholde:
> at the nether ende were twoo broade arches vpon

1 **face**
2 a gambling game with dice

thre Antike pillers all of gold burnished swaged[1]
and graven full of Gargills and Serpentes . . . In
this chamber was thre ewry bordes,[2] one for the
kynge, another for the quene, and the third for the
princes: the fyrst bourde had ix. greate ewers,
and basins all gilt, and playne, the seconde bourde
had seaven greate gilt basins chased, and thre paire
of covered basyns, chased all gilt with Cuppes of
assaie,[3] they were so greate that euery Lorde
grudged to beare theim. The third ewery had ix.
basins and two payre of coveryd Basines and
cuppes of assaie; thys ewery was all of gold, and
the Basins were so massye that thei troubled sore
the bearers . . .

Hall then describes a second, more elaborate house for games and
shows.

These two houses . . . the kyng commaunded should
stand still for thre or foure daies, that al honest
persones might see and beholde the houses and
riches . . .

In Court to serve

serve]

Wyatt entered Court service at the age of 13,
when he became a glorified page boy, obliged to
serve at table at ceremonial banquets. There is
a list, dated 1516, giving 'the names of the King's
officers and servants admitted and sworn to attend
in his grace's most honorable Chamber', in which
we find these entries:

Cupbearer for the King: Sir Fras. Brian
and among the Sewers extraordinary:
Th. Wyet.

fresh array]

In Francis Pilkington's *First Booke of Songs or
Ayres* (1605) there is a song entitled *Musicke,
deare sollace*, which has the lines:

1 with ornamental grooves
2 tables for pitchers containing water for washing hands after meals
3 for tasting

> I doe nimbly clime from Loues secluse
> Vnto his Courts, wher I in fresh attire
>   attire my Muse.

sugared meats]   Normally the words for *sweetmeats*, varous forms of confectionery. But that it might also refer to highly-spiced food is suggested by some lines in Henryson's *The complaynt of Creseyde*:
> The swete meates serued in plates clene
> With sauery sauce of a good facioun . . .

feeling . . . repast]   'Savouring the rich food', as in *Mine own J.P.*:
> I am not now in France to judge the wine,
> With savoury sauce the delicates to feel . . .

banquets]   In the seventh chapter of his translation of Guevara's *Menosprecio*, Sir Francis Bryan wrote:
> For euery man knowes well what excessiue expences are accustomed to be wasted in the court, & specially in these dayes that the great apparellyng of bankettes is suche that they be well worthy to be reformed.

play]   The connotation was wide, as the introduction suggests.

press . . . lordly looks]   The same phrase is found at the opening of *Mine own J.P.*:
> And flee the press of courts whereso they
>   go
> Rather then to live thrall under the awe
>   Of lordly looks . . .

It is possible that the meaning of 'press' is more than 'crowd' and includes the sense of suffering distress. Wyatt may have known a version of Chaucer's *Truth* beginning:
> Flye ye fro ye prease & dwel with soth-
>   fastnesse
> Suffyse vnto the good if it be smal
> For horde hath hate/ and clymbyng tykel-
>   nesse
> Preace hath enuye . . .

where 'press' might have the meaning 'aristocratic arrogance'.

bitter taste]   In addition to the remarks in the introduction, there is an interesting parallel in the fifteenth

chapter of Sir Francis Bryan's translation of
Guevara's *Menosprecio*:

> The propertie of this vicious libertie, or
> better to cal it, this mischeuous subieccion,
> is, that at the beginnyng it semeth somewhat
> pleasaunt but in the ende al conuertes to a
> bitternes, sorow and lamentacion.

Erasmus in his *Epicureus* has:

> ... *quantum amaritudinis admixtum sit istis*
> *falso nomine voluptatibus* ...

which Ph. Gerrard translated:

> how great peyne is intermyngled wyth these
> false and wrongly named pleasures ...

but Erasmus meant *bitterness*, as is clear from an
earlier remark:

> *ut etiamsi quid incidat dulce protinus*
> *amarescat*
> that if any pleasaunt thing chaunce them,
> forthwith it waxeth bitter ... in like maner
> as where the welle hed is corrupted and
> stynketh, there the water must nedes be
> vnsauery.

chains of gold]   Wyatt seems to have been drawing on one of
Erasmus' *Adagia*, entitled *Aureae Compedes*,
Golden Fetters, which, he said, summed up the
splendid slavery of the normal life of a courtier.
Wyatt's epigram gains in point from the actual
habit of court display and the wearing of massy
chains of gold. Hall in his account of 1513–
1514 reports on a typical instance:

> The xi. day of August beyng thursday, the
> kyng lyeng at the siege of Tyrwyn, had
> knowlege that Maximilian themperour was
> in the toune of Ayre. The kyng prepared
> all thinges necessarie to mete with themper-
> our in triumphe. The noble men of the
> kynges campe were gorgeously apparelled,
> ther coursers barded of cloth of gold, of
> damasko and broderie, theire apparelle all
> tissue cloth of gold and syluer, and gold
> smithes woorke, great cheynes of balder-
> ickes of gold, and belles of bullion ...

Erasmus, as usual, was sarcastic in his *Praise of*
Folly:

> And now (on gods name) geue hym a
> chayne about his necke for token that all
> vertues shoulde agreeablie be enchayned in
> hym . . .

If this poem is convincing evidence of the vehe-
mence of Wyatt's feelings about the servitude of
a courtier's life, we may look back and say that
he took to heart something he translated from
Plutarch's essay on true quiet of mind. The phrase
is to be found or *sig. c. ij. verso*:

> Truly now men are nat ledde with enuy of
> the craft or order of their felowes/ but
> riche men with enuy of lerned men/ nobles
> of riche men . . . and at the last/ free and
> noble men of auncient famyles dasyng for
> wonder at the good fortunes of men of
> bondage in the courtes of kynges . . . [*ser-
> uorum in aulis regum*]

There is an interesting prolongation in Guazzo's
dialogue on *Ciuile Conuersation*. In the third book
Anniball says, in G. Pettie's translation, 1586,
p. 166:

> . . . the distinction which may be made
> between Gentlemen Courtiers which serue
> Princes, and the base sort, which serue
> gentlemen, is, that the chaines or fetters of
> the baser sort are of yron, and those of the
> Gentlemen, of Golde.

which allows Guazzo to make the quip:

> I hold well with that difference, & I make
> good moreover, that the chaines of gold
> binde more strongly then those of yron. . .

Throughout the world

Wyatt's procedure here is similar to that we must posit when we relate
Duncan's remark in *Macbeth*:
> There's no Art
> To finde the Mindes construction in the Face

to Juvenal's *frontis* [in Shakespeare's text *fronti*] *nulla fides* — you can't
trust a face — if we suppose that the commonplace emerges in this form in
Macbeth in part as a result of Shakespeare's personal experience of the topic

in particular circumstances. At any rate Wyatt had before him a similar grand commonplace which had taken many proverbial forms. Ultimately, it is the opposition between saying and doing, between the meaning to be constructed from words and the intention in the speaker's mind. One expression of this general truth is:

> Say well is good but doe well is better.

But the saying which gave Wyatt his start is a bitter denial of the claim in *Ecclesiasticus*:

> The tre of the felde is knowne by his frute, so is the thought
> of mans hert by his wordes . . .

such as this from Hawes' *Passetyme* (85/2173), where the careful maiden reproaches the lover:

> For men saye well/ but they thynke full yll.
> Though outwarde swetenes your tonge doth enlarge
> Yet of your hert/ I neuer can haue charge . . .

One of the oldest forms of this cynical view of mankind can be traced back to the *Book of Job*:

> [ye] can speake many wordes in the wynde.

Wolsey in his darkest hour complained to Cromwell:

> I have had fair Wordes, but littlc comfortable Deedes.

This passed into ordinary speech in the form, *wordys be but wynde*, and, as the sixteenth century passed into the seventeenth, we find, *words are winde*. Words therefore are worthless. 'Good words (or Fair words) are good cheape' was the traditional form. Only a fool would take them at face value, as in the proverb, *fair words maketh fools fayne*, which occurs in *Greeting to you/22*. In this sense *fair words* was used for promises made to deccive or to keep the hearer happy. There is a good example in Thomas Starkey's dialogue between Cardinal Pole and Thomas Lupset, where he speaks of defrauding a client:

> wych by hys dyssymulatyon and fare wordys was inter-
> teynyd in long sute . . .

Wyatt used the phrase when reporting his impression that Charles V was trying to string him along, or, in his idiom, to 'entertain the king':

> Agayne in brynging in the faire wordes wher with he hath
> long entertainid your maiestie at that he kekid[1] saying he
> holdyth no man with faire wordes . . .

That an *accord* between words and deeds was thought to be something exceptional emerges incidentally from a *Ballade* Lydgate wrote on a lady possessing all tho virtues:

> Yee beon the myrrour and verray exemplayre
> Of whome that worde and thought acorde in deed . . .

---

1 kicked, objected strongly

For all these proverbs it is possible that Wyatt had the use of a handbook closely resembling a little schoolbook which survives from the early seventeenth century. In his *Paroemiologia Anglo-Latina* John Clarke 'marshalled, ranked, and digested under the Heads of [Erasmus'] latine *Adages*,' a collection of English Proverbs, 'parallel'd with them, and sorted together . . . all along this worke'. For it is striking that all the proverbs discussed in this introduction and used by Wyatt find their place in this little book, most of them coming under *Adulatio* and *Magnifica Promissa*.

Throughout . . . find] The whole expression may have been proverbial by Wyatt's time. It survives in the ballad formula 'you may seek the wide world over but you will never find.' Spenser used it in a dedicatory poem 'To all the gratious and beautifull Ladies in the Court':

> If all the world to seeke I ouerwent
> A fairer crew yet no where could I see . . .

The rival translator of *Rotta è l'alta colonna* has:

> Like of my loss no age shall ever find
> Though the world's eyes a-seeking all ways
> went.

good cheap . . . nought] As the proverbs show, the meaning here is 'in great plenty', 'cheap and nasty', 'costing no effort to produce'.

substance . . . wind] Wyatt may have had the whole of Chaucer's *Second booke of fame* in mind, and, in particular, the lines:

> . . . euery speche . . .
> In his substaunce is but eyre . . .

well . . . mean] Referring to the proverbs involving 'say well' and 'do well', meaning both 'to express pious principles', 'to make promise of good to another' and to intend to fulfil them.

sweet accord] The agreement of what was said with what was intended. Wyatt may be playing on the musical meaning of 'accord' as 'pleasing harmony', as in the farmyard, according to Chaucer's *Nun's Priest's Tale*:

> But suche a joye it was to here hem synge,
> Whan that the bright sonne gan to sprynge,
> In swete accorde . . .

Surrey wrote something similar in *Ecclesiastes*

IV/51-52:
> In humble spryte is sett the temple of the
> Lorde/ wher yf thow enter loke thy mouth
> and conscyence may accorde.

seldom seen]   A proverbial expression for 'extremely rare', as
we find it, for example, in Cavendish's *Life of
Wolsey* 5/3:
> he was made en bachelor of art at xv yeres
> of age/ wiche was a rare thyng And seldome
> seen . . .

It is perhaps worth recording the impact made by the theme of this poem
throughout the anthology known as *The Paradyse of daynty deuises*. The
original compiler, Richard Edwards, who died in 1566, has a poem entitled:
> *Faire woordes make fooles faine*

in which a father advises his son:
> . . . when thou art become one of the Courtly trayne,
> Thinke on this prouerbe olde (qd he) that faire woordes
>   make fooles faine.

The fourteenth poem has for title:
> Most happy is that state alone,
> Where woordes and deedes agree in one.

Erasmus wrote the following comment on Cato's distich: *sic ars deluditur
arte*:
> *Erga eum qui fuco utitur, tu item contra utere fuco, &*
> *iuxta prouerbium Cretiza contra cretensem . . .*

which R. Burrant translated in his *Preceptes of Cato* (1560) as follows:
> Vse gile with him that vseth gile to thee, for it is better to
> entertaine such a fayned frende with fayre words, then
> vtterly to make him thy enemy . . .

Stand whoso list

The version in the Arundel manuscript, which all modern editors print, may
well be Wyatt's revision of an earlier poem, namely that printed by Tottel's
editors:
> Stond who so list, vpon the slipper whele,
> Of hye astate and let me here reioyce,
> And vse my life in quietnesse eche dele,
> Vnknowen in court that hath the wanton toyes.
> In hidden place my time shall slowly passe
> And when my yeres be past withouten noyce
> Let me dye olde after the common trace

> For gripes of death doth he to hardly passe[1]
> That knowen is to all: but to him selfe alas,
> He dyeth vnknowen, dased with dreadfull face.

It seems not unreasonable to regard the differences as a clear case of improved second thoughts. Both versions correspond to Wyatt's known habits. In the first place, the germ of both poems may lie in the last line, which implies that Wyatt may have had one particular victim at one particular execution in his mind's eye. At the same time in both poems Wyatt has come unusually close to the text of a passage from Seneca's *Thyestes*, which was a popular commonplace. The Tottel editors rightly entitled their poem: *Of the meane and sure estate*. From this it would follow that Wyatt's victim was one who had fallen from high position.

Some editions fancy that this poem was written at the same time as one beginning *Who list his wealth*, which has these lines:

> The bell tower showed me such sight
> That in my head sticks day and night
>   There did I learn out of a grate
> For all favour, glory or might
>   That yet *circa Regna tonat.*

The coincidence that in the Spanish Chronicle Wyatt was said to have watched the execution of Anne Boleyn's supposed lovers from a window above the gate of the Tower has convinced some that there is a parallel between a poem based on Seneca's *Phaedra* and one based on his *Thyestes*.
Here are the lines Wyatt had before him:

> *stet quicunque uolet potens*
> *aulae culmine lubrico:*
> *me dulcis saturet quies,*
> *obscuro positus loco*
> *leni perfruar otio.*
> *nullis nota Quiritibus*
> *aetas per tacitum fluat.*
> *sic cum transierint mei*
> *nullo cum strepitu dies,*
> *plebeius moriar senex.*
> *illi mors grauis incubat*
> *qui notus nimis omnibus*
> *ignotus moritur sibi.* (391–403)

Let any one who wishes stand in power on the slippery roof of the court, let sweet quiet fill me full, let me be situated in a dim spot, there let me enjoy a life of luxurious ease. Let my life flow silently along unknown to the upper-class citizens of Rome, so that when

---

1 The rhyme-scheme requires a word like *fele.*

my days have passed with no disturbance I may die like any old plebeian. Death falls heavy on the man who known too much by the world dies unknown to himself.

To show how closely Wyatt was translating, I have given references to the following Latin-English dictionaries:

The Dictionary of syr Thomas Eliot knyght (1538)
Bibliotheca Eliotae Eliotis Librarie (1548)

Stand whoso list]	A literal translation following the Latin order: *stet quicunque uolet.*

slipper]	Elyot *Dictionary* (1538); *Lubricus* slypper. It was a common epithet for Fortune, as in Caxton *Eneyidos* vii/32:
	    fortune . . . thyng slypper & lubrik
	and in Sir Thomas More's *Fortune*:
	        Thus dowble Fortune, whan she list reuerce
	        Her slipper fauour . . .
	Wyatt used the word to translate *precarias* in the phrase: I knew I had slypper riches

top]	Elyot *Bibliotheca* (1548): *Culmen* The toppe of any thynge.

court estate]	I have not found the phrase elsewhere, but the thought occurs in Grenewey Tacitus *Ann.* I/xv. 29:
	        the higher he should clime, the slipperer his estate should be . . .
	The most likely meaning is: 'The position of eminence of a prominent courtier'.
	Sir Francis Bryan in his translation of Guevara's *Menosprecio de corte* introduced the phrase off his own bat:
	        it was tyme for him to leaue the daungerous estate of the court . . .

use me quiet]	'Pursue an untroubled existence'.

let or stop]	'Without interference from others'. A set phrase. When composing his version of Psalm 102, Wyatt first began:
	        Lord, hear my prayer, and let my cry pass
	            Unto thee, Lord, withouten stop or let
	and later crossed out the last three words and wrote in: *impediment.*

Unknown]	Elyot *Dictionary* (1538): *Obscurus* hydde . . . vnknowen

brackish]

Used properly of the salty taste of sweet water that has gone off and become salty. Wyatt wrote, translating Budé.

the draught of our lyfe was not euyn and leuel but rather brackish and sower . . .

where he may have thought that *salebrosus*, rough, was derived from *sal*, salt.

The thought was presumably taken from *In court to serve*:

Hath with it joined oft times such bitter taste That whoso joys such kind of life to hold. . .

Underlying both passages there may be a reminiscence of Erasmus in his *Epicureus*:

animus illorum impurus est, & cupiditatum fermento vitiatus, ut etiamsi quid incidat dulce, protinus amarescat, quemadmodum fonte vitiato non potest non esse liquor insipidus.

which Ph. Gerrard translated:

. . . their mynde is vile, and corrupted with the sauour and taste of noughtie desires, in so muche that if any plesaunt thing chaunce them, forthwith it waxeth bitter, and is nought set by, in like maner as where the welle hed is corrupted and stynketh, there the water must nedes be vnsauery.

withouten noise]

Elyot *Bibliotheca* (1548): *Tacitus* without noyse. The possible meanings here include 'in a quiet manner, without any display, secretly', as in Gower's *Tale of Florent*:

In clos him hield, and schop his rode On nyhtes time, til the tyde That he cam there he wolde abide, And priuely withoute noise

*ugly female monster

He bringeth this foule grete Coise* To his Castell . . .

after . . . trace]

'Following the path trodden by the common people'.

grippeth . . . crop]

'Seizes by the throat'.

unknown]

Elyot *Dictionary* (1538): *Ignotus* vnknowen.

dazed]

'Stunned, bewildered'.

dreadful]   'Terrified'. Also possible is 'frightening', as in
this quotation of 1447:
> The blessed and dredeful image of our Lord
> Jesu in his most fereful and last dome.

This is the meaning in *The pillar perished.*

Luck, my fair falcon

It is a golden rule when trying to understand Wyatt to consider whether, at the very time when he seems to be reflecting on his own particular circumstances, the poem does not turn on a large commonplace in which the particular event is subsumed. Everything about the poem suggests that personal bitterness is giving shape and edge to the phrasing, and Wyatt's public career was such that on certain occasions the loss of friends might have been critical or even fatal. But Wyatt also had available to him, and drew on, the traditional wisdom about true and false friendship, somewhat as Shakespeare did when giving Polonius words to advise his son:

> The friends thou hast, and their adoption tride,
> Grapple them to thy Soule, with hoopes of Steele . . .

Neither Wyatt nor Shakespeare need be thought of as having only one 'source' here, but by one route or another we may suppose that the wisdom of *Ecclesiasticus* had reached them, and in particular, in the sixth chapter:

> *Si possides amicum, in tentatione posside eum*
> Yf thou gettest a frende, proue him first . . . For some man is a frende but for a tyme, and wyl not abyde in the daye of trouble . . . in the day of nede he contynueth not.

The meaning of 'prove' here is well brought out in Chapter 27/6:

> *Vasa figuli probat fornax,*
> *Et homines iustos tentatio tribulationis*
> The ouen proueth the potters vessell,
> so doth tentacion of trouble trye righteous men.

Just as it could be said of a sure friend:

> Yf thou suffre trouble and aduersite, he is with thee

so it was not cynical to observe that:

> whan the poore man falleth, his friendes forsake him.

But the thought of the poem as a whole appears to come from a passage at the beginning of one of Plutarch's essays on the distinction between a true friend and a flatterer, a passage that Wyatt would no doubt have come across in a translation made by Erasmus. Here is the version of Mr Tullie, Sub-Dean of York, as he was described in the 1694 edition:

> . . . so never saw we Flattery the Attendant of the poor, the inglorious and inconsiderable Plebean, but of the Grandees of the World, the Distemper and Bane of great Families and Affairs, the

Plague in Kings Chambers, and the Ruin of their Kingdoms: Therefore it is a Business of no small importance, and which requires no
ordinary circumspection, so to be able to know a Flatterer in every
shape he assumes, that the counterfeit Resemblance sometime or
other bring not *true Friendship* it self into suspicion and disrepute.
For Parasites, like Lice, which desert a dying Man, whose pall'd
and vapid Blood can feed them no longer, never intermix in dry
and insipid Business, where there's nothing to be got; but prey upon
a nobler Quarrie, the Ministers of State, and Potentates of the Earth,
and afterwards lowsily shirk off, if the greatness of their Fortune
chance to leave them. But it will not be Wisdom in us to stay till
such fatal Junctures, and then try the Experiment, which will not
onely be useless, but dangerous and hurtful; for 'tis a deplorable
thing for a Man to find himself then destitute of Friends, when he
most wants them, and has not an opportunity neither of exchanging
his false, his faithless, for a fast and honest Friend. And therefore
we should rather try our Friend, as we do our Money, whether or no
he be passable and current, before we need him.

The poem, however, could not be born until the theme of false friends
abandoning Wyatt could be contrasted with his falcons who remained faithful
to him. This could well have been a reflection that might have been made
when Wyatt was by royal command confined to Allington Castle and went
hawking as weather permitted. It is, however, possible that there were also
literary links. For example, in the Plutarch passage Erasmus wrote of the
behaviour of false friends when their rich patrons come to grief:

sed ijdem rebus commutatis statim auolant

but when their fortunes change they immediately fly away.
In *Ecclesiasticus* we find these words:

Like as one that letteth a byrde go out of his honde can not take
her agayne: Euen so thou, yf thou geue ouer thy frende, thou
canst not get him agayne: Yee thou canst not come by him, for he
is to farre of.

A great deal depends on the interpretation of one line in the poem:

How well pleasant it were your liberty!

Are we to understand that in some sense Wyatt himself was a captive when he
wrote that? If so, were the birds to be envied for their comparative freedom?
If that were so, it would be no accident that the Latin for this line:

quam sit dulcis libertas

is both the title and the theme of one of the Aesopic fables in which the
liberty of the free-roaming wolf is contrasted with the servitude of the
pampered house-dog.[1]

---

1 Further comment on this poem may be found in *The Cambridge Quarterly*, Volume
VII Number 4, pp. 281–296

Luck]

If we had reliable information about the names commonly given to trained falcons in Wyatt's day it might be possible to determine whether *Luck* and *Lux* were possibilities or out of the question. There is nothing that absolutely compels us to say that in this poem Wyatt saw the birds as symbols of Fortune. But it is conceivable that Wyatt might call such a bird *Lady Luck*. This would be a homelier version of *Dame Fortune*.

How well]

F.T. Prince suggests (T.L.S. 29 July, 1983) that we take the sense of the line to be, 'However pleasing your freedom would be to you'. For a comparable use of 'how' in the sense of 'however', see note on *how foul* in *Miserere mei* (page 200).

fair . . . fall]

'In order that you may prosper'. The common phrase for wishing good luck in Wyatt's day was, 'Fair fall thee!'

sometime]

'Formerly'.

lice]

Wyatt is translating from the words of Erasmus:
Nam pediculi discedunt a morientibus & corpora relinquunt . . .
for lice depart from people when they are dying and leave their corpses . . .
It may be to the point to recall the experience of the monks whose duty it was to prepare Thomas Becket's body for the tomb. When they stripped him, they found he was wearing a tight hair shirt and close-fitting drawers of the same material, all so heavily infested with lice that there was no spot free from the little beasties [*bestiunculis*].

proof . . . adversity]

The meaning is not clear. Wyatt may have had the same proverb in mind as was used by Sir Thomas Elyot in the *Bankette of Sapience* sig. B 1 *recto*:
good men be proued in tyme of aduersitie
perhaps in one of the many forms in which it was given in the collection of *Sententiae Pueriles* made by Leonhardus Culmannus, such as:
Amici in rebus aduersis cognoscuntur

It is in adversity that you find who are your friends.

Among the *Sententiae* taken from the Mimes of Publilius Syrus we find:

Secundae amicos res parant, tristes probant.

Adversity puts to the test the friends procured by prosperity.

Caue amicum credas, nisi si quem probaueris.

Do not call any man a friend before you have put him to the test.

But Wyatt's phrase is not so clear as any of these. It is possible that by *light adversity* Wyatt was saying that it would not have involved serious hardship for his friends to prove their loyalty, and by *what a proof* he was complaining that his friends had failed to stand up to this very slight trial.

bells]

A bell was attached by means of a leather strap or buckle to each leg of the birds. The purpose was, as Turbervile reported in his book of falconry, 'to make the Falcon fine'. Dame Juliana Berners said in 1486 that the bells should be arranged to give a matching, musical chime:

* sonorous
* giving a clear note

Looke ... that thay be sonowre* and well sowndyng and shil* and not both of oon sowne: bot that oon be a semytoyn vnder a noder.

Since the topic was evidently near to Wyatt's heart, it may be an advantage to see the whole situation in which these bells had a function. The last song in *A Handefull of pleasant delites*, 1584, touches on all the matters arising in Wyatt's poems on birds.

The Louer compareth him self to the painful Falconer.

The soaring hawk
from fist that flies
her Falconer doth constraine
sometime to range
the ground vnknown

to find her out againe:
and if by sight
or sound of bell
his falcon he may see,
wo ho, he cries
with cheerful voice,
the gladdest man is he.

By Lure then
in finest sort
he seeks to bring her in,
but if that she
ful gorged be,
he cannot so her win . . .
wo ho, he cries,
awaie she flies,
and so her leaue she takes.

Later, however, he comes upon her:
His heart was glad,
his eies had seen
his falcon swift of flight:
wo ho, he cries,
she emptie gorgde
vpon his Lure doth light.

The Falconer then *swam in blisse*. The Lover
makes his application:
My deer likewise
beholde thy loue
what paines he doth indure:
and now at length
let pitie moue
to stoup vnto his Lure.
A hood of silk
and siluer belles,
new gifts I promise thee:*

---

* ct. *The Paradise of daintie deuises*, 1576 p. 63:
  A. By skilfull meanes I her reclaime, to stope vnto my luer
  B. Suche hagard haukes will sore awaie, of them who can be suer?
  A. With siluer bells and hoode, my ioye was her to decke.
  B. She was full gorgd, she would the soner giue the checke.
  A. The more is my paine.
  B. Her loue then refraine . . .

wo ho, I crie,
I come, then saie,
make me as glad as hee.

Wyatt may have been thinking the contrary: that the luck or fortune he enjoyed as a falconer was not matched as a courtier.

WYATT AND CROMWELL

The pillar perished may well be a unique poem in the Wyatt *corpus* in that it may tell us of a historical event and so throw a light both on Wyatt's part in it and on the whole career of another person, the Thomas Cromwell who rose in Henry VIII's service to become the Earl of Essex only to end on the scaffold on July 28, 1540 a confessed malefactor. The interest of these facts is alone great enough to make it desirable that such a reading should be capable of being shown to be the only right one.

One complicating factor is that in some respects this poem must also be read as a translation of part of a famous sonnet in Petrarch's collection. It is a comparatively minor complication that Wyatt may have made two related but dissimilar attempts to use Petrarch's sonnet. But the apparent digression of dealing first with the relation to Petrarch's sonnet is only apparent, since the likeness and difference of the two English versions strongly support the suggestion that Wyatt in our poem went further away from mere translation because of something not in Petrarch's sonnet yet very likely in the historical events already hinted at.

The following is a modernised version of Sonnet No. CCLXIX:

> *Rotta è l'alta colonna, e 'l verde lauro*
>   *Che facean ombra al mio stanco pensero;*
>   *Perduto ò quel che ritrovar non spero*
>   *Dal borea a l'austro, o dal mar indo al mauro.*
>
> *Tolto m'ài, morte, il mio doppio thesauro,*
>   *Che mi fea viver lieto, e gire altero;*
>   *E ristorar nol pò terra né impero,*
>   *Né gemma oriental, né forza d'auro.*

Ma se consentimento è di destino,
  Che posso io piú, se no aver l'alma trista,
  Umidi gli occhi sempre, e'l viso chino?

O nostra vita ch'è sí bella in vista,
  Com perde agevolmente in un matino
  Quel che'n molti anni a gran pena s'acquista!

For the purposes of this introduction a rough, line-by-line version
will serve:

  Smashed is the tall column, smashed the green laurel
    Which gave cooling shade to my weary thought;
    Lost is that I do not expect to find again
    From North to South, from East to Western sea

  Taken you have, Death, my two treasures from me,
    Which made me glad to walk with a high head;
    And bring them back to me can no land, no realm,
    No Eastern jewel, no mountain of gold.

  But if such is the will of destiny,
    What else can I do more than have a sorry mind,
    Eyes ever dropping tears and head bent to ground?

  This life of ours which seems so fine,
    How easily in a brief morning you lose
    That which was gathered together with great pains over
        many years!

It is evident that Petrarch was here mourning a *double* loss. The
preceding poem in the *Canzoniere* would make it clear that one
loss was of his Madonna, Laura. Every edition of the poems would
explain that the 'column' was Petrarch's patron, the Cardinal
Giovanni Colonna.

The following is a modernised version of the sonnet taken from
a manuscript containing many poems which from other sources we
have the right to include in the work of Wyatt and Surrey:

  The precious pillar perished is and rent
    That countenanced life and cheered the wearied mind,
    Like of my loss no age shall ever find
    Though the world's eyes a-seeking all ways went.

Death hath me reft the world's chief glory here,
  Who made the mind with life the more content;
  And now, alas, no gold, no land empire,
  Nor gift so great can that restore is spent.

But if the cause proceed from the upper place,
  What can I more than mourn that am constrained
  With woeful tears to wail that woeful case?

O brittle life, with face so fair y-stained,
  How easily lost thou art in a moment space
  That many years with much ado attained!

Nobody to the best of my knowledge has claimed this poem for either Wyatt or Surrey. Nobody has expressed astonishment that there should have arisen a third poet capable in these years so easily of rivalling or even outmatching the two poets whose reputation with later generations rested on their translations from Petrarch. This is not, however, the place to investigate the authorship of this poem. The sole purpose of the confrontation is to enforce a point about *The pillar perished*. There is one feature of similarity which will bring out the kind of and the significance of the difference. Both poems make no attempt to render the main point of Petrarch's sonnet. Both deal with only *one* loss:

    the world's chief glory here
and
    Of all my joy the very root and rind.

Both deal (though obscurely) with the opposition between fate and fortune. But there the resemblance ends. For Wyatt's poem then turns to bitter reflection on his own behaviour. In this context Petrarch was capable of saying 'I no longer love myself now Laura is gone' but no *ò in odio me stesso*, 'I hate myself'. That reflection occurs in the different context of *Pace non trouo*, where Wyatt rendered the line as:

    I love another and thus I hate myself.

This very reflection, however, has been treated by some editors as good grounds for rejecting the hypothesis that Wyatt was here writing about a political figure. The Tottel editors entitled the poem 'The louer lamentes the death of his loue'. But this may have been prudent camouflage for a poem which might have come to the notice of Cardinal Pole, who had shown a keen (but, of course, quite different) interest in the execution of Cromwell. Modern editors, who feel that Wyatt is here giving sincere expression to his love and high regard, cannot reconcile these sentiments with their conception of Cromwell's character and his dealings with Wyatt. The poem seemed to them incompatible with what they read into Cromwell's hard-faced portrait. Wyatt, they were sure, could not have loved a man of whom it was said by one biographer:

> Cold and cynical in the face of death as he had been in life, he knelt down. The executioner obeyed his orders.

It is therefore clear that if the poem is to contribute to history, it will need some prior historical support both for the tenor of the relations of Cromwell and Wyatt during the years 1536–1540, and for what was said and done on Tower Hill on July 28, 1540, the supposed precipitating cause of the poem. Unfortunately, on the latter point the historical record is far from clear. While execution was undoubtedly done and seen to be done on that fateful July day, there is some doubt about the actual words Cromwell pronounced just before his death. Did he in fact say what was printed by the government for publication at home and abroad in the form of a speech in which he both acknowledged his guilt and abjured all heresies? Cardinal Pole was told that there was some discrepancy. What is disturbing for the hypothesis that Wyatt was present at the execution is that none of the serious historical accounts mentions him at all. Both Hall in his *Triumphant Reign* and Foxe in his *Acts and Monuments* print what has been taken for the full text of the government hand-out. There is, however, a manuscript version of Cromwell's last words in the commonplace book kept by Richard Cox, then Bishop of Ely, which continues past the text in the printed version to say:

> & after this prayer he stode vp agayne & sayed, praye for our prince & for all the Lordes of the cownsaylles & for all the comunaltie, & now I praye you ons agayne that ye wyll praye for me, & he turned him abowt & sayed farewell Wyat & gentell Wiat praye for me.

What looks like the draft made for the printer of the hand-out, for it goes on to complete the document with 'God Saue ye kyng!' and the printer's name, has turned up in a Harley manuscript.[1] It has in the identical words this closing reference to Wyatt. This makes it reasonable to recall the existence of a document, fortunately containing an account of the execution, which states that Cromwell in fact so addressed Wyatt before he died. The manuscript has not been treated with the respect it here deserves since, taken as a whole, it is not a serious historical work, and contains a great deal of false reporting and downright romancing. But one or two of the Spaniard's — although his name is not known, he is thought to have been a merchant resident in London during these years — stories seem to have come to him from either Richard Cromwell, the statesman's nephew, or from the poet's son. Whatever his source, he gives the very same words that we find in the hand-out:

> Among these courtiers around the scaffold, Cromwell caught sight of Master Wyatt — he was the gentleman who had been in love with the Queen, Anne Boleyn — and he called to him and said, 'Farewell, Wyatt, and gentle Wyatt, I pray you to pray God for me.'

The Spaniard then broke off his narrative to remark:

> There had always been great love between him and this Master Wyatt.

In addition to the evidence of the poem we have several letters written to Wyatt by Cromwell showing an unbroken concern for his material welfare. It is also significant that Wyatt's father held Cromwell in the same high regard and asked Cromwell to stand *in loco parentis* to his son when he died. A few words from a letter Wyatt's father wrote to Cromwell in June 1536 will give the tone of their relations:

> And ffurther on my blessing I have chargid hym not only to ffolowe your commaundementes ffrom tyme to tyme, but also in euery point to take and repute you as me, and if whilst he livith he have not this for sure printyd in his hart than I refuse hym to be my son. I besech you to

1 Ms. Harl. 3362 *fo. 79 recto.*

contynewe vnto hym as ye have bene . . .

The Spanish Chronicler gives a circumstantial account of how Cromwell saved Wyatt's life during this crisis of 1536. When the King wished to 'frame' Anne Boleyn, he had all suspects rounded up and put in the Tower:

> It appears that the King sent to Cromwell telling him to send for Wyatt and have him examined. When he reached London, Wyatt was taken aside by Cromwell, who said to him, "Master Wyatt, you well know how great is the love I have and always have had for you, and now I would have you know that it would grieve me to the guts if you were to be found guilty in a matter I am going to tell you of." He then told him all that had been happening. Master Wyatt was astounded to hear of it, and replied with some spirit. "My Lord, I swear by the love I owe to God and the King, my master, that I have nothing to fear, for I have not wronged the King either in deed or even in thought, as his Majesty well knows from what I told him before he married the Queen." Then Cromwell said to him, "Well then, Master Wyatt, it has been decided that you must go to the Tower, but I promise to be a good friend to you."

For the narrative of what happened after Cromwell spoke to Wyatt on the scaffold we have to rely exclusively on this Spanish chronicle. It sounds to me more like history than romance:

> And Wyatt could not answer him, for his tears came too fast.
>
> Those courtiers were all surprised to see Wyatt betraying so much feeling. This did not excape Cromwell's notice, and as he was a wise politician, he said in a loud voice, "Wyatt, do not weep for me: if I were no more guilty than you were when you were arrested, I should not now be standing where I am." As all those gentlemen were very fond of Wyatt, they pretended

they had heard nothing, for otherwise he might have been put in prison to get out of him whether he knew of any treasonable act that Cromwell might have plotted.

Some commentators pick and choose what they consider the history in this poem. If any part is historical all must be. Therefore we must take Wyatt literally when he says he hates himself. We do not need to conclude he thought himself guilty or in any way responsible for Cromwell's downfall, but there must have been some circumstance to have prompted such strong language.

The pillar perished

The pillar]

It is noteworthy that Wyatt used the same language when expressing his dependence on God, as in these lines in *From depth*:

> Thy holy word of eterne excellence,
> Thy mercy's promise, that is alway just,
> Have been my stay, my pillar, and pretence.

Spenser used the phrase in a poem to Lord Grey of Wilton:

> Most Noble Lord the pillor of my life . . .

Cooper under *Columen* has: the stay and succour of a thing.

Both Petrarch and Wyatt would know that Horace used the word of his patron in *Od.* II/17/3-4:

> *Maecenas, mearum/grande decus columenque rerum.*
> Maecenas, the great glory and support in my affairs.

perished]

Perhaps 'brought to a violent end'.

whereto I leant]

The meaning 'rely on' was normally expressed in contemporary prose by 'lean to'.

It is possible that Wyatt read his Petrarch in an edition where the second line of the sonnet ran:

> *Ove s'appoggia il mio stanco pensero*
> Whereon my weary thought leans or rests.

stay]

'Support', *i.e.* what you can safely lean on.
N. Udall *Apophthegmes* p. 219:

> [Athens] the foundamente, the staye or ye leanyng poste of all Grece . . .

The word was used in a similar context to Wyatt's by Sir Thomas More at the beginning of his *A Dialogue of Cumfort*:

> But that may be your great cumfort, good Uncle, syth you depart to God: but vs here shall you leaue of your kinred, a sort of sorie cumfortlesse Orphanes, to all whome your good helpe, cumfort and counsel hath long bene a great stay, not as an vnkle vnto some, & to some as one farther of kinne: but as though that vnto vs al you had bene a natural father.

unquiet]   'Restless, uneasy, troubled'.

still]   'Always'.

seeking]   As in *Throughout the world if it were sought*.

unhap]   Many of Wyatt's contemporaries lumped together all the words, hap, chance, Fortune, Destiny, for the forces affecting man's prosperity. They come together in *The Demaundes of holy Scripture* (1577) by Thomas Becon:

> *What is fortune?* It is fate, or destiny chaunsing to any man by the will of God, without mans prouidence.

rent . . . rind]   Among the expressions for 'the sum or totality', corresponding to 'from A to Z' are the phrases applied to trees, 'crop and root', 'root and rind'. Chaucer in the Fifth Book of his *Troylus* has:

> As man that hath his ioyes eke forlore
> Was waytyng on his lady euer more
> As she that was sothfast croppe and more
> Of al his lust or ioyes here tofore . . .

and   O Pandarus
> nowe knowe I croppe & roote
> I nam but deed . . . .

and in the Second Book we find:

> . . . ye that ben of beaute croppe and rote

Wyatt has a similar expression in *The wandering gadling*:

> . . . sitting by her side
> That of my health is very crop and root . . .

Root and rind is an exactly parallel expression: both were used adverbially, e.g. of a bush:

> hewe hit downe crop and rote

and of a king:

> destroie him rote & rynde

The phrase was commonly used with *rend*:

Lydgate *Assembly of Gods*/66:

> He breketh hem asondre or rendeth hem
> roote & rynde
> Out of the erthe

Root and rind was used for 'the whole source or origin', e.g. of envy or of pity. It also stood for the pulp, the pith, the true substance, as contrasted with the mere outer appearance when contrasted with *bark and rind*. The OED gives a good example:

> You're my better in bark and rine, but in
> pith and substance I may compare with you.[1]

assigned]

It appears that Wyatt regularly used this word in the sense of *allotted* for what the inscrutable powers have assigned to man as his lot. The word is used by Wyatt for what God assigns as well as for the operation of Fortune. A poem where this vocabulary is fully displayed begins *Give place all ye*. That Wyatt did not distinguish the two words may be seen from *My mother's maids*:

> Thy self content with that is thee assigned,
> And use that well that is to thee allotted...

Daily to mourn]

Presumably on his knees.

it relent]

'Soften it'.

by destiny]

Petrarch *Ma se consentimento è di destino*

> But if consent is by destiny.

Wyatt knew a solemn account given in Chaucer's *Knight's Tale*:

> The destenye mynster general
> That executeth in the worlde ouyr al
> The purueance that god hath seyn byforn
> So straunge it is that though the world hath
>   sworn
> The contrary of a thyng by ye or nay
> Yet somtyme it shal falle vp on a day
> That fallyth not eft in a thousand yeer
> For certenly our appetitis heer
> Be it of pees hate warre or loue
> Al is rewlide by the sighte aboue.

---

1 This contrast is brought out in the *Romaunt of the Rose* 7168ff.

woeful heart . . . full of smart]	These same phrases occur in *Thou sleepest fast.*
My pen . . . plaint]	'I am bound to use my pen only to lament'.
careful]	'Full of sorrow'.
dreadful]	'Inspiring fear', as, possibly, in *Stand whoso list.*
ease]	*A Handefull of plesant delites*, 1584, has the phrase: til dreadful death/ do seek to ease my paine . . .
doleful]	'Miserable'.

Sighs are my food

The dramatic situation is of confinement in a prison cell. The evidence in the Commentary would support the conjecture that the circumstances are those of Wyatt in 1541 when he was put in the Tower and treated as guilty before his trial. It can hardly have been composed after March 1541, when Wyatt was again employed in the king's service.

The form of the poem may indicate it is one of a group in which Wyatt wrote of his personal affairs to members of an intimate circle of friends. Such a poem is *The flaming sighs*:

But you that of such like have had your part
  Can best be judge: wherefore, my friend so dear,
  I thought it good my state should now appear
To you, and that there is no great desert.
And whereas you in weighty matters great
  Of Fortune saw the shadow that you know,
  For tasting things I now am stricken so
That though I feel my heart doth wound and beat,
  I sit alone . . .

Metrically, it is close to a poem beginning *Sometime the pride*, which may be a dedicatory preface to a translation of a Psalm made for Cromwell. Surrey wrote similar dedicatory poems to close friends to whom he sent his Psalm versions. He virtually vouches for the authenticity of *Sighs are my food* in a short dedicatory poem beginning 'My Ratcliffe . . .', and ending:

Yet Solomon said, the wronged shall recure,
But Wiat said true, the scar doth aye endure.

Sighs]	It is possible that Wyatt wrote *Syghis*, and scanned the word as having two syllables. A similar scansion seems likely for the word in line 16 of *Lord,*

hear (Psalm 102 in the A.V.):

> And ffor my plaintfull syghis and my drede

my food]

Although Wyatt may have been familiar with the story of Orpheus as told in Ovid's *Metamorphoses*, Book X, where occurs the line:

> *cura dolorque animi lacrimaeque alimenta fuere*

care, pain of mind, tears were his food,

I fancy that the various similar expressions in the Bible may have come to his mind, and, in particular, the Vulgate Psalm 79/6. Joye has:

> In stede of bodely foode thou feddest vs withe teres/ thou madeste vs drinke plentuously oure owne teres.

crave]

The noise of the fetters would call for the accompaniment of sighs and tears.

away it wears]

I assume that Wyatt was very familiar with *The Complaynt of Creseyde,* which has the line:

> Al welth in erthe/ as wynde awaye it weares

In the Declaration Wyatt composed for his defence in 1541 he wrote:

> I besyke you humbly be my good lordes and lett not my lyf were awaye here [in the Tower]

There is a similar passage in the poem beginning *What rage*:

> Lo, see, mine eyes swell with continual tears,
> The body still away sleepless it wears.
> My food . . .

A Handefull of plesant delites, 1584, has:

> For still in teares,
> my life it weares,
> And so I must remaine . . .

Innocency]

Wyatt's word for 'innocence'. In his Declaration of 1541, when on trial for his life, he wrote:

> for Chrystes charite weigh in this myne innocency . . .

Malice . . . save]

Wyatt is saying that his innocence ought to have saved him from his enemies' ill-will. There is a

similar word order, object, subject, verb, to
> that righteousness should save

in Wyatt's Seventh Psalm:
> Before thy sight no man his right shall save . . .

that is, in the sight of God no man shall be saved
by his own righteousness.

Wyatt was probably referring to his political
enemies, as in his Declaration:
> . . . I shall sincerlye declare vnto you the
> mallice that hathe moved them . . .

heal . . . remain]

Wyatt has given an original twist to the proverbial
thought that although the wounds inflicted by
envy and malice can be healed, they mark you for
ever. Caxton in his *Fables of Avyan* p. 184 had:
> And yf hit were a stroke of a spere hit
> myght be by the Cyrurgyen heled/ but the
> stroke of an euylle tongue may not be
> heled.

But, judging by other similar borrowings Wyatt
made from the translations of Erasmus from
Plutarch's Moral Essays, I think it likely that here,
too, he may have found the proverb in this translation made by Erasmus:
> *docens etiam, si quis morsus sit, uulneri*
> *medeatur, cicatricem tamen calumniae re-*
> *linqui . . .*

> he taught, too, that though there are cures
> for all other bites, the scar left by the bite
> of slander remains for ever . . .

The phrase turns up in this Declaration of 1541:
> These men thynkethe yt inoughe to accuse
> and as all these sclaunderers vse for a generall
> rule, whome thou louest not, accuse. For
> tho he hele the wounde yet the scharre
> shall remayne . . .

cf. *The flamyng Sighes*/13–14:
> The wound, alas, happ in some other place
> Ffrom whence no toole away the skarr can
>
> race.

What rage/10:
> To curid skarre that neuer shall retorne . . .

DISPRAISE OF THE COURTIER: MINE OWN J.P.

Although, as will appear in due course, *Mine own John Poyntz* might well be classified along with Wyatt's other verse translations from Italian sources, many people have felt that the choice of such a piece to translate must have had a deeper cause than the desire to experiment in adapting into English a difficult Italian metre. Some people go further than merely imputing a standing dislike of the court in which Wyatt was forced to live, and suppose that some particular occasion made him long for an opportunity to express himself in verse. He then, it is supposed, recalled a very similar 'occasional' poem he had known for some time, and used the act of translation as a mask.

This would be nothing new for Wyatt. There is therefore every reason for enquiring when in Wyatt's life there had been an appropriate occasion to cause him to feel so strongly about the darker side of court life. What was known in Wyatt's day as 'his first putting into the Tower' was an obvious choice,[1] since everybody at the time said, and Wyatt in later years admitted, that he 'grudged at' his treatment there. This was in May 1536, when he was arrested and put in the Tower of London, apparently in connection with the investigations into the supposed adulteries of the Queen, Anne Boleyn. It is certain that Mark Smeaton, a lute player, was made to confess his guilt. Several of Wyatt's friends were convicted without confessing their guilt. It is also certain that the first sign for the public that something odd was under way occurred on May 1st, when May Day was being celebrated by a tournament at Greenwich. It is also certain that Wyatt was arrested at this time. What is not certain is whether Wyatt was imprisoned at this time on account of Anne Boleyn.

Nobody doubts that the conduct of the adultery enquiry was in Cromwell's hands. It is therefore worth hearing an account of the events affecting Wyatt for which Cromwell's nephew is the most likely authority. The following is an extract from the chronicle of the Spanish merchant:

> The Secretary immediately wrote to the King and
> sent him Mark's confession by his nephew, Richard

1 But nothing in this discussion excludes the imprisonment of 1541 as the possible occasion.

Cromwell. This is what was in the letter:

Be it known to your Majesty that, having observed certain things going on in your palace, and grieving for the damage to your honour, I made up my mind to find out the truth. Your Majesty will recollect that Mark has not yet been a good four months in your service and his wages barely come to one hundred pounds *per annum*. Yet the whole court has witnessed his extravagant way of living, and for the jousts of to-day he has spent a great deal of money. This has aroused some suspicion at Court, and I myself have examined him. Enclosed you will find his written confession.

When the King read it, he found it hard to digest, but like a brave prince he hid his feelings, and ordered his barge to be got ready at once and went to Westminster. He also gave orders that the tournament should go on as planned, but that as soon as it was over, Master Norris, Brereton, and Master Wyatt should be quietly arrested and taken to the Tower. . . . So the tournament took its course and Master Wyatt came off best.

This Master Wyatt was a very graceful nobleman, there was no prettier fellow at Court. When the jousts were finished, and they were taking off their armour, the Captain of the Guard came up and summoned Master Norris and Master Brereton, and told them the King wanted to see them. So they went off with him, and there was a boat waiting, and without drawing attention to themselves they were immediately conveyed to the Tower.

Then Cromwell's nephew, Richard, said to Master Wyatt, "Sir, my master, Cromwell, sends to you to request you to come and have a talk with him in London since he is slightly indisposed." And Wyatt went off with him without delay.

It appears that the King sent to Cromwell telling him to send for Wyatt and have him examined.

Thomas Cromwell wearing his chain of gold.
From a Holbein miniature.

But all unbeknown to the Spanish Chronicler, there was a quite
different crisis under way during these days both for King Henry
VIII and for Thomas Wyatt. Our evidence comes from letters
written by and to Wyatt's father, Sir Henry. On May 7, he wrote
to his son urging him to rally round the throne 'in this dangerus
tyme, that his grace hath suffered by ffals and vntreu Traitors',
by giving 'to his grace dewe attendaunce nyght and daye'. Two
days later Sir Henry was informed by Cromwell that his son had
been arrested and was being punished. But the crime is not named.
The father hoped that it would be made clear to his son 'that
this ponishement that he hath for this matter ys more ffor the
displeasure that he hath done to god otherweise. Wherein I beseech
you [Cromwell] to aduertise hym to fly vice and serue god better
than he hath done'.

What Wyatt had done to call for punishment was equally

unknown to Anne Boleyn. While she was in the Tower she neither showed any resentment on hearing of Wyatt's arrest nor said anything to incriminate him. A little light on Wyatt's offence can be won from another letter from his father to Cromwell, which shows that, whatever it was, Wyatt had been released by the middle of June with a warning against future lapses. The father told Cromwell he had spoken to his son and 'not only commandyd hym his obediens in all pointes to the kinges pleasure, but also the leving of such slaunderous ffacon, as hath engendered vnto hym both the displeasure of god and of his maister'. But although we are blocked in our search for an explanation of these events of 1536, inspection of the poem would favour a date of composition during the time when Wyatt was under house arrest and his father's supervision at Allington Castle, the family home in Kent. There was no parallel in the Italian for the restriction on his freedom implied in the line:

Save that a clog doth hang yet at my heel.

By the same token we ought to consider the implication at the opening of the poem that beside the desire to get away from 'lordly looks', his positive aim in retiring to the country was to learn to set a law to will and lust, which makes it seem likely that he had failed to do so and had been punished for that.

There is still one further line of enquiry that might be tried. If we do not tie the answer too close to the situation of imprisonment followed by subsequent release and, almost immediately after that, distinguished public employment (as experienced by Wyatt in both 1536 and 1541), it may be possible to detect a lasting cause of deep resentment coming to a head because of this situation but having a different origin. It is not easy to give a name to something which, as will be seen, could not by definition be brought to the surface. The simplest term would be 'hatred of tyranny' and, specifically, condemnation of Henry VIII as the slave-master, as the man who poisoned the wells of life at court and gave rise to the image Wyatt twice used of 'bitter taste' and 'brackish joys'. It may be plausibly conjectured that two, at least, of Wyatt's contemporaries would have been able to give the term full definition: Erasmus and More. And it would be in keeping with Wyatt's practice if the particular *grief* were presented in a mass of general observations on the drawbacks for an honest man of living in a Tudor court.

This line would be to ask what reasons Wyatt had, first, for turning to Luigi Alamanni, then, for taking his satires, and thirdly, for selecting the particular satire Alamanni addressed to his friend, Thommaso Sertini. A vicious circle cannot be broken altogether, since there is no written statement by Wyatt (or traceable back to Wyatt) giving his reasons — even though they must have been powerful ones, since no English poet would take on the challenge of making an equivalent of the Italian *terza rima* without some strong incentive. But a little breach in the circle may be made by inspecting the Italian poem and noting why Alamanni wrote it, and then making a close study of the parts Wyatt has translated almost literally, those he has ignored altogether, and those that he has remodelled to suit his own conditions.

It is of interest to note that Luigi Alamanni was a contemporary, born a few years before Wyatt and surviving him. Since he was for most of his adult life an exile at the court of the French kings, it would have been possible for the two poets to have met[1] or to have had acquaintances in common. But what is of far greater interest is the fact that Alamanni was a life-long republican, and spent his whole time in exile because he hated the 'tyranny' in his native Florence. From his early years he had been brought up to see contemporary events in terms of classical precedents. Consequently, his and his party's attempts to murder the Medici ruler were ennobled by likening them to the republican conspiracy which culminated in Caesar's murder during the Ides of March.

The Satire Wyatt chose was first published in 1532 in Alamanni's first volume of *Opere Toscane*. The reader is invited to pause over the text of this poem and, if desired, the rough translation I have added to bring out the salient points.

À Thommaso Sertini

Io ui dirò poi che d'udir ui cale,
Thommaso mio gentil, perch'amo, et colo
Piu di tutti altri il lito Prouenzale,

---

1 Alamanni was present at the interview between the Kings of France and England in October 1532, to which Wyatt had to go. (See the commentary on *Sometime I fled*). In his *Opera Toscane* Vol. II there is a sonnet beginning *Avventuroso il di che sorge il seme* which refers to this meeting, and another beginning *Io volea visitar* indicating a desire to visit England.

Et perche qui cosi pouero & solo,
  Piu tosto chel seguir signori & Regi
  Viua temprando il mio infinito duolo.
Ne cio mi uien perch' io tra me dispregi
  Quei, ch' han dalla fortuna in mano il freno
  Di noi, per sangue, & per ricchezze egregi.
Ma ben è uer ch'assai gli estimo meno
  Chel uulgo, & quei ch'à cio ch'appar di fuore
  Guardan, senza ueder che chiugga il seno.
Non dico gia che non mi scaldi amore,
  Talhor di gloria, ch'io non uo mentire
  Con chi biasmando honor, sol cerca honore
Ma con qual pie potrei color sequire
  Chel mondo pregia, ch'io non so quell'arte
  Di chi le scale altrui conuien salire.
Io non saprei, Sertin, porre in disparte
  La uerità, colui lodando ogni hora
  Che con piu danno altrui dal ben si parte.
Non saprei reuerir chi soli adora
  Venere & Bacco, ne tacer saprei
  Di quei chel vulgo falsamente honora.
Non saprei piu ch'à gli immortali Dei
  Rendere honor con le ginocchia inchine
  À piu ingiusti che sian, fallaci, & rei.
Non saprei nel parlar coprir le spine
  Con simulati fior, nell'opre hauendo
  Mele al principio, & tristo assentio alfine.
Non saprei no, doue'l contrario intendo,
  I maluagi consigli usar per buoni,
  Dauanti al uero honor l'util ponendo.
Non trouare ad ogni hor false cagioni
  Per abbassare i giusti, alzando i praui,
  D'auaritia, & d'inuidia hauendo sproni.
Non suprei dar de miei pensier le chiaui
  All' ambition, che mi portasse in alto
  Alla fucina delle colpe graui.
Non saprei'l cor hauer di freddo smalto
  Contro à pietà, talhor nocendo a tale,
  Ch' io piu di tutti nella mente esalto,
Non di loda honorar chiara immortale

Cesare, & Sylla, condannando a torto
  Bruto, & la schiera che piu d'altra uale.
Non saprei camminar nel sentier corto
  Dell' impia iniquità, lasciando quello
  Che reca pace al uiuo, & gloria al morto.
Io non saprei chiamar cortese & bello
  Chi sia Thersite, ne figliuol d'Anchise
  Chi sia di senno, & di pieta rubello:
Non saprei chi piu'l cor nell' oro mise
  Dirgli Alessandro, e'l pauroso & uile
  Chiamarlo il forte, ch'i Centauri ancise.
Dir non saprei Poeta alto, & gentile
  Meuio, giurando poi che cotal non uide
  Smirna, Manto, & Fiorenza ornato stile.
Non saprei dentro all'alte soglie infide
  Per piu mostrar amor, contr'à mia uoglia
  Imitar sempre altrui se piange, o ride.
Non saprei indiuinar que'l ch'altri uoglia,
  Ne conoscer saprei quel che piu piace,
  Tacendo il uer che le piu uolte addoglia.
L'amico lusinghier, doppio, & fallace,
  Dir non saprei gentil, ne aperto & uero
  Che sempre parli quel che piu dispiace.
Non saprei l'huom crudel chiamar seuero
  Ne chi lascia peccar chiamarlo pio,
  Ne che'l tyranneggiar sia giusto impero.
Io non saprei ingannar gl'huomini & Dio
  Con giuramenti, & con promesse false,
  Ne far saprei quel ch'è dun'altro mio,
Questo è cagion che non mi cal, ne calse
  Anchor gia mai, di seguitar coloro
  Ne quai fortuna piu chel senno ualse.
Questo fa chel mio Regno, el mio thesoro
  Son gl'inchiostri, et le carte, & piu ch'altroue
  Hoggi in Prouenza uolentier dimoro.
Qui non ho alcun, che mi domandi doue
  Mi stia, ne uada, & non mi sforza alcuno
  A gir pel mondo quando agg[h]iaccia, & pioue
Quando eglie è'l ciel seren, quando egli è bruno
  Son quel medesmo, & non mi prendo affanno,

Colmo di pace, & di timor digiuno.
Non sono in Francia à sentir beffe & danno
* S'io non conosco i uin, s'io non so bene*
* Qual uiuanda è miglior di tutto l'anno.*
Non nella Hispagna oue studiar conuiene
* Piu che nell'esser poi nel ben parere,*
* Oue frode, & menzogne il seggio tiene.*
Non in Germania ou' el mangiar' el bere
* M'habia à tor l'intelletto, et darlo in preda*
* Al senso in guisa di seluagge fere.*
Non sono in Roma, oue ch' in Christo creda,
* Et non sappia falsar, ne far ueneni,*
* Conuien ch' a casa sospirando rieda.*
Sono in Prouenza, oue quantunque pieni
* Di maluagio uoler ci sian glingegni*
* Lignoranza el timor pon loro i freni,*
Che benche sian d'inuidia & d'odio pregni
* Sempre contro i miglior per ueder poco*
* Son nel mezzo troncati i lor disegni.*
Hor qui dunque mi sto, prendendo in gioco
* Il lor breue saper, le lunghe uoglie*
* Con le mie Muse in solitario loco.*
Non le gran Corti homai, non l'alte soglie
* Mi uedran gir co i lor seguaci a schiera,*
* Ne di me hauran troppo honorate spoglie*
Auaritia, et liuor, ma pace uera.

To Thomas Sertini

Since you care to know, my dear Thomas, I
will tell you why I love the shore of Provence and
prefer it above all others, and the reason why I
had rather live in poverty and solitude moderating
my endless grief there than follow the progresses
of princes and kings. It is not because I privately
think meanly of those to whom Fortune has given
the power to govern us either on account of their
birth or for their great possessions. But it is very
true that I think far less of them than do the
common people who are taken with outer appearance and judge only by that, ignoring what is
hidden in the heart. That is not to say that I am

not fired from time to time with a love of glory.
I refuse to join the liars who speak ill of public
honours while seeking nothing else. But how could
I possibly follow those the world values since I
have not mastered the art of climbing the right
back stairs?

I could never manage, Sertino, to set aside the
truth and praise the man who is always far from
the path of right to the hurt of mankind. I could
never feel deep respect for a man who worships no
other gods than Venus and Bacchus. Nor could I
hold my tongue when I heard men earning un-
deserved honour from the common people. Nor
could I myself bend the knee to worship more
than the immortal gods unjust, treacherous and
wicked people. I could not in my words cover
thorns with false flowers, begin my plots with
honey first and end with bitter gall. I could not
where I mean the opposite, give bad advice as if
it were good, putting expediency before the truly
moral honourable act. I could not be always
inventing bad reasons for bringing down the just
and exalting the wicked, spurred on by greed and
envy. I could not surrender the keys of my thoughts
to an ambition which might carry me up to the
place where serious crimes are forged. I could not
have a heart hardened against pity, which would
let me harm those I value in my mind more than all
others. I could not honour with bright, immortal
praise the dictators, Caesar and Sulla, while wrongfully condemning the republican, Brutus, and the
company which has no peer in worth. I could not
walk the narrow path of godless wickedness
and leave the way that brings peace to the living
and glory to the dead.

I could not call a man courtly and refined who
was a Thersites, nor a true son of Anchises, one
who had broken away from good sense and piety.
I could not call a man an Alexander whose heart
was all for money, nor name after the hero who

slew the Centaurs a man who was a despicable coward. I could not say that Maevius was a great, distinguished poet, and swear that an equally polished style had never been found in Smyrna, Mantua or Florence.[1] In the treacherous high halls of the mighty I could not try to show devotion by going against my inclination and crying when my masters cried or laughing when they laughed. I could not guess another's secret wishes nor find out what most he wanted, nor keep my mouth from telling the truths that most often give offence. When I find a friend a false, two-faced flatterer, I could not call him well-bred, nor praise for his truth and openness one who is always saying the most disagreeable things. I could not praise a bloody-minded man for his proper strictness or call pious him who turns a blind eye on sin nor say that tyranny is the right way to govern a country.

I could not cheat God and men by oaths and false promises nor convert another's property to my own use. That is why I have never cared yet and do not care now to follow those for whom Fortune carries more weight than does true judgement. That is the reason why my kingdom and my treasure are my ink and writing paper, and that is why I nowadays prefer to live in Provence rather than anywhere else. There is nobody here to ask me where I live or where I am going, nobody to drive me out of doors when it is cold or raining. It is all the same to me whether the skies be clear or dark. Nothing agitates me, I have peace in plenty and a scarcity of fear. I am not in France, where I am made to feel the smart of jibes when I fail to identify the wines or do not know which foods are in season at any time in the year. Nor am I in Spain, where one must concentrate rather on seeming than being good, where fraud and lies sit in the seat of justice. Nor am I in Germany, where I would be in danger of losing my wits through

1 where Homer, Virgil, and Dante lived

excessive eating and drinking, where people behave like wild animals whose brains are sacrificed to the gratification of their sensuality. I am not in Rome from where a Christian goes home full of sighs if he cannot forge documents and make up poisons.

But I *am* in Provence, where, although the locals are full of malice, their evil efforts are kept within bounds by their ignorance and fear. Much as they are for ever bursting with hatred and envy of their betters, their wicked plots are frustrated by their shortsightedness. So here I dwell in solitude with my Muses, mocking the yokels' lack of wit and slow desires. Henceforth the courts of the great and their palaces will not see me crowding in among their followers. Greed and envy will take no tribute, will not triumph over me. I shall know true peace of mind.

If it seems an absurd hypothesis to find resentment against 'tyranny' in a man who in the next month after the supposed date of composition (either 1536 or 1541) of this poem and for years after was active in the 'tyrant's' service, we have an exact parallel in the poems and epigrams of Sir Thomas More. The paradox is complete. An 'autobiographical' topic arising out of his epigrams is one that struck Erasmus at the time and strikes everyone today: the extraordinary number of poems against the arbitrary powers of kings. Erasmus reports that it was in fact a passion of More's — this hatred of the New Power which returned to the king with the accession of Henry VII. One of More's first acts in Parliament, his opposition to the crown over taxes, puts him in a great tradition. This would not be so significant if More had been, as it were, born to opposition, but he was the reverse. He accepted to the full the current doctrine that the King's service was God's service. More's greatness as a martyr depends in part on this deep loyalty to his king.

I have tried to expound in the Commentary[1] what may be the significance of the prominence given to *Cato Uticensis* in Wyatt's poem. The distinction between Luigi Alamanni's Brutus, the man

1 and in an article in *The Cambridge Quarterly*, Volume Seven Number Two, 'Wyatt's Greatest Adventure?'.

who killed the 'tyrant', and the man who killed himself rather than be beholden to that same tyrant cannot be without a meaning. But the real weight of the suggestion lies in the reader's accceptance of the possibility that Wyatt was *deeply indebted to Erasmus* in all things, secular and religious, and, in particular, in his attitude to the 'splendid slavery' of the life of a courtier. Erasmus, too, continued as the Emperor's servant all his life.

The historian who is unwilling to believe that Henry could have aroused in his courtiers the disgust it is easy for us at a safe distance of centuries to feel has to recall that there is one historical fact which must never be forgotten in reading the poems of courtiers: the absolute power of life and death in Henry's hands. The proverb on everyone's lips in Henry's reign was:

> *Indignatio regis nuntij mortis*
> The kynges displeasure is a messaunger of death,
> but a wyse man wyl pacifie him.

Writers were driven to wit, irony, or any masking devices to avoid that messenger.

Supposing for the moment that 1536 was the date of composition, and the animus in the poem was directed at Henry VIII, I would advance a conjecture that, even if Wyatt had been content to assist in the process of getting rid of Anne Boleyn, he might well have shared the *popular indignation* at Henry's behaviour during the days when he was enjoying his new mistress, and his wife was confined to the Tower. My authority for calling the indignation popular is not impeccable, since it comes from a letter Charles V's ambassador wrote on May 19, 1536:

> Another thing that did not go down very well with the people was to see the said king after undergoing such disgrace and dishonour showing himself to be very much more cheerful after the imprisonment of the aforesaid whore (*putain*) than he had ever been before. There was hardly a night when he did not go a-banquetting with the ladies in some house or other, and sometimes he stayed out after midnight, and on his returns by water he was often accompanied by divers instruments of music, and the singers of his privy chamber did their duty there.

The general view of this is that it exposes the
king's joy at having got rid of a skinny, ageing,
nasty harlot (*bague*) and his hope of starting up a
fresh campaign, which is something the said king
has always been fond of.

At any rate it seems not altogether fanciful to feel an undercurrent
of unavowed resentment running beneath the surface of the poem
and lifting the catalogue of general vice from prose declamation
into something like dramatic, passionate song.

Mine own J.P.
(The Italian references are to Alamanni)

Mine own John Poyntz]   *Thommaso mio gentil* My gentle Thomas
There is no other record of the friendship, but
there is an expressive drawing of the head by
Holbein.

The causes]   In favour of this reading we might cite Juvenal's
Third Satire, line 315:
His alias poteram et pluris subnectere causas
More I cou'd say; more Causes I cou'd show
For my departure . . .

flee the press]   The phrase may well mean more than 'run away
from the crowd', for Wyatt has, in the poem
beginning *In court to serve*:
The life in banquets and sundry kinds of play
Amid the press of lordly looks to waste . . .

whereso they go]   The court made regular progresses during the
summer, and was at all times going from one
Royal Palace to another. The phrase, however,
was commonly used by Chaucer to end a line with.

Rather than]   *Piu tosto chel seguir signori & Regi*
Rather than follow lords and kings

lordly looks]   The bitterness of 'thrall' and 'under the awe of'
is all Wyatt's, and makes it as certain as anything
of this sort could be that it was in the same mood
that he wrote *In court to serve*, where he spoke
of the bitter taste which came from wasting life
Amid the press of lordly looks.

wrapped . . . cloak] As he reflected on his condition in retirement, it would be appropriate if Wyatt had recalled Horace's *mea uirtute me inuoluo*. Elyot gave *wrapped* as the meaning of *inuolutus*. The context of this phrase in *Odes* III/29:

> *resigno quae dedit [Fortuna] et mea*
> *uirtute me inuoluo probamque*
> *Pauperiem sine dote quaero.*

is as much in keeping with this poem as it is in the passage in *A spending hand*:

> Content thee then with honest poverty . . .

Horace is saying, 'I give up whatever Fortune gave me, wrap myself in the cloak of my own sense of worth, and take up with the honest maiden of modest means, even though she brings me no dowry.'

will and lust] A collective phrase for the unruly side of our nature, the passions.

set a law] The sense order is: learning to set a law to my will and lust. Two meanings are conflated, 'to lay down a law, like God', as in Lydgate's *Pilgrimage/52*:

* Nature
> To al pylgrymes kynd* hath set a lawe . . .

thus regulating the conduct of the passions, and 'mark the limits', saying to the passions, 'thus far and no farther'.

Spenser used similar language in his *Faerie Queene*: IV.ix.19.8:

> And lawlesse lust to rule with reasons lore

IV.viii.30.8:

> And each vnto his lust did make a lawe

VI.xi.6, 3:

> Fearing least he at length the raines would lend
> Vnto his lust, and make his will his law . . .

Richard Tauerner *Proverbes or adagies*, 1539, A .ij. *recto*:

> And also bycause that a man must fyrst rule hys owne lustes, and be hym selfe obedient to ryght reason, ere he can well gouerne other

It is not for because] *Ne cio mi uien perch'io tra me dispregi*
Nor do I do this because I inwardly scorn
Wyatt used the form *forbicause* for *because* in

My mother's maids.

scorn or mock]

A set phrase, as in Lydgate's *Pilgrimage*/14645:
> I am she that ful wel kan
> Scorne and mokke many a man . . .

Elyot *Dict.* (1538) *Deridere* to laughe to scorne:
Udall *Apoph.* p. 174 *verso*: to mocke
> with hissyng mocke and skorne hym . . .

to whom Fortune]

Quei, ch'han dalla fortuna in mano il freno

Charge over us]

'Power to govern us'. Coverdale used the phrase to translate the Vulgate version of Psalm 90/11:
> *Quoniam angelis suis mandauit de te,*
> *Ut custodiant te . . .*
> For he shall geue his angels charge ouer the[e]

of right]

A contemporary translation of *iure, merito*, for which Cooper in his *Thesaurus* offered the translation, *worthily, of good right, lawfully*. Wyatt used the words in *O Lord, since*/30.

strike the stroke]

'Have the supreme authority'. The ordinary phrase was 'to bear the stroke', as in Cavendish's *Life of Wolsey* 43/17:
> wherin the Cardynall bare the stroke

Erasmus *Apophthegmata* tr. N. Udall p. 16 8 *recto*:
> all suche persones . . . as beare any rewle,
> stroke or autoritee in the commonweale . . .

But the phrase Wyatt uses here must have been current, for it turns up in James Calfhill's *An Aunswere to John Martiall's Treatise of the Crosse*, 1565 *sig.* A.ij. *verso*:
> But mans lawe striketh so great a stroke with you, that . . .

But true it is]

Ma ben è uer But it is very true

Less to esteem]

assai gli estimo meno/ *Chel uulgo*
I think very much less of them than common people do.

the common sort]

As contemporary dictionaries show, this was the regular phrase for the Latin *uulgus hominum*, the generality of mankind.
Erasmus in his *Epicureus* has:
> *Non sunt igitur uera bona, quae uulgus*
> *hominum per fas nefasque uenatur?*

which Ph. Gerrard translated:
> bee not those good that the commune sorte
> seeke for, they care not howe?

The note of faint contempt is found in one of Wyatt's letters to his son:
> I meane not that honestye that the comen
> sort callith an honist man . . .

Of outward things] *quei ch'à cio ch'appar di fuore/Guardan*
those who base their judgement on what appears outwardly

Ph. Gerrard *ibid.* has:
> the commune people seeke too haue a
> pleasaunt life in outwarde thynges . . .

in their entent] A common tag at the end of a line in the Chaucerian corpus, as here:
> But vndirstonde in thyn entent (*RR* 2187)

The meaning is like the *tra me* used by Alamanni in the phrase *io tra me dispregi*, where a verb of mental action is accompanied with 'inwardly' or 'in my own mind'. The phrase can be illustrated from Henry Bradshaw's *The Life of Saint Werburge*, Book I/5:
> I rose vp shortly . . .
> Aboute mydnyght and cast in myne intent
> How I myght spende the tyme . . .

Without regard] *senza ueder che chiugga il seno*
without seeing what is hidden in the breast.

I grant sometime] *Non dico gia che non mi scaldi amore*
> *Talhor di gloria*
I do not deny that I sometimes burn to win
> honour

Both poets may have recalled Valerius Flaccus: *Argonauticon* I, 76:
> *tu sola animos mentemque peruris/Gloria*
you alone, Glory, burn the mind and the
> spirits.

report Blame by] 'Find fault with'.
> *io non uo mentire*
> *con chi biasmando honor sol cerca honore.*
I do not want to join the liars who while finding fault with worldly honour seek nothing else but that.

But how]

> *Ma con qual pie potrei*
> But how could I bring myself to.

black-a-lyre]

> Black cloth from Lire or Liere in Brabant, used at this time for making expensive hoods. The OED offers a quotation of 1479 referring to a mayor of Bristol:
>> in . . . his scarlat cloke, furred with his black a lyre hode, or tepet of blak felwet;
> Wyatt is giving a contemporary twist to a proverb in Pliny's *Natural History* 8.73, para.193:
>> *lanarum nigrae nullum colorem bibunt*
> which Heywood in his *A Dialogue*, 1556, The seconde part, The ix chapiter *sig*. F.iiii *recto*, tr.
>> they saie, blacke will take none other hew.
> If Wyatt had, as I have supposed, Juvenal's Third Satire before him while he was composing this, he may have been attempting a witty variant on line 30:
>> *maneant qui nigrum in candida uertunt*
>> Knaves who in full Assemblies have the knack
>> Of turning Truth to Lies, and White to Black.

My Poyntz]

> *Io non saprei Sertin porre in disparte/ la uerità*
> Sertin, I could not lay the truth aside.

frame . . . feign]

> In this context *frame* must have the sense 'fashion so as to deceive'. Whether 'tongue' or 'tune' should be read here is hard to determine, since both were idiomatic. Spenser's use of the phrase would be in favour of *tune*: *e.g.*:
>> Well couth he tune his pipe and frame his stile . . . frame my pype . . . glozing speaches frame . . .

cloak . . . desert]

> The general sense appears to be 'to conceal the unfavourable facts and instead praise undeservedly'

vice . . . retain]

> The meaning of *retain* may be 'keep in their service'. *Maintain* would be easier, in the sense 'practise habitually'.

I cannot . . . long]

> *Non saprei reuerir chi soli adora*
>> *Venere & Bacco*
> I could not venerate those who worship as gods only Venus and Bacchus.
> The phrase 'sets their part with' is not clear. It may mean no more than 'side with'.

hold my peace]

> *ne tacer saprei Di quei*
> nor could I be silent about those people

That this is how Wyatt saw himself behaving in real life is suggested by a passage in his Declaration of 1541:

> The emperour had myche a doe to save me and yet that made me not holde my peace when I myght defende the kinges deede agaynste hym . . .

crouch nor kneel]

Although, taken by itself, the phrase means to bend the body in an act of worship, it was often, as here, used to describe the obsequious motions of a flatterer, as in Sir Thomas More's poem on Fortune:

> Yet for al that we brytill men ar fayn,
> So wrechid is owr nature & so blynde,
> As sone as Fortune list to lawgh agayn
> With fayre contenance & deceytfull mynde
> To crowche & knele . . .

Spenser in *Mother Hubberds Tale* said that the noble courtier

> Will not creepe, nor crouche with fained face . . . 737

worship . . . alone]

> *Non saprei piu ch'a gli immortali Dei*
> *Rendere honor con le ginocchie inchine*
> I could not bend the knee to pay honour more than is due to the immortal gods.

That 'worship' and 'honour' could be synonyms may be seen from Tyndale's *Answere* Fo: xxxiij *verso*:

> Concerninge worsheping or honouringe (which .ij. termes are both one) . . .

Wyatt has given the passage a slightly more Christian turn than Alamanni's immortal gods, in keeping with English usage, as here, in Sir Thomas More's *Cumfort* (1573) p. 154 *recto*:

> [false flatterers] make a brittle man . . . take himselfe . . . for a God here vpon earth . . .

and in Sir T. Elyot *The Image of Gouernaunce* p. 15 *recto*:

> [The Emperor Alexander Severus] compelled the senate and people to worshyp hym, as god . . .

Wyatt may also have been glancing at the treatment of Henry VIII as God's image on earth. See, for example, the dedication of Thomas Paynell's translation of Felicius's *Conspiracie of Lucius Catiline* for 'his ymage in erthe, a kynge' and 'his veray image in erthe'.

Erasmus in his *Colloquies* uses the phrase of those who bear the stroke in France:

Persuadent sibi, se deos esse, suaque causa mundum hunc esse conditum . . .

They think they are gods, and that the world was made for them . . .

wolves . . . lambs]   Another traditional, English twist, perhaps derived from the Bible, as in *Matt*. x.16:

Beholde I sende you forthe as shepe amonge wolues . . .

Wyatt was referring to hypocrites, as was Erasmus in his *Adages* tr. R. Taverner (1569) p. 21 *verso*:

. . . whiche beare owtwarde signes and badges of great holines as though they were lambes, but inwardly they be rauenous Wolues . . .

Surrey wrote in his translation of Psalm 55:

Friowr, whose harme and tounge presents the wicked sort

Of those false wolves with cootes which do their ravin hyde . . .

Here 'silly' probably means 'helpless, defenceless'.

with my words]   *Non saprei nel parlar* I could not in my speaking.

turn . . . gone]   If Wyatt meant 'turn back', he may have been thinking of a Horatian tag from the *Art of Poetry*:

nescit uox missa reuerti

a word once out cannot be turned back.

The second half of the phrase may owe something to these lines from Chaucer's *Manciple's Tale*/353:

But he that hath missayde I dar wel sayn

He may by no way clepe his worde agayn.

Thyng that is sayde is sayd & forth it goth . . .

But more probable is the sense 'twist, writhe, wrest, wrench the original meaning to something quite different'.

look right as a saint]   A traditional description of a hypocrite, as in

A. Barclay's *The Shyp of Folys* (1874) p. 113:
> Many them selfe fayne as chaste as was
> saynt Johnn . . .
> Some lokyth with an aungels countenance
> Wyse sad and sober lyke an heremyte
> Thus hydynge theyr synne and theyr mys-
> gouernaunce
> Vnder suche clokys lyke a fals ypocryte . . .

Use . . . counsel]

If the three phrases are formed on the same principle, each contains one good and one bad element. *Wiles* will then be 'deceit', *craft*, 'cunning', and *wit*, 'good sense', and *counsel*, 'sound advice'.

still]

'All the time'.

paint]

Here, as often, 'to flatter or deceive with specious words'. Palsgrave 655/2:
> I peynt, I glose or speke fayre

wrest]

'Pervert'. The language is Biblical, as in *Deuteronomy* 16.19 (Coverdale 17.2):
> Thou shalt not wrest the lawe

fill . . . coffer]

A traditional phrase, as in Skelton in *The Image of Ipocrysy* writing of the 'Antychryst of Rome':
> By bryve* or els by bull*
> To fill his coffers full.

    * Papal brief
    * Papal bull

innocent blood]

A Biblical phrase. Wyatt may have had this passage especially in mind: *Salomons Prouerbes*. The .VI. Chapter:
> There be sixe thinges which the LORDE hateth, & the seuenth he vtterly abhorreth: A proude loke, a dyssemblynge tonge, handes that shed innocent bloude . . .
> (*manus effundentes innoxium sanguinem*)

to feed myself fat]

The phrase occurs in *A spending hand*:
> Feed thyself fat and heap up pound by pound . . .

allow]

As always in Wyatt, it means 'praise', 'approve of'.

state]

The meaning is the same as 'estate' in *Whoso list*, 'high dignity'.

him, Caesar]

* agreement

Cato to die]

There are two instances of this turn in Chaucer's *Knight's Tale*:

> Thys was the forwarde* playnly to endyte
> Betwyx duke Theseus and hym arcyte . . .
> (1209)
> And Venus sleeth me in that other side
> For jalousye and feer of hym arcyte (1333)

And there are two similar instances in Douglas' *Eneados*:

> II.v.47 clad with the spulye of hym Achillys
> VI.xiii.75 all the famyl of hym Iulius

It is not clear what Wyatt is saying here. In Alamanni he found *condannando a torto Bruto* 'while wrongfully condemning Brutus'.

The impossibility for the honest speaker must lie in approving of Julius Caesar as Head of State and disapproving of the republican Cato and his decision to escape from the dictator by suicide, but could Wyatt have thought that *damn to die* stood for *disapprove of his suicide*?

If the reference is to *Cato Uticensis*, who fought against Julius Caesar, and killed himself rather than submit to the victor after the battle of Thapsus (46 B.C.), Wyatt knows far more than is stated in the surviving summary in Livy. Some of Wyatt's facts could have been found in Plutarch, as Sir T. Elyot reported in his *Boke of the Gouernour*:

> . . . Cato Uticensis . . . whanne he in the Senate egrely defended the publike weale . . . Who can sufficiently commende this noble man Cato/ whan he redeth in the warkes of Plutarche of his excellent courage and vertue . . . where Cato for the conseruation of the weale publike . . . [Fo: 223]

The point of Cato's escape from Caesar's hands was made by Seneca in his treatise on Providence:

> Caesar's soldiery stands outside the city gates. Yet Cato has his escape route sure, he can still find the high road to freedom by one movement of his hand . . . Can we doubt that the Immortals were well pleased with the spectacle of their nursling making such a wonderful escape from Caesar, and finding

by his self-inflicted death a sure place in history?

But it is quite possible that Wyatt derived all the material he uses in this poem from a few lines of Erasmus' *Apophthegmata*:

> *Postquam... Cato uictus sibi necem Vticae conscisset, Inuideo, inquit Caesar,*[1] *o Cato tibi mortem istam, quando tu mihi salutem tuam inuidisti. Caesar existimabat sibi summae gloriae futurum, si uir tantus, quum bello uictus esset ipsi uitam deberet. At Cato maluit honestam mortem quam oppressa publica libertate cuiquam seruire.*

N. Udall translated the passage as follows:

> After that ... *Cato* beeying vanquyshed by *Caesar* had killed hymself at *Vtica*, these were the woordes of *Caesar*: I enuie to the o *Cato* this death of thyne, sens thou hast enuied vnto me the sauyng of thy life. Caesar thought it a thyng like to redounde highly to his honour and renoume, if suche a noble manne as Cato hauyng been ouercomed in battaill should bee bound to hym and no man els for his life. But Cato rather chose death with honour, then after the oppressyng of ye publike libertee and freedome to bee as a bondeseruaunte to any persone. (p. 269 *verso* –270 *recto*)

scape ... From Caesar's hands] The phrase is frequent in Caxton's *Aesop*, e.g. in the *Life* p. 69:

> he scaped out of theyr handes

and in *The Fables of Alfonso* p. 203:

> And fro his hands I had not scaped ...

If Livy do not lie] Nobody, so far as I know, has found anything odd about this reference. One editor refers to 'Livy's story'. But Livy's account of this moment in Roman history is lost. All Wyatt could have had is *one sentence*:

> *Cato audita re cum se percussisset Uticae et interueniente filio curaretur, inter ipsam curationem rescisso uulnere expirauit, anno aetatis quadragesimo octauo.*

When the news of this defeat reached him

---

1 Plutarch, *Life of Julius Caesar* 54.

at Utica, Cato used a knife on himself. But his son broke in on him, and had the wound looked after. Cato, however, tore off the bandages before the wound could heal, and so died in his forty-eighth year.

It is odd that Wyatt should refer to this sentence when he had access to a full life by Plutarch, and numerous references in Seneca's writings. He could not have written as he does in this poem if all his knowledge of Cato was that one sentence.

It is a minor problem that Wyatt should use a a mediaeval tag, excusable only in an age of ignorance, as if he were not sure of his facts about Cato, whereas if he knew only Erasmus' references to Cato, he could have no such doubt.

The real oddity thus reduces itself to this: how did this tag find its way into all our surviving texts of this poem? If the motive was censorship, it would not be the first instance. The original line in *If wacker care*, where we now read:

> sure since I did refrain
> Brunet that set my wealth in such a roar . . .

was:

> her that did set our country in a roar

which may have been censored for fear of referring too openly to Anne Boleyn. So here Wyatt may have written something like:

> . . . free from his tyranny . . .

the common wealth]   That is, the common weal, the welfare of the state, and also the state itself, *respublica.*

apply]   'Diligently attend to'. As this use is rare outside authors of the Early Tudor period, it may be as well to give some illustrations. Wyatt had used the verb in this way in his translation of Plutarch's essay on true quiet of mind on *sig.* viij. *recto*:

> Aplyeng thy priuate busynesse

as a translation of Budé's

> *circa tua priuati negocia satagens.*

The same passage in Plutarch was translated by Sir T. Elyot in his *Banket of Sapience* p. 39 *recto*:

> Arte thou put from thyn office? thou shalte be the more at home, and the better applye

thine owne businesse.

The almost exact parallel for Wyatt's phrase is to be found in Sir T. Elyot's translation of Plutarch's essay on the education of children on *sig.* D.ij. *recto*:

> let vs endeuour our selfes, that the commune weale may be applied ...

Ph. Gerrard in 1545 translated the opening of Erasmus' Colloquy, *Epicureus*,

> *Quid venatur meus Spudaeus, quod sic totus incumbit libro ...*

as follows:

> What meaneth mi *Spudeus*, too applye hys booke so ernestlye ...

It is therefore likely that Wyatt was translating from Erasmus' *Apophthegmata*:

> ... *Catonem, qui totum diem reipublicae negotijs dabat,*

which N. Udall translated as:

> ... Cato, who bestowed all ye whole daye vpon the affaires of ye commenweale ...

singing as the swan] It was a literary convention that swans had musical voices, as we see from Erasmus, who in his *Adagia* maintained:

> *Cygnos canoros esse, omnium poetarum scriptis celebratum est.*

That swans are good singers is mentioned in the writings of every poet.

Nor ... most] 'Call the bravest of all animals the greatest coward'.

as the cat can.] There are two passages in Plutarch where something similar is said. Erasmus had translated one:

> *uidesne simiam? non potest custodire domum ut canis.*

Do you see the monkey? It cannot protect the house as a dog can.

Wyatt himself translated Budé as follows:

> So that if one be troubled for that a mighty lyon may nat be norisshed in a womans lappe as well as a lytell whelpe/ surely he is a gret fole.

dieth for hunger] A set phrase from Chaucer's time.

gold]

The reference is to a tag in Virgil's *Aeneid* 3/57:
> *quid non mortalia pectora cogis*
> *auri sacra fames!*

It was incorporated by Erasmus into his *Adagia*, and from there translated by Thomas Paynell as:
> what is it that the cursed hunger & desire of golde doth nat constraine mortal folkes to do?

Alexander]

Dirgli Alessandro say he is Alexander.

The character traditionally given to Alexander was well expressed by Plutarch in the phrase, 'being more intent upon action and glory than upon either pleasure or riches'.

Pan]

In his *Praise of Folly* Erasmus remarked that everybody knew the story of Midas, who preferred Pan's singing to Apollo's. Ovid in his *Metamorphoses* Book XI/171 ff. tells how Apollo would not allow such thick ears to retain their human shape.

Passeth]

'Surpasses'. Cooper in his Thesaurus gave for *excedere*: to passe or excede. Skelton in his *Phyllyp Sparowe*/ said of the Roman satirist, Sulpicia, that her
> name regystred was
> For euer in tables of bras,
> Because that she dyd pas
> In poesy to endyte . . .

Savonarola:
> thou passest without compairison al creatures in gentlenes

This meaning is preserved for Bible-readers in II *Sam.* 1/26:
> passing the love of women

noble tale]

A deliberate use of Chaucer, *e.g.* in the Prologue to the *Miller's Tale*:
> I can a nobyl tale for the nonys

Wyatt is taking for granted that his reader will recall in the *Canterbury Tales* that the pilgrims all thought the knight's tale 'a noble storie', but when Chaucer attempted a tale of the knight, Sir Thopas, in verse, he was interrupted by the Host with:

No more of this, for goddis dygnyte.

counsel] 'Sober advice'.

drunk of ale] Common in Chaucer's *Canterbury Tales.*

Grin . . .pale] Wyatt is applying to his special theme,the afflictions of a courtier in the company of his superiors, the commonplaces on the topic of the flattering parasite. If he and Alamanni had a commonplace book, under *Adulator* they would find the following extract from Plautus' play *Amphitryo*:

> atque ita seruom par uidetur frugi sese
> > instituere:
> proinde eri ut sint, ipse item sit: uoltum e
> > uoltu comparet:
> tristis sit, si eri sint tristes: hilarus sit, si
> > gaudeant . . .

And this is how I think an honest servant ought to behave. He ought to be just like the masters, his face like theirs. If they are sad, he should be sad, too. If they are in a jolly mood, he ought to be glad.

While Alamanni wrote:

> Imitar sempre altrui se piange, o ride

Always do what the other man does, laugh or cry

Wyatt may have known this passage from A. Barclay *The first egloge* 1177 ff.:

> What he commaundeth that nedest do thou
> > must
> Be it good or ill/ rightwise or uniust,
> Laugh when he laugheth all if thine heart be
> > sad,
> Wepe when he wepeth be thou neuer so glad
> . . .
> And shortly to speake thou must all thing
> > fulfill
> As is his pleasure and nothing at thy will.
> None of thy wittes are at thy libertie,
> Vnto thy master they needes must agree.

The ultimate source for all who wrote on flatterers was Juvenal's Third Satire, and, in particular, these lines:

> natio comoeda est: rides, maiore cachinno
> concutitur; flet si lacrimas conspexit amici,

> *nec dolet . . .*
> All *Greece* is one Commedian. Laugh and they
> Return it louder than an Ass can bray:
> Grieve, and they Grieve; if you Weep silently,
> There seems a silent Eccho in their Eye:
> They cannot *Mourn* like you, but they can
> > Cry.

pale]

Wyatt might have found in his commonplace book
under the heading of the Flatterer or False Friend,
a quotation from Horace's *Art of Poetry*:
> *pallescet super his, etiam stillabit amicis*
> *ex oculis rorem . . .*
> > he will turn pale over them [your poems],
> > he will even distil some tear drops from his
> > eyes to prove his friendship . . .

On others' . . . day]

Wyatt could have found among Erasmus' *Adagia*
a remark taken from Aristotle's *Rhetoric*:
> It is the mark of a free-born soul to refuse
> to live at another's will [*alterius arbitratu*].

He could also have found in an edition made by
Erasmus of the *Sententiae* of Publilius Syrus:
> *Miserrimum est arbitrio alterius uiuere*
> > There is no condition more wretched than
> > to have one's life depending on another's
> > whim.

'Hang' suggests our 'hanger-on at court', *i.e.*
not 'suspended' but 'completely subservient to'.
Wyatt may be translating *ex nutu alterius pendere*
in the spirit of Tyndale's translation of *pendere*
de nutu dominae: to be made to the lure & be
obedyent at a becke, nor dare do any thing except
she nod or wagge her heed . . .
Cooper translated *pendere ex arbitrio alterius*:
To be subiect to an other mans will and pleasure.
If Wyatt knew from the text of Lucretius Book
IV the lines 1131–1134 quoted in the opening
remarks (*Wyatt and the Court*) to *In court to*
serve, he must have known line 1122:
> *adde quod alterius sub nutu degitur aetas*
> > add that their whole life is passed at another's
> > will.

This may have induced Wyatt to add: *both night*
and day.

lust] 'Lust' here means 'will or good pleasure', which is how Cooper in his *Thesaurus* translated *Nutus.*

points] One manuscript, the best of a bad lot, reads here:
None of these, Poyntz, will ever frame with me . . .

frame with] That the meaning here is 'go down well with', 'suit my character' is suggested by these quotations from the OED:
1550 Now I could not frame with it, nor it liked me not in no sauce . . .
1582 So frames it with mee now, that I . . .

asken help] 'To have resort to the assistance of'.

colours] The fundamental meaning is things 'which serve to conceal or cloak the truth, or to give a show of justice to what is in itself unjustifiable' (OED III/11) and leans towards III/12:
fair pretence, pretext, cloak'.

device] Taken with 'colours', the word means 'underhand trickery'. Sir Thomas More has a similar use in his life of Richard III (1513):
But now was al the labour & study, in the deuise of some conuenient pretext, for which the peple should be content to depose the prince & accept the protector for kinge. In which diuerse thinges they deuised.

join . . . vice] Wyatt may have had the following passage from Book I Ch. 13 of Castiglione's *Book of the Courtier* in mind:
. . . in everie thing it is so hard a matter to know the true perfection, that it is almost unpossible, and that by reason of the varietie of judgements. Therfore many there are, that delight in a man of much talke, and him they call a pleasant fellow. Some wil delight more in modestie, some other will fancie a man that is active and alwaies dooing: other, one that sheweth a quietnesse and a respect in everie thing . . .
And thus doth euerie man praise or dis- praise according to his fancie, alwaies

* nearest

covering a vice with the name of the next* vertue to it, and a vertue with the name of the next* vice: as in calling him that is sawcie, bold: him that is sober, dry: him that is seelie, good: him that is vnhappie, wittie; and likewise in the rest.

mean . . . extremity]

The phrase is well explained in the OED, which points out that the word *extremity* is used for each end of a scale of which the middle point was called the *mean*. This refers to the scheme introduced by Aristotle when defining 'virtue' as a mean between deficiency and excess, as set out in his *Nicomachean Ethics*. The dictionary also supplies some contemporary references. Justice, for instance, considered as the right amount of punishment, could have at the deficient end, negligence, refusal to punish when punishment was a duty, and, at the excessive end, cruelty, a vicious delight in inflicting pain where it was not right.

the next . . . vice]

We here find the definition of a new meaning for *cloak*. In this context the word was a translation of the Latin *pallium*. We may see from Cooper's *Thesaurus* that his word for *pallium* was *a cloke*, and for the verb *pallio*, *To conceale, hide, or couer*. According to the OED it was only in the seventeenth century that *palliate*, in the sense of *extenuate*, took over the new meaning of *cloak*, which was used by Wyatt and some of his contemporaries for the practice of softening a vice, that is an extreme of too much or too little, by calling it the mean, the just right amount or degree. Wyatt calls this *mean*, the *nearest* term to the two extremes.

Erasmus in a similar passage (*Enchiridion*, 1533, p. 32) wrote:

we must beware of this onely that we cloke not the vice or nature with the name of vertue/ callynge heuynes of mynde grauite/ crudelite iustice/ enuy zele/ fylthy nygg-yshnes thryfte/ flatering good felowshyp/ knauery or rybaldry/ vrbanite or mery spekyng.

There is a similar run of thought in Lydgate's
Pilgrimage/22431, which I have modernised:

> It is the regular practice of flatterers, intent
> on deceiving by subtle tricks, to call virtuous
> those who are most enslaved to vice, to say
> that mean, grasping and rapacious people
> are liberal, and to call worthy of fame and
> renown those who extort illegally and plun-
> der other's goods; and people who are worth-
> less fools are described as wise.

to purpose . . . fall]

The meaning might be 'when a similar opportunity for this despicable act next presented itself',
as in Chaucer, *Troylus and Criseyde* III/1131:

> and sayde
> As fyll to purpose for his hertes reste

The commonest use in Chaucer, however, is in the
sense, 'when the appropriate moment in a conversation occurs', as in *Troylus and Criseyde*
III/1366:

> Sone after this they spake of sondrie thinges
> As fyl to purpose of this auenture.

Wyatt uses the phrase in this sense in *My mother's
maids*.

press . . . rise]

'Press down'. Wyatt may have had in mind the
passage in Alamanni's poem which runs:

> *Non trouare ad ogni hor false cagioni*
> > *Per abbassare i giusti, alzando i praui . . .*
> I could not be always finding bad reasons for
> bringing down the just and exalting the
> wicked . . .

Wyatt's argument may be paraphrased as follows:
'Just as vice, at both outer edges on Aristotle's
moral scale, is palliated by calling it by the name
of the mean, the right virtuous quality, so virtue
is not allowed its true name, but is degraded and
lost to view by being given the name of one or
other of the vices at the extreme ends of the
scale.'

drunkenness]

Wyatt in a letter to his son in Egerton MS. 2711
fol. 72v.:

> Trust me that honist man is as comen a
> name as the name of a good felow, that is
> to say, a dronkerd, a tauerne hanter . . .

friendly foe]

That the oxymoron may be a symptom showing that this general observation had some particular bitterness for Wyatt is made plausible by a parallel instance where Wyatt took up the theme of the 'bosom serpent' from Chaucer's *Summoner's Tale*:

> Be waar of her that in thy bosom slepyth
> Ware fro the serpent that so slily crepyth
> Undyr the gras ande styngeth ful subtylly. . .

and turned it to his own purposes in the following poem:

> Right true it is, and said full yore ago:
> Take heed of him that by the back thee
>   claweth,
> For none is worse than is a friendly foe,
> Though thee seem good all thing that thee
>   delighteth,
> Yet know that well that in thy bosom
>   creepeth,
> For many a man such fire oft times he
>   kindleth
> That with the blaze his beard himself he
>   singeth.

false and double]

All the manuscripts read:

> The friendly foe with his double face

which, as the Tottel editors saw, is a syllable short. They proposed *his fair double face*. I think *false and double* a better guess, on two grounds. First, Alamanni offered Wyatt *doppio & fallace* double and false. Secondly, *false and double* was a set phrase, as in Hawes' poem *The Example of Vertu* Cap. primum/111:

> flaterers be . . . euermore fals and double . . .

Lydgate *Isopes Fabules* II/260 has

> thou art false & double.

The force of 'double' is well brought out in Rolle's *Psalter*:

> Dubbil hert: when a fals man thinkis an
> & says a nother.

Behind this was the sense of 'two-faced', or, as it was put then: *she had two faces in one hode.* (Hawes *Passetyme*/3035)

gentle]

Dir non saprei gentil.

I could not call him gentle.

gentle and courteous] A set phrase, as in the Chaucerian *Romaunt of the Rose* 2020:

For I am of the silf manere,
Gentil, curteys, meke, and fre.

N. Udall *Apophthegmes* p. 154 *verso*:

> When *Plato* gaue a greate laude and praise to a certain person for this poynte & behalf, that he was excedyng gentle and courteous towardes all folkes . . .

Favell] It is clear from this and a handful of similar incidental references in contemporary writings that by this time Favell had become a well-understood figure, especially as a personification of flattery, although the history of the word is obscure. It clearly had special reference to life at court. This emerges from Skelton's *Bowge of Court*, where we meet, in close association with *Fauour*,

> Fauell, full of flatery,
> Wyth fables false that well coude fayne a tale.

More instructive is a reference in *The Arte of English Poesie*, where *curry-favell* is linked to the topic Wyatt is treating at this point of the poem:

> But if such moderation of words tend to flattery, or soothing, or excusing, it is by the figure *Paradiastole*, which therfore nothing improperly we call the *Curry-fauell*, as when we make the best of a bad thing, or turne a signification to the more plausible sence: as to call an vnthrift, a liberall Gentleman: the foolish-hardy, valiant or couragious: the niggard, thriftie . . . and such like terms moderating and abating the force of the matter by craft, and for a pleasing purpose, as appeareth by these verses of ours teaching in what cases it may commendably be vsed by Courtiers.

That these conditions obtained at the court of Henry VIII is shown by the following quotation, which is a reflection made on a proverb in Erasmus *Adagia*:

> *Obsequium amicos, ueritas odium parit.*
> Telling the truth breeds hatred, it is flattery that gets you friends.

Taverner in his *Prouerbes* (Fol. xlvij. *verso*) translated this, and added a comment of his own:

> Flatery & folowing of mens myndes getteth
> frendes, where speakyng of trouth gendreth
> hatred. Suche is now and euer hath ben the
> fascion of the worlde, that who telleth the
> trouthe, is for moost parte hated, and he
> that can flatter and saye as I saye, shalbe
> myne owne whyte sonne.

In his 1569 ed. (p. 44 *verso*) he went on:

> Our Englishe Prouerbe agreeth with the same.
> He that will in Court dwell, must needes
> * curry favell   currie fabel.* And ye shal vnderstand that
> fabel is an olde Englishe worde, and signi-
> fied as much as fauour doth now a dayes.

goodly grace]

The two words were near allied. 'Goodly' here
means 'excellent'. cf. OED, 1430:

> Holden he was for oon of the wise,
> And of spech most goodeliest.

*cruelty . . . Zeal of
justice*]

The same thought is found in *Pilg. Perf.* Fo:
lxxx. *recto* (list A) 1526:

> if our zele be so feruent in any cause of
> religion as in correction or such other/
> so that it begyn to growe in to crueltie

where we also find on Fo: C.v. *recto*:

> in the zele of iustice he shulde be strong
> . . . to feyght

It is possible that Sir Francis Bryan recalled this
passage when he came to translate Guevara's
Menosprecio de corte:

> O dissemblyng heart that vnder a pretence
> to be clere and loyall, make men to iudge
> that hypocrisy is deuotion, ambicion nob-
> ilitie, auarice husbandrye, crueltie zele of
> iustice . . . *sig.* d.i. *verso*.

change . . . time . . . place] Presumably the plea that circumstances alter cases.

suffers . . . blame]   An innocent victim of violence.

pitiful]   'Contemptible'.

true and plain]

ne aperto e vero nor open and true.
In *My mother's maids* Wyatt wrote:
> Make plain thine heart

The OED offers 'open in behaviour, free from duplicity or reserve'.

raileth]

Chi sempre parli quel che piu dispiace
who always speaks what most offends.

reckless]

'Without caring about its effect'.

lie and feign]

A set phrase, as in the *Romaunt of the Rose/* 3871:

> Wikked-tonge, that false espye,
> Whiche is so glad to fayne and lye . . .

lecher]

All the manuscripts have:

> The lecher a lover, and tyranny

which has ten syllables but gives an awkward accent. The form *lecherour* occurs in Sir Thomas More's *Confutacyon* Book VIII [Yale edition p. 920/18]

The thought may have been taken from a translation of an essay by Plutarch on how to distinguish a flatterer from a friend, which Erasmus made:

> *eum qui foedis amoribus est deditus appellatum comem & amantem*
> him who is given up to filthy amours they call a friendly and a loving man

This would favour an emendation: *the filthy lecher.*

right rule]

All the manuscripts have:

> To be the right of a prince's reign

This has the twofold defect of being a syllable short and not being contemporary usage. In favour of *right rule* is Alamanni's line:

> *Ne che'l tyrannegiar sia giusto impero*
> Nor that playing the tyrant is a just rule

and similar contemporary expressions, such as *Isaiah* Ch. 32:

> *Ecce in iustitia regnabit rex:*
> . . the kinge shal gouerne after ye rule of rightuousnes,

and in Erasmus *Apophthegmata* Lib. I/Aegidis primi 88:

> *ad recte gubernandam rempublicam necessariae*

necessary for the right ruling of the state
According to G.R. Elton in *Reform and Renewal*
(1974) p. 60, Moison wrote to Cromwell in 1538
a letter containing the phrase:
> Taking this as a right rule and trial of a
> friendship, to love ever . . .

cause]

Questo è cagion che non mi cal, ne calse
> *Anchor gia mai . . .*
This is the reason why it does not and has never
yet bothered me . . .

yet]

Probably pronounced 'yit'.

Hang . . . sleeves]

The meaning of the phrase is given by Cooper in
his *Thesaurus* when he translated the phrase discussed above in the note on *At other's lust*:
pendere ex arbitrio alterius to hang on an other
mans sleeue. J. Heywood has in *The fyrst hundred
of Epigrammes* (1562) No. 19:
> *Two arme in arme*
> One said to an nother takyng his arme,
> By licence freend, and take this for none
>   harme.
> No sir (quoth the other) I geue you leeue
> To hang on my arme, but not on my sleeue.

weigh . . . chip . . . wit]

The sense intended may be derived from Alamanni's
line:
> *Ne quai fortuna piu chel senno ualse*
> In whose case fortune counted more than
>   good sense
It is possible that Wyatt knew a proverb of the
form (taken from Cotgrave under *Sagesse*):
> An ounce of lucke excells a pound of wit
and inverted the sense. If so, the sense requires a
balance of *a pound of wit* against a small quantity
in weight of luck or chance or fortune. It is just
possible that *chip* could mean a small amount, but
there is no good parallel. (Its meaning is always
basically a fragment of a whole.) Nor does any
other word immediately step in if 'chip' is rejected.
If the contrast intended was between a pound and
a *grain*, the smallest unit of weight, and a grain of
corn, a word like *chep* or *chef* might be considered,

if there were such variants of *chaff*. But there is no good parallel for these words either.

hunt and hawk] A set phrase, as in Chaucer's *Clerk's Tale*/81:
> As for to hauke and hunte on euery syde. . .

at my book] A Chaucerian phrase, as in the *Canon Yeoman's Tale*/841:
> Though he sitte at his book day and nyght

and in *The House of Fame*/656:
> And also dombe as a stone
> Thou syttest at another boke . . .

But there is no reason to suppose that the phrase thereby acquired a special, literary flavour. When Ph. Gerrard found in Erasmus' *Epicureus*
> *Tu igitur malles ieiunus incumbere libro*

he translated it:
> Then you had leuer sit fastyng at your booke . . .

In frost and snow] *quando agghiaccia & pioue*
whenever it freezes and rains

bow to stalk] If Wyatt had deer hunting in mind, as in J. Russell *Book of Nurture*/21:
> his bowe he toke in hand toward the deere to stalke,

we must suppose that he was thinking of the common practice of using a *stalking horse* to get within range without alarming the deer. This could be an actual animal or an artificial contrivance.

No man doth mark] *Qui non ho alcun, che mi domandi doue*
> *Mi stia, ne uada*

Here I have nobody to ask me where I live or where I am going.

ride or go] On horseback or on foot. A Chaucerian phrase, as in *The Knight's Tale*/1350:
> But in pryson muste he dwelle alway

*Arcite
> That other* where hym lyst may ryde or goo . . .

Tyndale in his translation of Erasmus' *Enchiridion*, (edition of 1533 *sig*. L.vj. *recto*) has:
> Let be a farre of from the eares of lytle bodyes wanton songes of loue whiche christen men synge at whom & where soeuer they ryde or go.

lusty lees] 'Pleasant pastures where a colt might run free'. Chaucer in his *Troilus and Criseyde* Book II/753 has:

> I am myne owne woman wel at ese
> I thanke it god/ as after myne estate
> Right yonge/ and stonde vnteyd in lusty lese
> Withouten ielousye/ and suche debate

And of . . . woe] I take the meaning to be something like this: 'And of what has just happened to me I feel no good or ill ensuing to me. I am indifferent'. But the meaning 'what has just been *reported*' cannot be ruled out.

clog] A heavy object tied to a prisoner's foot. *Paston Letters*/II/48 has:

> I am with the gayler, with a clogge vpon my hele for suerte of the pees . . .

Here it is more likely to be a reference to Wyatt's confinement to his father's house than to the fetters of *Sighs are my food*.

No force] 'It does not matter a bit'. Chaucer has *Therof no fors, No fors of that, No force for that*.

hedge and ditch] That it continued to be a set phrase we may see from passages in Spenser's *Faerie Queene*:

> Ne hedge ne ditch his readie passage brake . . .
> Nor hedge nor ditch, nor hill nor dale she staies,
> But ouerleapes them all . . .

in France . . . wine] *Non son in Francia à sentir beffe & danno*
S'io non conosco i uin
I am not in France to receive mocks and loss
if I don't know the wines.

savoury sauce] *cf.* the picture of luxury in Henryson's *The complaynt of Creseyde*:

* embroidered
tapestries

> Where is thy chambre wantonly be sene
> With burly bedde and bankers brouded* bene
> Spyces and wyne to thy colatioun
> The cuppes al of golde and syluer shene
> The swete meates serued in plates clene
> With sauery sauce of a good facioun . . .

delicates] 'Exquisite, tasty food', as in *My mother's maids*:

By sea, by land, of delicates the most
Her cater seeks . . .

to feel] 'Savour', as in *In Court to serve*/2:

Of sugared meats feeling the sweet repast

Tyndale in his *Answere* (Fo: xxi. *recto*) has the argument that there is no man so good but that at times he feels in himself no more faith or love to God than 'a sycke man oftymes feleth the tast of his meate which he eateth.'

him incline] 'Dispose himself.

be . . . seem] *Non nella Hispagnia oue studiar conuiene*
Piu che nell'esser poi nel ben parere
Not in Spain, where one must study to seem rather than *be* good.

The antithesis became proverbial in the distinction drawn by Sallust between Caesar and the elder Cato: the latter, he said:

esse quam uideri bonus malebat

preferred to be rather than to seem a good man.

Wyatt made this distinction between 'being' and 'seeming' in a letter to his son:

. . . if you wil seme honist, be honist, or els seme as you are . . . he that huntith only for [an honest name] is like him that had rathir seme warme then be warme and edgith a single cote about with a furre.

Spenser's comment on courtiers in *Mother Hubberds Tale*/649 is similar:

For not by that which is, the world now
deemeth,
(As it was wont) but by that same that
seemeth.

wits . . . fine] Sir Francis Bryan made a similarly sarcastic remark in his translation of Guevara's *Menosprecio de corte* Ch. XI *sig.* h ij. *recto*:

the wittes of the courtiers are so fine, that they knowe not onely what one sayeth but what he thinketh . . .

The shades of sarcasm may be judged by the Spanish original *ingenios tan delicados* (such delicately fine wits) and a French version which has *d'esprits subtils & delicats, voire peruers & malins* (delicate and subtle, that is to say, perverse and cunning, wits).

Flanders cheer]

The food the people of the Netherlands were so fond of. Alamanni makes a similar remark in another of his satires.

lets not]

'Does not prevent'.

deem . . . black and white]

Erasmus has among his *Adagia*:

> *Persuadebit album esse nigrum*
> He will argue that white is black
> *Hoc dicto non est aliud hodie uulgo tritius apud Gallos, qui sua lingua dicunt: Il me fera à croire que le blanc est noir.*
> This is one of the commonest expressions in modern French, 'he will try to make me think white is black'.

It had passed into English before Wyatt, as we may see from this snippet of Skelton:

> So we be in the plyte
> That losing of oure sight
> We know not black from whyght
> And be thus blinded quyte . . .

The following quotation from OED 1581 shows the continuation:

> He is not able to deeme white from blacke, good from badde, vertue from vice . . .

takes my wit away]

> *Non in Germania ou'el mangiar' el bere*
> *M'habia à tor l'intelletto*

I am not in Germany, where eating and drinking could take away my wits.

beastliness]

Erasmus in *Epicureus* has:

> *sed leuius miseri sunt, quos natura genuit brutos, quam belluinis cupiditatibus ob- brutuerunt*

which Gerrard rendered as:

> yet thei be lesse miserable whom nature hathe made verye brutes, then those that walowe theim selues in foule and beastly lustes.

Alamanni offered:

> *in guisa di seluagge fere*
> like wild beasts

given in prey]   'Sacrificed'. Alamanni had:
                       et darlo in preda al senso
                       and give it in prey to the senses

treason]   'Betrayal of trust'.

Kent and Christendom]   In his commentary in Spenser's *The Shepherd's
                       Calendar* E.K. wrote on the proverbial phrase:
                       Nor in all Kent, nor in Christendome:

> This saying seemeth to be strange and
> vnreasonable: but indede it was wont to be
> an olde prouerbe and comen phrase. The
> original where of was, for that most part of
> England in the reigne of king Ethelbert
> was christened, Kent onely except, which
> remayned long after in mysbeliefe and
> vnchristened, So that Kent was counted no
> part of Christendome.

Drayton in his *Polyolbion* (1613) p. 184 speaks of:

> our vulgar by-word *Nor in Christendom, Nor
> in Kent*

and refers us to Richard White's *History of Britain*
Book 7, Note 24, where after telling of a battle
after which the Britons ran away to London, he
added:

> *Vnde suspicor ortum illud commune vulgi
> dictum, nec in Christianitate, nec in Cantio,
> quasi nunc a Christianis Britonibus eo loco
> penitus relicto Saxonibus paganis.*

> This, I suspect, is the origin of that popular
> saying, 'neither in Kent nor in Christendom',
> for when the Christianised population ran
> away, the place was left to the pagan Saxon
> invaders.

When J. Ray incorporated this proverb in his
collection he took a similar line, supposing that
Kent was pagan when the rest of England was
Christian.

The positive phrase as we find it in Wyatt remained colloquial in the time of Lyly and Nashe.

Among the Muses]   Wyatt's lines might well have been written at
                       Allington Castle, his home in Kent. Alamanni
                       wrote:

> *Con le mie Muse in solitario loco . . .*

> With my Muses in a lonely spot.

Spenser *Mother Hubberds Tale*/753 ff.:

> Thus when this Courtly Gentleman with toyle
> Himselfe hath wearied, he doth recoyle
> Vnto his rest, and there with sweete delight
> Of Musicks skill revives his toyled spright . . .
> Or lastly, where the bodie list to pause,
> His minde vnto the Muses he withdrawes. . .

Alamanni, it may be supposed, would be familiar with this use of 'Muses' to stand for the study of philosophy as carried out by literary-minded politicians forced into temporary or permanent exile. The archetype of such men was Cicero. In one of his letters to Atticus he writes:

> *Interea . . . cum Musis nos delectabimus . . .*
>
> In the mean time we shall take our pleasure
>   with the Muses . . .

and in his *Tusculan Disputations* he explicitly defines the phrase *cum Musis*:

> *id est, cum humanitate et cum doctrina*
>
> that is, with literary and philosophical studies.

This use may ultimately derive from a phrase in Plato's *Republic* (548b), where he speaks of commerce with the 'true' Muse as 'the practice of discussion and philosophy'. But for Wyatt we might conjecture that the decisive passage was the dramatic opening of Boethius' *Consolation*, where the unhappy exile thinks first of consoling himself with the Muses of Poetry only to be confronted with Philosophy herself:

> *sed abite potius Sirenes usque in exitium*
> *dulces meisque cum Musis curandum sanan-*
>   *dumque relinquite.*

This is how Chaucer put it:

> But goth nowe rather awaye ye mermaydens/
> whiche that ben swete tyl it be at the laste/
> & suffreth this man to be cured and heled
> by my muses/ that is to saye/ by my noteful
> sciences.

Where . . . to come]   This is Wyatt's witty adaptation of the turn at the close of Juvenal's Third Satire, lines 318–322:

> *ergo uale nostri memor, et quotiens te*

Roma tuo refici properantem reddit Aquino,
me quoque ad Heluinam Cererem uestramque
                                        Dianam
conuerte a Cumis . . .
Farewell; and when, like me, o'rewhelm'd
                                    with care,⎫
You to your own *Aquinum* shall repair,   ⎬
To take a mouthful of sweet Country air,   ⎭
Be mindful of your Friend; and send me
                                        word,
What Joys your Fountains and cool Shades
                                    afford:
Then, to assist your Satyrs, I will come:
And add new Venom, when you write of
                                        Rome.
                                    (Dryden)

THE COURTIER'S DILEMMA: COUNTRY VERSUS TOWN

Whether poems, as some poets have thought, *make* civilisation
must remain a matter for debate. What is certain is that some
poems *embody* a great civilisation, express what lies at the heart
of a civilisation, and so make it clear to us what is the essence,
the civilised thing about the thousands of elements contributing
to make a civilisation. It seems to me equally certain that one such
poem is the sixth *sermo* in Horace's Second Book. For there he
'sets' the values which give relish to human existence. Civilisation,
as the word suggests, depends on the city, a concentration of
living effort which nevertheless seems to stultify life; yet, without
submission to its harsh necessities, the erosion of what is human in
us, no noble and great civilisation can arise. In the city, people
are busier than is humanly good for them, the pulse and tempo of
life are faster, the number of contacts every day greater than any
human being can stomach.

Yet if the phrase 'heart' may be properly used of a civilization,
we cannot deny the term as the right one for the capital, the
metropolis. Wordsworth's admiration for the 'mighty heart' of
London was for an organ with no blood in its arteries. Johnson
spoke for civilisation when he claimed that the full tide of human

existence was to be found in a certain part of London. Yet the crowds who make the blood running through the arteries have always been loud and stinking. The heart is ever a filthy organ. It is not a note of nineteenth-century machine-and-factory culture to speak of:

> *fumum et opes strepitumque Romae.*
> The Smoke, and Wealth, and Noise of *Rome.*

Yet there we have the actuality of the functioning heart.

Moral filth accompanies the physical. We have no sense of time or place changing if we pass rapidly from the Rome of Horace to the Paris of Boileau or of Baudelaire, to the reports of our present London police authorities, and back to the *London* of Johnson and the third satire in Juvenal's collection. No reader of Dickens will need me to go on, but a perhaps less familiar classic of the topic may serve to focus what it is that enables poems to embody the heart of civilisation. If Boileau in his Sixth Satire was able to give us a Christianised Juvenal, a poem which covers the very same points in language nearer to us can be found in Baudelaire's *Le Crépuscule du Soir*:

> *Cependant des démons malsains dans l'atmosphère*
> *S'éveillent lourdement, comme des gens d'affaire,*
> *Et cognent en volant les volets et l'auvent.*
> *A travers les lueurs que tourmente le vent*
> *La Prostitution s'allume dans les rues;*
> *Comme une fourmilière elle ouvre ses issues;*
> *Partout elle se fraye un occulte chemin,*
> *Ainsi que l'ennemi qui tente un coup de main;*
> *Elle remue au sein de la cité de fange*
> *Comme un ver qui dérobe à l'Homme ce qu'il mange.*
>
> *On entend çà et là les cuisines siffler,*
> *Les théatres glapir, les orchestres ronfler;*
> *Les tables d'hôte, dont le jeu fait les délices,*
> *S'emplissent de catins et d'escrocs, leurs complices,*
> *Et les voleurs, qui n'ont ni trêve ni merci,*
> *Vont bientôt commencer leur travail, eux aussi,*
> *Et forcer doucement les portes et les caisses*
> *Pour vivre quelques jours et vêtir leurs maîtresses.*

Paris in the Gloaming

It is also the time when evil spirits begin to spread like diseases through the twilight air. They heave themselves clumsily out of bed like tired business men, and stub their wings against window panes and shutters. You can see street-walkers beginning to jerk into action by the light of the lamps which dance a madder St. Vitus in the wind. Their ant-hill has unbolted all its exits: from each the creatures file silently into the darkness, as confident of their objectives as predators on a night raid. They grub their way into the heart of the filthy city, and pop up like maggots that have lodged in a man's daily bread before he can get his own teeth into it. In different parts of the town you can hear noises of various pitch: hissing steam from hotel kitchens, yaps and yelps from theatres, deep booms from concert rooms. Cafés and restaurants begin to fill up; gambling rather than the menu is the main attraction there, and the whores' clientele provide the card-sharpers with their victims. The working day will also soon be beginning for the professional burglars whose war on society knows neither truce nor peace. They will soon be at it, gently forcing our doors and sweetly picking the locks of our treasure chests. Each so prolongs his own existence for a few days more and acquires the wherewithal to buy his fancy woman a new frock.

The fable of the two mice cannot embody the most delightful and profound of contrasts unless the 'city' case is taken for granted. Civilisation is something we 'buy full dear', but we cannot refuse the bargain. Something smug or merely 'week-end' emerges if the longing to escape from the big city is not made by a soul whose choice to partake of civilisation has begun to seem *tragic*. The contrast is sickly if it is thought of as merely that between two environments, say, Cheapside and the countryside. The classic poem begins to interest us deeply when it is in the name of true civilisation that the poet longs to get away from the centre. And the moment the point is made with reference to Horace's *sermo,* we realise that Wyatt is both miles away and centuries away from a classic poise.

Horace, I take it, is defining for us the circumstances which make it possible for human beings to be truly serious, the conditions which permit and encourage 'the Flow of Soul' in civilised intercourse. A glimmer of his powerful meaning will force its way even through a crude prose paraphrase:

> As the long day wastes on, I feel depressed, and yearn for home — my little bit of land with a garden and running stream and a few trees — and wonder how long I must wait before I can get back to my old books, to doze and do nothing, and forget the worries of city life. And eat my home-grown food, dining like a prince in front of my own hearth, with my cheeky, home-grown, too familiar servants around me. Or inviting friends of an evening with no formal etiquette to govern our drinking: the one who likes his whisky neat next to the other who sips his sherry and mellows at his own speed. And the talk that comes of it! We don't discuss our richer neighbours or their smart, modern residences, nor what is on at the Old Vic. We talk about things which really concern us, things it is bad not to make up your mind about: what makes people happy? money, or their own inner worth? what holds friends together? the advantages each gets from having the other, or an impersonal bond, an ideal? We exchange views about what 'good' really means, and what is the supreme aim in life . . .

Although this account has been much loved and imitated, Horace's poem is not yet the classic embodiment of civilisation. This only begins to happen when after mention of the ultimate questions of ethics, the word is passed to the *raconteur* of a fable. Here less damage is done by the crudities of paraphrase, for this part of the poem could have been enjoyed by all the slaves who overhear the city gentlemen talking. Only the elegance of the verse-making would be reserved for the connoisseur. Horace risks everything on our taking the tale of the two mice to heart.

Once upon a time there was, they say, a country mouse who had to put up a town mouse in his agricultural hovel. It was a case of old friends meeting, and the need to show hospitality forced the country mouse, for once, to break his parsimonious habits and bring all his hoard of beans and oats out of the larder. He became a generous and attentive host and served a dried raisin for dessert and a piece of half-nibbled bacon for a savoury – anything to get the pampered town mouse to eat. But he hardly touched a single course, even with his front teeth. He found the whole thing too nauseating, even though his host had put down fresh straw, and was letting him have the best bits and keeping the coarser items (spelt and darnel) for his own plate. The town mouse tried to remain urbane, but came out in the end with,"I can't see the point of your struggle for existence on this frontier. Can you honestly say you prefer the backwoods and their fauna to the town and civilised people? My dear old friend, haven't you made an . . . unfortunate mistake? You had better come with me. You can't get away from the fact that we mice, unlike cats, have only one life, and a short one. 'All flesh shall perish together.' You remember Solomon? 'What hath man of all his labour . . . there is nothing better for a man than that he should eat, drink, and be merry,' " These Biblical quotations made such a deep impression on the country mouse that he at once decided to leave home. The two friends travelled by night, eager to creep through a hole in the city walls.

Night now commanded the heights of heaven when the two came into a rich man's house. Ivory couches, scarlet covers, and the leavings of a sumptuous five-course dinner were found conveniently piled up in baskets. The town mouse offered his friend a plush-covered chair while he bustled around him like a well-trained waiter tasting each dish first to see whether it was fit for his guest to eat. The country mouse lolled back, and was congratulating himself on his decision to leave home, and trying to live up to his 'posh' surroundings, when a tremendous banging on the outer doors shot them both out of their chairs. They lost their heads and scuttled down the enormous length of the dining-room. When they heard the barking of dogs echoing through the high-ceilinged set of rooms, they were as good as dead. "Good-bye", said the country mouse, "this is no life for me. My meals in my agricultural hovel in the backwoods may be nothing but bitter vetch, but at least I can satisfy my hunger there without this sort of interruption."

No word follows. Either the simplicities and complexities of life have met and joined or all we have is a fable which has not been worked up for its own sake, for there is not much imaginative insight into animal behaviour or the humours proper to the animal fable.

So there was room for a different treatment by Henryson, who must have had at his disposal the independent tradition of what may be called the 'Aesopic' fable of the two rats or mice, which reached back to Greco-Roman times, and developed in its own way in countless prose and verse treatments, mostly in Latin, but later in vernacular versions. Henryson deserves to take a momentary precedence of these because he has made a *poem* out of this matter, and it is quite possible that in some way Wyatt came across this poem before he composed his own.

The Taill of the Uponlandis Mous, and the Burges Mous has no central bearing on the quality of civilisation. Its great charm comes from a few flashes of common life which have concentrated power by having to pass through the narrow confines of the animal scale. For example, when the well-to-do mouse scoffs at the meagre fare offered by the country mouse, and says:

My gude friday is better nor your Pace[1]

we are powerfully reminded of the Christian year and its contrast

1 Easter

between the days of abstinence and feast days, an impression reinforced when the two mice cry out when feasting together:

> 'haill yule, haill'.

It is *real* country the mice travel through, and it is a real early morning

> or the Laverok sang

as they at last reach the town. And a whole household world flashes in the phrase about the Burges mouse running to safety in her hole

> as fyre on flint.

But the central impact of the poem is made by turning the mice into *sisters* who once lived together but have found themselves separated in later life by wealth and poverty, and yet retain the bonds of family love. We forget that they are mice when we hear:

> The hartlie joy, God! geve ye had sene,
> Beis kith[1] quhen that thir Sisteris met;
> And grit kyndnes wes schawin thame betwene,
> For quhylis they leuch,[2] and quhylis for you thay gret[3]
> Quhyles kissit sweit, quhylis in armis plet[4]

The distinctively mediaeval limitation becomes evident when we discover that the fable is being offered as a moral lesson:

> Freindis, ye may find, and ye will tak heid,
> In to this fabill ane gude moralitie.

Since Wyatt here resembles Henryson, I shall postpone discussion. It is plain that both poets have drawn heavily on their 'Aesop'. We therefore need to have Caxton's version (made from a French translation) before us in order to appreciate the originality of the two poems:

> The xij. fable is of the two rats
> Better worthe is to lyue in pouerte surely than to
> lyue rychely beyng euer in daunger/ wherof
> Esope telleth such a fable/ There were two rats/

1 is shown
2 laugh
3 weep
4 fold

wherof the one was grete and fatte/ and held hym in the celer of a Ryche man And the other was poure and lene/

On a day this grete and fatte rat wente to sporte hym in the feldes and mette by the way the poure rat/ of the whiche he was receyued as well as he coude in his poure cauerne or hole/ and gaf hym of suche mete as he had/ Thenne sayd the fatte ratte come thow wyth me/ And I shalle gyue the wel other metes/ He went with hym into the toune/ and entred bothe in to the celer of the ryche man/ the which celer was full of alle goodes/ And whan they were within the grete rat presented and gaf to the poure rat of the delycious metes/ sayeng thus to hym/ Be mery and make good chere/ and ete and drynke Ioyously/

And as they were etynge/ the bouteler of the place came in to the celer/ & the grete rat fled anon in to his hole/ & the poure rat wist not whyther he shold goo ne flee/ but hyd hym be-hynd the dore with grete fere and drede/ and the bouteler torned ageyne and sawe hym not/ And whan he was gone the fatte rat cam out of his cauerne or hole/ and called the poure ratte/ whiche yet was shakynge for fere/ and said to hym/ come hyder and be not aferd/ & ete as moche as thou wylt/ And the poure rat sayd to hym/ for goddes loue lete me go oute of this celer/ For I haue leuer ete some corne in the feldes and lyue surely than to be euer in this torment/ for thou arte here in grete doubte & lyuest not surely/ And therfore hit is good to lyue pourely & surely. For the poure lyueth more surely than the ryche.

While this is enough to establish Wyatt's complete independence, there are a few places in Caxton's version which appear to have found their way into Wyatt's poem. At any rate the meaning of *poor surety* in these lines:

That had forgot her poor surety and rest
For seeming wealth wherein she thought to reign . . .

is made clear by reference to Caxton's moral:

> Better worthe is to lyue in pouerte surely than to
> lyue rychely beyng euer in daunger . . .

It is unlikely that Wyatt would have derived the phrase from the Latin:

> *Fabula quod sit melius in paupertate securum*
> *uiuere quam in diuitiis taedio macerari.*
> A tale with the moral: it is better to live in poverty
> but free from fear than in riches to be wasted away
> with disgust.

The force of this remark will become apparent when it is appreciated that Wyatt has taken several phrases from extant Latin versions of the fable. Since Wyatt does not seem to have followed any one version throughout his poem, there is no need to go into the history and ramifications of the 'Aesopic' fable from Roman days down to the versions produced in Wyatt's youth. The topic has been exhaustively treated by Léopold Hervieux in the five volumes of his *Les fabulistes latins* (1884–1889), and in the commentary I shall refer to this work to give the references of Wyatt's borrowings, or coincidental phrases.

The coincidences, though few, are striking. The mere fact that the country mouse was said to feed on barley and beans is common to so many versions that there is little point in giving references. But the closeness of:

> Sometime a barley corn, sometime a bean . . .

to:

> *Quandoque durae fabae et quandoque sicca grana*

suggests on Wyatt's part that he knew that version. Similarly, the lines:

> The towny mouse fled, she knew whither to go.
> The other had no shift, but wonder sore
> Feared of her life . . .

both recall Caxton, who had written:

> & the poure rat wist not whyther he shold go . . .

and one of the Latin versions:

> *Urbanus nota facile se abscondit cauerna*
> (It was easy for him to hide; he knew his cave well)

Other Latin versions say that the poor thing *mortem metuit* and *usque ad mortem timuit* (feared death, feared unto death).

The impression that Wyatt inherited a far richer fable tradition than the extant records tell us of is strengthened if we turn to the other source for fables about mice, the various poems set to music which entered popular tradition. Although the commentators are probably right to warn us that Wyatt's homely reference to his mother's maids spinning in the big house and singing as they worked was a deft *literary* touch, and therefore to remind us of a similar literary device in Shakespeare's *Twelfth Night*, when the Duke ordered the Clown to sing:

> O fellow, come, the song we had last night:
> Marke it, Cesario, it is old and plaine;
> The Spinsters and the Knitters in the Sun;
> And the free maides that weaue their thred with bones,
> Do vse to chaunt it . . .

nevertheless there is a certain natural curiosity aroused about what Wyatt may have heard on such occasions. We may wonder whether he introduced any element of these songs into his poem.

Our curiosity is increased by the persistence to our day of something not too different from what we may reasonably conjecture was to be heard in the early years of the sixteenth century. Children are still singing versions of 'A frog he would a-wooing go!', where the little creatures speak like humans:

> Pray, Mrs. Mouse, are you within?
>   (Heigh ho! says Rowley)
> O yes, kind sirs, I'm sitting to spin
>   (With a rowley, etc . . .)

This seems to be very close to 'The Marriage of the Frogge and the Mouse' in the *Country Pastimes* section of Ravenscroft's *Melismata* (1611), where we find the singers imitating the sound of the spinning wheel:

> When [at] supper they were [s]at,
>   humble dum, humble dum
> The Frog, the Mouse, and euen the Rat,
>   tweedle, tweedle twino:

> Then came in gib our cat,
>   humble dum, humble dum,
> And catcht the mouse euen by the backe . . .

And the oral tradition contains a song with these lines:

> But Lady Mouse baith jimp and sma',
> Crept into a hole beneath the wa';
> "Squeak!" quo' she, "I'm weel awa'!"

Nevertheless, even if all this 'oral' material could be magically restored to us, I should expect that there would be much in the poem we should still judge to be quintessential Wyatt. Yet not Wyatt at his most complex. There does not seem to be much *point* in the fable he has rendered so vividly. Here I am contrasting him not so much with Horace as with Chaucer, the Chaucer of that part of the *Nun's Priest's Tale* which has to do with the confrontation of the Cock and the Fox, the part Wyatt seems to be consciously drawing on when his mice are surprised. There is so much more mental play in Chaucer's Tale that we are prepared sadly to find that Wyatt's 'moral' is both incoherent and feeble. It is not so feeble as Caxton's 'the poor are safer than the rich', but in part it is identical with Henryson's:

> The sweitest lyfe . . .
> Is sickernes with small possessioun.

The truth is, there is a mediaeval as well as a classical Horace. Though Wyatt's poem is a warning to us not to oppose too sharply the mediaeval to the renaissance enjoyment of the classical author, nevertheless we can see that on the theme of *honesta paupertas* and *paruo uiuitur bene* Horace made a sense congenial to the times. And it was mediaeval, too, to deepen the negative wish to be 'sicker', 'free from danger' to the more inward desire for true *vita quieta*. For Wyatt may have had as a schoolbook the 1503 edition of *Aesopi fabulae metrice cum commento*, where one of the moral remarks was:

> *Dat pretium dapibus uita quieta meis.*
> (It is the quiet life I enjoy which makes my meals
>   precious.)

These remarks rest on more than mere surmise, for there was a mediaeval poem which fits so exactly the moral Wyatt was drawing that it might have been his model. Like Henryson's Fable, it was not in print in Wyatt's day, but it is now included among Chaucer's poems under the title of *The Former Age*. A few extracts will justify the conjecture that Wyatt had it before him: for example, people of the former age

> . . . eten mast, hawes, and swich pounage,
> And dronken water of the colde welle.
> . . .
> Ther poverte is . . .
> Ther as vitaile is eek so skars and thinne
> That noght but mast or apples is therinne.
> . . .
> In caves and in wodes softe and swete
> Slepten this blissed folk withoute walles,
> On gras or leves in parfit quiete.
> Ne doun of fetheres, ne no bleched shete
> Was kid to[1] them, but in seurtee they slepte.

And the closing moral is introduced with:

> Allas, allas! now may men wepe and crye!

But it is just here that Wyatt entered into his own, for he had clearly taken to heart the essay by Plutarch he himself had put into English prose under the title of *Plutarkes boke of the Quyete of mynde*. His developments via Seneca and Persius are in the Christian Humanist vein.

It is now time to deal with the charge of incoherence. It is in part a complaint about the uncertainty of address. Wyatt seems a trifle too vehement and hectoring as he adjures his friend, Poyntz, to observe his various morals. But Wyatt's mind appears to wobble, and he threads in and out with references to 'wretched minds' and other unspecified plurals. Nothing prepares us for the vicious close where Wyatt virtually curses 'these wretched fools', for it is impossible to see where Wyatt was heading and what his 'moral' amounted to.

My mother's maids

for because]   'Since', 'in as much as'.

1 available for

livelihood]

Wyatt might have spelled the word *liflode*, and scanned it as having two syllables.

thin]

From Chaucer's day a common epithet for food, diet, etc.

Maskell Vol. III quotes from a primer of 1545:
> Thynne diet, of drynke and meate,
> Of the fleshe to cool the heate.

John Heywood in *The fyrst hundred of Epigrammes* No. 46 writes of two university students:
> Kept in thinne diet, after scolars rate . . .

Wyatt could have found in an 'Aesopic' version (Hervieux II/506):
> *ad macram nemoris dietam*
> the meagre diet of the woods.

enured]

All our manuscripts have *endured*. It is tempting to take the sense of the whole line as an explanation of what has gone before: 'because she thought she had endured too much pain'. But if it prefaces the account of the 'pain' of her normal existence in the various seasons of the year, 'endured to' must be taken in the sense of 'hardened to'. If this is so, the word Wyatt wrote might have been *indured*, in the sense of 'indurate'. This word would be familiar to the scribes in a moral rather than a physical sense. My conjecture *enured* is the regular contemporary word in this context, as may be seen, for instance, from Caxton's *Fayttes of Armes*, Ch. xiij. p. 47:
> To enure hem self so to peyne and trauayll

and Udall's *Apophthegmes* Fol. 3 *verso*:
> . . . to endure houngre and thirst, he had purposely exercised & enured hym self.

swimmed]

The OED quotes this line of Wyatt's as the first English instance of the sense 'to be covered or filled with fluid', and gives as the second a 1560 translation of verse 6 of Psalm 6. In our Psalter we find:
> every night wash I my bed: and water my couch with my tears.

But in our Authorised Version we have:
> all the night make I my bed to swim.

Wyatt, in his own version, followed Campensis:

euery nyght haue I wesshed my bedde and
watred my couche with my teares.

It is possible that Wyatt at some time looked at
a version of the Psalms published by Pellicanus
in 1527, where, commenting on this line, he
wrote:

*donec lectulus madefieret & rigaretur, immo
dissolueretur, & ut Iudaei dicunt, nataret.*

until the little bed is drenched and watered,
nay dissolved, and, as the Jews say, swims.

Wyatt certainly knew a translation of Savonarola's
Meditatio contained in the *Prymer* of 1534, where
we find:

I shall water my bedde . . . with my teares,
so that it shall swym in them . . .
sig. U .iii. *recto* in the 1535 edition.

lie . . . sorry plight]
The phrase sounds Chaucerian, but is recorded
only in Gower's *Confessio Amantis*, e.g. P III/
200:

In sori plit and povere he lay

bare meat]
Could the meaning be, 'her larder contained the
very minimum of food'? The OED offers under
BARE 10d: *Simple, without luxury*, but has a
quotation from Stubbes, *Anatomy of Abuses*
II/72, which might support the conjecture:

Better it is to haue bare feeding than none
at all . . .

R. Burrant *Preceptes of Cato* 1560 *sig.* C.viij.
verso:

it shall . . . make thy liuinge full bare

house . . . dight]
Griselda's labour to get her house ready for her
successor in Chaucer's *Clerk's Tale*/974 gives the
general sense:

she gan the hous to dight,
And tables for to sette, and beddes make

Wyatt may here have been thinking of drying out
as well as putting in order. The detail occurs in
one of the 'Aesopic' versions: (Hervieux II/389):

aedem commodat
puts the house in order

*Sometime . . . corn
. . . bean*]
Hervieux II/773 prints a version with this line:

Quandoque duras fabas et quandoque

> *sicca grana*
> sometimes hard beans and sometimes dry corn.

These items occur in all the 'Aesopic' versions, e.g. (Hervieux II/608):

> *Duras fabas, sicca grana frumenti vel hordei comedo*
> I eat hard beans, dry corn of wheat or barley

harvest time]

She was like the Ant in *The Prouerbes of Salomon* The VI. Chapter:

> in the sommer she prouideth her meate & gathereth hir foode together in ye haruest.

go and glean]

Wyatt's phrase suggests actual everyday practice. At any rate there is a passage in Langland (C.ix.67) where Piers promises that all those who helped him get in the harvest:

> Shal haue leue by oure lorde to go and glene after . . .

Are we to recall the story of *Ruth* Ch. II?

wellaway!]

Deliberate Chaucerian colouring? Wyatt in his own person uses only 'alas!'

clean]

'Utterly'.

fain]

'Happy' in the sense of 'content'.

beguile]

'Cheat', 'charm away'.

hence . . . mile]

Is this an attempt to give a rustic air to the country mouse's speech? If not a folk turn of speech, it may be a literary reminiscence, since it occurs in Chaucer's *Troilus and Criseyde*, Book Five/403:

> nat hence but a myle . . .

lieth warm]

Wyatt in *A spending hand*/64 has:

> Yet where thee list thou mayest lie good and warm . . .

bed of down]

A similar remark is found in *A spending hand*/15:

> And might'st at home sleep in thy bed of down . . .

Wyatt treats this feather bed as an item of luxury, as it is in *The Former Age*.

labours not as I]

The provident mouse seems to be recalling a rebuke in *The Gospell of S. Mathew* The vi. Chapter:
> . . . be not carefull for your lyfe, what ye shall eate, or what ye shall drincke . . . Considre the lylies of the felde, how they growe. They labour not nether spynne . . .

rich man's]

In Caxton's version of the fable the mice are caught 'in the celer of a Ryche man'.

crave nor cry]

The two words make up one idea,
> 'cry bitterly for',

as in *The Wife of Bath's Prologue*/517:
> . . . what thyng we may nat lightly haue Therafter wyl we crye al day and craue . . .

By sea . . . spareth]

A cluster of similar words but in a different context is found in *The Pilgrimage of Perfection* (1531 Fo: 2 *verso*):
> They . . . spared no labours neyther by see ne yet by lande

delicates]

'Exquisite, tasty food'. There is a passage in the same book on Fo: 701 *verso* which contains this:
> to be admytted to the kynges owne table and to taste of his deyntye delycates . . .

the most]

We must supply 'dainty' or 'delicate'.

cater]

'A buyer of provisions or "cates", in large households the officer who made the necessary purchases of provisions'. (OED)
An example of their employment is given by Cavendish in his *Life of Wolsey* 68/7:
> they sent forthe all ther Cators/ purveyours & other persons to prepare of the fynnest vyandes that they cowld gett other for mony or frendshyppe . . .

spareth . . . parail]

Wyatt would pronounce the word *parell*. This has given rise to a misunderstanding since *parell* could also stand for our *peril*, and the phrase was common in this sense. A good example occurs in *A Myrroure for Magistrates* near the end of a poem on Edmund, Duke of Somerset:
> Constant I was in my Prynces quarell, To dye or lyue and spared for no parell.

I think, however, that the Cater spared for no *cost*, as in Cavendish's account:

> And nother to spare for expences or trauell
> to make them suche tryhumphante chere . . .

I take the word 'parail' to be an aphetic form of *aparayle* 'expensive preparation of all kinds and especially meals'. An example can be found in Lydgate's *Isopes Fabules* III/460:

> And what ys worthe all the apparyll
> Of diuerse deyntees to a mannys lust

* thirsty

> When aftyr mete men gon awey a thrust?*

boiled]

The whole passage is discussed in *A Guide to the Commentary*. The town mouse is thought to enjoy all the main forms of cooking meat practised in a rich household. This is the claim that Henryson's rich mouse makes, that she fares like a lord:

> With all coursis that Cukis culd devyne . . .

When in the Prologue to his *Canterbury Tales* Chaucer describes the skill of his professional cook, Roger, we learn that:

* boil

> He coude roste sethe* broylle and frye
> Make mortrewys and wel bake a pye . . .

baken meat]

'Baked meat', in Chaucer's day known as *bake mete*, and described as *viande en paste*, baked in a pie. It was an item of high luxury, *most daynté*, as we may see from its position in the diet of the Frankeleyn,

> Epicurus owene sone

in the General Prologue to Chaucer's *Canterbury Tales*:

> Wythoute bake mete was he neuer in his hous
> Hys fissh hys flessh and that so plentuous
> It snewede in hys hows of mete ande drynke
> Of alle deyntees that men couthe thynke.

Wyatt's whole phrase may in fact have been a formula, for Erasmus wrote of

> cibi elixi, ussi, coctiquo

boiled, roast and baked meats
and Malory wrote of venison that was

> rosted baken and soden.

By contrast, *boiled bacon* was the lot of the *poor* in classical and modern times. Chaucer's poor widow in the *Nun's Priest's Tale*, who had to be

content with many a slender meal, enjoyed
        Seynde bacon, ande somtyme an ey or tweye.

charge . . . travail]   In *Troylus and Criseyde* Book III/522 we find:
        And nyther lefte for coste ne for trauayle
The meaning here may be 'neither trouble nor exertion'. There is a similar line later in this poem:
        Ye do mis-seek with more travail and care

liquor . . . grape]   Chaucer in his *Pardoner's Tale*/452 has:
        I wol drynke the licour of the vyn
If Wyatt had *Numbers* VI/3 in mind, it can only be because he knew Olivétan's 1535 translation:
        ne de toute liqueur de raisins
which did not appear in an English Bible until the Geneva edition of 1560: nor shal drinke anie licour of grapes . . .
cf. Surrey *Ecclesiastes* Ch. 2/38:
        What fancies in my hed had wrought the licor of the grape

glad her heart]   This is a Chaucerian phrase, as in the Prologue of the *Nun's Priest's Tale*/4001:
        Tel vs suche thynge as may our hertis glade
and in *The Franklin's Tale*/968:
        So that I wyste I myght your herte glade

of . . . makes . . . japes]   It seems to be English idiom to scoff and jape *at*, but to make a scoff or jape *of* something, when the meaning is 'make light of'.

part . . . shape]   Perhaps 'arrange for her share to be'.

keep . . . health]   Since Wyatt used 'health' as co-extensive with the Latin '*salus*', the meaning here might be 'so long as she could live there without danger to life'.

live a lady]   Henryson/ I fair alsweill as ony Lord.

life . . . last]   A common formula in mediaeval literature, as in Chaucer's *Troilus and Criseyde* Book IV/677:
        She wolle ben his, whyle that her lyfe may last

scrapes]   Both 'scratches like an animal' and 'makes an unobtrusive signal' at the door.
The Tale of Beryn/481 has:
* like a dog   And scrapid the dorr welplich*

appear]   'Come out of hiding', as in *Some fowls*:

And some [fowls] because the light doth
them offend
Never appear but in the dark of night . . .

asked] To be scanned as having two syllables.

"Peep "] Part of the mouse fable tradition, as in
Gesta Rom. I xlv. 364:
The Cate come beside, and herde the mouse
Crie in the barme, pepe! pepe!
In Henryson's version of the fable we find:
How fair ye sister? Cry peip, quhair euer ye
be!

fair and well] A set phrase, as in Chaucer's *Canon Yeoman's
Tale*/1113:
And he hem leyde faire and wel adoun . . .
And in Lydgate *Pilgrymage*/884:
ffor thow shalt passe fayre & wel . . .

by the Rood!] The reference to the Holy Cross had little more
effect than to strengthen a 'yes' or 'no'.

joy it was] A regular phrase, used here as in Book Three of
Troilus and Criseyde/1228:
Criseyde, al quyte from euery drede and tene
As she that iuste cause had hym to tryste,
Made him suche feest, it ioye was to sene . . .
The Early Tudor variant may be seen in:
Lord Berners *Huon* p. 157/20:
but the erthe was so fayre and grene that
ioy it was to se it . . .
Caxton:
ete and drynke Joyously . . .

clear] A necessary condition for drinkability, as is shown
by the following examples. *Gest. Rom.*/337-8:
The fadir said, "yeue me of another tonne
of wyne," than the sone seid, "nay, for it
is not clere ynogh; and yf it shuld now be
touched, the wyne myght be troubled;
and therfore I wille not touche it, tille I
se it clere ynow."
Sir Fr. Bryan *A Dispraise* Chapter III:
None wyl . . . drynke the wyne, if it be not
clere . . .

to purpose]   A similar line occurs in Wyatt's *Mine own J.P.*:

> And as to purpose likewise it shall fall . . .

See the commentary on that line for Chaucerian uses. Here the sense might be, 'when the appropriate moment in the conversation occurred'.

cheered]   To be scanned as having two syllables.

How]   Probably an exclamation of encouragement, as in Chaucer's *Miller's Tale*/3577:

> How, Alison! how, John!
> Be mery

It might also be the equivalent of Henryson's

> How fair ye, sister?

what cheer!]   A common phrase both of greeting when meeting (as at the opening of *The Tempest*) and of encouragement, a shorter form of 'be of good cheer!'

a sorry chance]   A possible reference to Book II of *Troylus and Criseyde*/463:

> And with a soroufull sygh she sayd thrie
> Ah lorde what me is tydde a sory chaunce!

but the *situation* is similar to the discovery of the fox in the cabbage patch in Chaucer's *Nun's Priest's Tale*.

looked askance]   'To one side'. Palsgrave 831/1:

> A scanche *De trauers en lorgnant*

steaming]   'Glowing', 'flaming', as in Chaucer's Prologue to the *Canterbury Tales* 201–202:

> Hys eyen steep and rollynge in hys heede

* cauldron

> That stemyde as a furneys of a leede* . . .

ears]   Wyatt wrote *erys*, a disyllable.

in France]   It was a traditional English joke that the French were all cowards.

feared]   'Terrified'.

th'unwise]   'The rash, foolish creature'. The phrase was used as *the fool* in our Psalm XIV:

> The fool has said in his heart . . .

e.g. in a mediaeval metrical version we find:

> The vnwise saide in hert his,
> Als a foele, that God noght is.

yseen]

The faulty scansion suggests as a possible emendation:

had not I sene suche a lyke beest before

since in *A spending hand*, where the reference to Chaucer was intended to be equally plain, we find:

as pandare was in such a like dede.

I take it that the deliberate archaism of *yseen* was Wyatt's way of reminding us of the feelings of Chaucer's cock (in the *Nun's Priest's Tale*) when suddenly confronted with the fox:

For naturelly a best desireth to fle

Fro his contrary yf he may it se

Though he neuer had seen it erst wyth his eye.

after her guise]

'As was her custom', 'Employing her usual instinctive way'. The phrase was common

knew whither]

This point is made in many versions of the fable, e.g.: *Urbanus nota facile se abscondit cauerna*

It was easy for the town mouse to hide: he was familiar with the cellar. (Hervieux II/125)

On the other hand, 'the poure rat', as Caxton put it, 'wist not whyther he shold go'. Wyatt would pronounce *whither* as one syllable.

no shift]

The meaning here is probably, 'Had no other means of escape'.

wondrous]

Wyatt may have written *wondrus*, but *wonders* or *wonder* are possible with the meaning 'very much', as we may see from Lydgate in his *Pilgrymage*/296:

wonder sore

or from *Gest. Rom.*/334 (of a prisoner in solitary confinement):

the knyght was wondir heuy

But Udall, *Apophthegmes* p. 271 *verso* has:

When he sawe his souldiours to bee woundreous sore a feard of . . .

Feared . . . life]

The OED offers c.1400 *Destr. Troy*/13842:

the kyng [was] of his lyfe feerd.

This point is made in many versions of the 'Aesopic' tale, *e.g.* in Hervieux II/125: *mortemque metuens* and p. 450: *timuit usque ad mortem*, which was what Wyatt had in mind.

tho]

'Then'.

The heaven . . . so]

A great deal is made of this distinction in Chaucer's *Nun's Priest's Tale*, lines 3234-3250. When events take a happy turn for his mice, Henryson has:
>   Bot as God waid it fell ane happie cace. . .

Wyatt probably wrote *thevyn* and pronounced the words as one syllable.

silly]
    * at a loss for
    * advice

'Unfortunate', as in Henryson:
>   . . . that selie Mous . . .
>   So desolate and wil off* ane gude reid*

recover]

'Get back on four feet'.

traitor]

'Treacherous'. The Fox in Chaucer's Tale is the great exemplar. Henryson treats the fox in his fable of the Wolf and the Fox in a similar way:
>   Seand this Wolff, this wylie tratour Tod . . .

by the hip]

Possibly a term of wrestling, 'catch at a disadvantage', as in *The Tale of Beryn*/1780:
>   Beryn he had y-caughte
>   Somwhat oppon the hipp, that Beryn had
>   the wers . . .

poor surety]

A difficult phrase made clear by reference to the opening of Caxton's fable of the two rats:
>   Better worthe is to lyue in pouerte surely
>   than to lyue rychely beyng euer in daunger

providing we take *surely* to mean 'free from anxiety'.

seek the best]

No doubt a commonplace, but see Chaucer's *Knight's Tale*/ 1266-1267:
>   We sekyn faste aftyr felycyte
>   But we goo wronge ful ofte trewly . . .

by error . . . stray]

The connection between the Latin and French, *err* and the earlier French borrowing, *stray*, may have been established before Wyatt, since by 1530 Palsgrave was giving as a translation of *je erre* 'I straye, I wander about and wot nat whyther I go', and Sir T. Elyot had under *Erratio* in his 1548 *Dictionarie* 'a goyng out of the waie, a wandryng, a straiying abrode'. But Wyatt seems to be the first to have used the phrase for moral

and spiritual matters. The first recorded liturgical
use is in the General Confession in the 1552 *Book
of Common Prayer*: We haue erred and strayed
from thy wayes, lykc loste shepe . . .
Wyatt used this image in his Psalm *O Lord, since*:
> The sheep that strays the shepherd seeks
> to see. I, Lord, am strayed . . . .

And no marvel] A mediaeval set phrase, as in *Pilg. Perf.* (1531
Fo: 2 *verso* :
> And no meruayle, For in the . . .

or in A. Barclay *The Shyp of Folys* Vol. I p. 237:
> And no meruayle, for it hath . . .

blind . . . guide] No English version of *Matt.* 15/14 has *guides*.
Wyatt may have been influenced by Olivétan's
Bible of 1535:
> *ilz sont aueugles/ conducteurs des aueugles.
> Si vng aueugle conduict vng aueugle/ ilz
> cherront tous deux en la fosse.*
> They are blind guides of blind mcn. If one
> blind man leads another, both will fall into
> the ditch.

On the other hand, when Tyndale translated the
Enchiridion, in a clear reference to this passage
in the N.T. he wrote (*sig. C.vj. recto*):
> these blynde capteyns or guydes of blyndc
> men . . .

out of the way] Tyndale tr. of the *Enchiridion sig.* L.iij. *recto*:
> Thou arte vtterly disceyued & cleane out
> of the way.

quiet life] The people in the former age, according to Chaucer,
slept 'in parfit quiete'. The moral of the fable in
one account (Hervieux II/390) ran
> *Dat pretium dapibus uita quieta meis*
> Quiet life gives value to my meals.

gold] Wyatt in his translation of Plutarch's essay on
quiet of mind has (*sig. d.ij recto*):
> So nouther gorgiousnesse of buyldtng nor
> weight of golde nor noblenesse of kyn nor
> greatnesse of empire nor eloquence & fayre
> spekyng brinketh [*sic*] so muche clerenesse
> of lyfe and so plesant quietnes as bringeth
> a mynde disceuered from trouble of busy-

nesse lyueng (as they say) with hym selfe
ferre from yll aduyse.

Sergeant]

Presumably a Sergeant at Arms, responsible to
the King for arresting traitors. He would have
a mace as a badge of his office. It is very likely
that here Wyatt is rewriting part of the Sixteenth Ode of Horace's Second Book. For the
moral of his fable appears to be a line from this
Ode: *uiuitur paruo bene*: the man who has little
lives best. This was also the moral drawn by
Henryson:
> The sweitest lyfe . . .

* absolute security

> Is sickenes* with small possessioun.

The last lines of the Ode include: *mihi parua
rura . . . Parca . . . dedui . . .* Fate has given me a
small place in the country.
The lines being rewritten here are:
> *non enim gazae neque consularis*
> *summouet lictor miseros tumultus*
> *mentis et curas laqueata circum*
> > *tecta uolantis.*

> The riches of the East will not bring you a
> quiet life. The consul's lictor cannot clear the
> mind of the unruly mob of cares that buzz
> round the ornamented ceilings of the great.

The Sergeant with his mace would be the modern
equivalent of the Roman lictor with his symbols
of office, the axe and the bundle of rods.

care . . . follow]

This, too, may come from the same poem:
> *scandit aeratas uitiosa naues cura*

which might be roughly modernised as:
> Climbing up the gangway after you into
> your luxury yacht a load of troubles will
> blight your cruise . . .

In Thomas Paynell's translation of Erasmus'
De contemptu mundi (1533) *sig.* C.2. *recto*
we find:
> Care dothe folowe the encreasynge of money

Wyatt may also have been thinking of the more
vigorous account in *Odes* III/1:
> *post equitem sedet atra Cura*

Black Care sits at the horseman's back.

Each ... fade]   Wyatt now turns to the obverse of his moral, the disgust produced by excess of pleasure. He has opened his commonplace book at the heading *Fastidium* or *Satietas*, in his English, *irksomeness. It irketh* was a translation of *fastidit mei*. There were many proverbs pointing out the speed with which pleasures pall. A well-known tag in Ovid's *Metamorphoses* VII/453 ff. is:

> *usque adeo nulla est sincera uoluptas*
> *sollicitumque aliquid laetis interuenit*

So true it is that there is no pleasure unmixed, and some trouble always intervenes and interrupts our joys.

Pliny in his *Natural History* 12.171 40. p. 81 has:

> *nulla uoluptas est quae non assiduitate*
> *fastidium pariat*

pleasures too long pursued and practised breed disgust.

Wyatt may have been thinking of the following passage from Cicero's *De Oratore* 3.25.98:

> *ea quae maxime sensus nostros impellunt*
> *uoluptate ... ab eis celerrime fastidio quodam*
> *et satietate abalienemur*

It is hard to say what the reason is why the very things which most strongly and most keenly strike our senses with immediate pleasure are the first we turn away from in disgust.

Wyatt returns to this thought a moment later for the lines:

> And yct the thing that most your heart
>   desires
> Ye do mislike with more travail and care.

A small ... appease]   The sentiment is found in Boethius *De Consolatione Philosophiae* II prose 5:

> *Paucis enim minimisque natura contenta est*

This is Wyatt's version of Horace's *uiuitur paruo bene.*

None ... briers]   Erasmus in his *Adagia* included this among his 'impossibilities', things which only a fool would attempt: *E spinis uuas colligere*, to gather grapes from thorns. But Wyatt seems to have gone back to the Bible, *Matt.* 7/6:

numquid colligunt de spinis uuas aut de tribulis ficus?
which Wyclif rendered:
Whether men gaderen grapis of thornys or figgis of breris?

hay]

Defined in the *Promp. paru.* as a 'net to catche conys wythe', that is, a rabbit-net.

conies . . . rivers]

Wyatt is recalling a passage from Plutarch's essay on true peace of mind, as he himself had translated it:

we accuse wicked fortune and our desteny/ whan rather we shulde dam our selfes of foly/ as it were to be angry with fortune/ that thou canst nat shote an arowe with a plou/ or hunt an hare with an oxe/ and that some cruel god shulde be agaynst them/ that with vayn indeuour/ hunt an hart with a dragge net/ and nat that they attempt to do those impossibilytes/ by their own madnesse and folysshnesse.

It is noteworthy that Wyatt has translated these impossibilities from Erasmus and not from Budaeus.

drag-net]

Cooper *Thes. Verriculum* A drag net. 'A net which is dragged over the bottom of a river . . . in order to enclose all the fish, etc.' (OED)

most . . . desires]

The seconde boke of the Testament of Loue (Usk) Fo: C C C xxxix *recto*:

Ah wicked folkes/ for your propre malyce/ and shreudnesse of your selfe: ye blame and dispyse the precioust thyng of your kynde/ and whiche thynges amonge other moste ye desyren . . .

plain]

'Open in behaviour; free from duplicity or reserve; guileless, honest, candid, frank.' (OED) 1399
wher the herte is plein withoute guile

knotted]

Could this mean 'bound like a slave', a touch of Stoic doctrine that true freedom lies in not being 'passion's slave'?

bare From all]

At the back of Wyatt's mind there may have been a phrase such as this: *liberatus omni perturbatione animi* (freed from all perturbation of mind) from Cicero's *Rep.* I/17/28.

affects]

The word was defined by Sir T. Elyot in his *Boke named the Governour* Fo: 131 *verso*:
> all motions of the minde/called affectes . . .

spotted]

'Morally stained', as in Sir T. More *Dialogue* Book 4 Ch. ii in *Workes* p. 270:
> All our onely iustice is all spotted . . . sore spotted with sinne. . . .

Sir T. Elyot (tr. of Plutarch) *The Education . . . of children sig.* F. ii. *recto*:
> company with no persone, whose maners be spotted with vice . . .

Thy self content]

Wyatt may have had the opening of Horace's *Satires* in mind:
> *Qui fit, ut nemo, quam sibi sortem seu ratio dederit seu fors obiecerit, illa contentus uiuat . . .*
> How does it come about that nobody is ever content with his lot, whether it was given him by his own deliberate choice or chance had thrown it in his path?

assigned . . . allotted]

For the meaning of these words, see the note on *assigned* in *The pillar perished*.

Taverner *Prouerbes* (1569) p. 62 *recto*:
> let euerie man be content with his allottement . . .

seek . . . out of thy self]

This may be Wyatt's deepest conviction in morals and religion. No doubt he knew the following formulations in Seneca's *Epistles*:

L/4: *Non est extrinsecus malum nostrum, intra nos est, in uisceribus ipsis sedet . . .*
> Our evil is not outside us, it is within, sitting in our very entrails . . .

XLI/1: *prope est a te deus, tecum est, intus est . . . sacer intra nos spiritus sedet . . .*
> God is near you, with you, inside you, the holy spirit is within us . . .

But the thought may have come from Boethius *De Consolatione Philosophiae II prose 4:*
> *Quid igitur, o mortales extra petitis intra uos*

positam felicitatem?
O ye mortal folke/ what seke ye than blysfulnesse out of your owne selfe; which is putte in your selfe?

continue . . . sore]   Perhaps 'cause your mental affliction to last any longer'.

gape . . . to come]   Wyatt appears to be recalling part of his own translation of Plutarch's essay on true quiet of mind, which he translated from the Latin version of the French Humanist, Budé:

Etenim insipientes bona quoque praesentia transmittunt: pereuntiaque negligunt: usque adeo ad futurum uergunt intentissime semper eorum curae.

For foles let good thynges passe tho they be present/ and regarde them nat whan they perisshe/ so moche doth their thoughtes gape gredily after thynges to come.

deep . . . more]   The general sense appears to be, 'it is equally mad to plunge deeper and deeper into unnecessary troubles and vexations'. Cooper in his *Thesaurus* gives *to diepe* for *immergere*.

all and some]   A dismissive phrase, similar in spirit to the brisk despatch of Arcite in Chaucer's *Knight's Tale*/2760:

Fare wel phisik! go bere the man to chyrche!
Thys is al ande som arcyte muste dye . . .

which has the effect of our 'that is the long and short of it. I have nothing further to say to these wretched fools than that . . .'
In Tottel's Miscellany and in a Cambridge University Library manuscript ff.5.14 there is a version of the opening of Lucretius Book II, which translates:

nonne uidere.
nil aliud sibi naturam latrare, nisi utqui
corpore seiunctus dolor absit, mente fruatur
iucundo sensu cura semota metuque?

Body deuoyde of grefe mynde free from care and dreede
Is all and some that nature craves wherwith our life to feede.

the great God]   This, and the remaining part of the poem, is a translation of the following lines from Persius III/35:

> *magne pater diuum, saeuos punire tyrannos*
> *haut alia ratione uelis, cum dira libido*
> *mouerit ingenium feruenti tincta ueneno:*
> *uirtutem uideant intabescantque relicta.*

> Great Father of the gods, when deadly lust, dipped in boiling poison, has stirred their spirits, be willing to punish inhuman tyrants in no other way than this: let them see Virtue [as she is] and rot away knowing that they have lost her for ever.

Given Wyatt's interest in *honesty*, as shown in his letters to his son, it is plausible to suppose that he would be familiar with Cicero's treatise on the subject, known as *De Officiis libri tres*. At any rate, there is a sentence in 1,5 which Wyatt may have been translating here:

> *Formam quidem ipsam, Marce fili, et tam-*
> *quam faciem honesti uides, "quae si oculis*
> *cerneretur, mirabiles amores",ut ait Plato,*
> *"excitaret sapientiae".*

> You now perceive, Marcus, my son, the whole configuration of honesty [ideal virtue] as if you were looking it in the face, about which Plato said, "if it could be seen with our eyes, it would give rise in us to a marvellous love for wisdom".

Whether Wyatt would have direct knowledge of the original Greek (Plato, *Phaedrus* 250 D) or a Latin translation, is not so sure. But all three 'sources', Persius, Cicero and Plato, were brought together by Milton in Book Four of his *Paradise Lost*:

> abasht the Devil stood,
> And felt how awful goodness is, and saw
> Vertue in her shape how lovly, saw, and pin'd
> His loss . . .

rage] Presumably Wyatt's translation of *dira libido*, the meaning of the word in Tyndale's *Answere* Fo: xx *recto*:

> And there be that can not attend to herken vnto the trueth for rage of lustes . . .

goodly fair and bright]   All three words were in common use to describe a woman's beauty. It is possible that *goodly* is here an adjective, as in *So unwarely*:
> a goodly face

in arms across]   'Embraced'. Surrey used the phrase in the poem beginning *O happy dames*:
> When other louers in armes acrosse
>   Rejoyce their chief delight . . .

An alternative phrase was 'in folded arms'.

mayest . . . might]   A formula of invocation similar to that in Chaucer's *Knight's Tale*/91:
> Now help me lady sithnes thou may and can

cf. the prayer to Mary as Queen of Heaven in Dante's *Paradiso*, Canto 33:
> *Ancor ti priego, regina che puoi*
> *ciò che tu vuoli . . .*
> And furthermore, O Queen, who can do whatever you wish, I beg you to . . .

Chaucer did not translate the phrase in his rendering of Bernard's prayer in *The Prologe of the Seconde Nonnes Tale.*)

fret inward]   Presumably Wyatt's translation of *intabescere*. Tyndale uses the verb to describe the action of syphilis: *Obedience* Fo: clix *verso*:
> it is lyke a pocke that freateth inwarde . . .

losing . . . loss]   Presumably, Wyatt's translation of *uirtute relicta* (virtue lost forever).

A spending hand

If we knew more of Wyatt's actual circumstances when he was writing this poem, I expect that we should relish the surface truth of his presentation of life at court. Consider, for example, how much it would help if we knew what all Wyatt's contemporaries would know of Kitson, who may have been the figure knighted in 1533,

> that in a long white coat
> From under the stall without lands or fees
> Hath leapt into the shop

and so know why it was pointed to single out the coat. We know just enough to have this expectation, but not enough to say whether any one topical remark is more pointed than another.

Of the addressee, Sir Francis Bryan, we can say with some assurance that Wyatt knew him as a boon companion, as a fellow-diplomat, and as a poet. The fragments of his poetry that have come down to us are not very prepossessing. There is a poem made up of proverbs loosely strung together, which contains one Wyatt himself uses in this epistle. Since it is not easy to come by, I here offer an extract:

> What availeth noble lineage and to use villany?
>> Or what reproach to a poor stock to use gentleness?
> He that boasts him of his ancestors of praises is unworthy.
>> Gentle fashion maketh the body to have quietness.
> An honourable life sheweth honesty.
>> A godly life it is wrongs to redress.
>>> What nobility, riches or puissance may be steadfast,
>>> Since God may make kings and kingdoms to waste?
>
> In realm not obedient there grows no good thing.
>> Better is obedience than lands and possession.
> He that resisteth authority resisteth his King.
>> Ye servants, obey your sovereign, for that is to be done.
> It is not lawful for subjects new laws in to bring.
>> Where commons will govern there reigns oppression.
>>> The laws of God we should at no time forsake,
>>> Nor against a King new laws for to make.
>
> The plant never proves* that is often times set.
>> The ball is soon worn that every man doth toss.
> He that is inclined to superstition shall never be quiet.
>> A rolling stone doth never gather moss.
> That body is in health that keepeth sober diet.
>> Search to have wisdom, the gain shall bear the loss.
>>> As fortune becketh, so favour enclineth.
>>> The fearful dog barketh sorer than he biteth.

*thrives [marginal note to *]

We also know that money had passed between the two men. Both were frequent borrowers and lenders. But the greatest smack of reality is given by these lines in the epistle:

> To thee therefore, that trots still up and down
> And never rests, but running day and night
> From realm to realm, from city street and town,
>> Why dost thou wear thy body to the bones . . .?

by our hearing Wyatt apply the same remarks to himself in 1541, in his Declaration, when he was in great danger of losing his life:

I, as God judge me, like as I was continually imagining and com-
passing what way I might do best service, so rested I not day nor
night to hunt out for knowledge of those things: I trotted continually up and down that hell through heat and stink, from coun-
sellor to ambassador, from one friend to another . . .

Similarly, those familiar with the seamy side of life either in the cloister or
at court could give chapter and verse for what seem the coarsest expressions
in the poem.

At the same time I subscribe to the general view that Wyatt was helped
to such vivid self-expression by the example of the Fifth Satire in Horace's
Second Book, which gives us a similar impression of having been drawn from
life as it was in Imperial Rome. At the very lowest, comparison with Roman
conditions would prevent Wyatt treating any of the goings-on at the court
of Henry VIII as extraordinary. At best, the Roman model would help Wyatt
to present his topical examples as modern instances of a common, unchanging
human nature. Yet Wyatt drew back from some of the exaggerations a true
satirist *must* make. Whereas he knew the contemporary habits that formed
the equivalent of Horace's

> *scortator erit: caue te roget: ultro*
> *Penelopam facilis potiori trade . . .*
> (Does the whoremonger lust after your own wedded lady? Oblige
> him by making him a present of her before he brings the subject up.
> After all, he is your better.)

he does not permit himself the extravagance of

> *anus improba Thebis*
> *ex testamento sic est elata: cadauer*
> *unctum oleo largo nudis umeris tulit heres*
> *scilicet elabi si posset mortua; credo*
> *quod nimium institerat uiuenti.*

(A wily old crone of Khartoum
Left her money by will to her groom
    With one stipulation: to dip
    Her dead body in oil and then strip
And carry her corpse to the tomb
On his back. You ask why? I aver
    She was hoping when dead to contrive
    To give him the slip whom alive
She had found much too grasping to bear.)

A spending hand]   Although the proverb must have been well-known,
                            it has not been recorded. The nearest thing I have
                            found is:

> He that owith mych & hath nowght,
> & spendith mych & gettith nowght,
> & lokith in his purse, & fyndith nowght,
> He may be right sory & say nowght.
> Dyboski No. 112 p. 140.

on the stone] See the opening remarks on p. 337 for Bryan's version of this proverb.

length of years] Chaucer *Troylus and Criseyde* Book IV/1681:
> And this may length of yeres nat fordo

force . . . waste] Perhaps 'destroy their validity' or 'weaken their impact'.

I thought forthwith] The poem beginning *The flaming sighs* has a similar remark:
> But you that of such like have had your part
> Can best be judge; wherefore, my friend so dear,
> I thought it good my state should now appear
> To you . . .

to counsel] If this epistle dates from 1540, these lines might be a compliment on Bryan's translation of a treatise by Guevara 'dispraising' the life of a courtier and praising life in the country.

trots still] See the opening remarks on p. 338 for similar language in his Declaration of 1541.

to the bones] *O Lord, since*/50:
> fret it to the bones
Tyndale *Obedience* Fo: clix *verso*:
> lyke a pocke that . . . consumeth the very mary of the bones . . .

bed of down] The equivalent of our 'feather bed'.

noppy] 'Having a good head', 'foaming'.

for the nonce] The pronunciation is given by the rhyme words. The phrase sometimes meant 'for the particular occasion' as Wyatt himself used it in Psalm 6/54:
> Here hath thy mercy matter for the nonce,
but the present use seems to fit the account of it given in the OED: 'a metrical tag or stop-gap with no special meaning, frequently riming with *bones* and *stones*'.

Feed . ... fat]   *Cf.* Surrey in his translation of the opening of *Ecclesiastes*, Ch. II:

> Then sought I how to please my belly
> > with much wine,
> To feed me fat with costly feasts . . .

heap . . . pound]   If Wyatt was thinking of money, this may have been suggested by Horace's satire, where Ulysses asks the prophet, Tiresias:

> *tu protinus unde*
> *diutias aerisque eruam, dic, augur, aceruos*
> Hurry up, you are supposed to be a fortune-teller, tell me where I can dig one up with heaps of brass.

groans]   'Grunts'. Palsgrave/917:

> A hogge groneth *ung pourceau grongne.*

chaw]   'chew'.

moulded]   I take this to be a rare form of 'mouldered', 'crumbled away'.

drivel: on pearls]   Refers to the flow of saliva from the pigs' mouths. The phrase goes back ultimately to the Bible, *Matt.* 7/6:

> nether caste ye youre pearles before swyne, lest they treade them vnder their fete.

It early became an English proverb. All three versions of *Piers Plowman* have a similar passage. The following is from C/xii/7:

> And seide *nolite mittere*, ye men, margerie-
> > perles
> a-monge hogges that hauen hawes at wille;

* hog's-wash

> thei don bote dreuele theron: draf* were
> > hem leuere

* gems

> than al the preciouse perreye* that eny
> > prince weldeth.

Henryson *The Taill of the Cok and the Iasp*/146:

> As does ane Sow, to quhome men for the
> > nanis

* trough * sow

> In hir draf troich* wald saw* precious
> > stanis . . .

A. Barclay *The Shyp of Folys* Vol. 2 p. 257:

> Cast precious stones or golde amonges swyne
> And they had leuer haue dreggis fylth or
> > chaffe.

No meruayle/ for they were norysshed vp
                                        with draffe.

in the manger]

Wyatt is saying that they are *hogs* in the manger.
The same association of hogs and dogs is found in
Sir Thomas More *Workes* p. 159D:

> such hogges and dogges as were not metely
> to haue those precious perles put vpon their
> nose . . .

and in Tyndale *Answere* Fo: xx *recto*:

> How be it there be [men like] swine that
> receaue no lerninge but to defile it. And
> there be dogges that rent all good learninge
> with ther teth . . .

and in Heywood's *A dialogue*, The seconde parte,
The ix chapiter:

> But you, to cast precious stones before hogs
> Cast my good before a sorte of cur dogs . . .

harp . . . ass]

This proverb is cast in the form of a story by
Phaedrus in his *Fables* Appendix 12. Erasmus
pointed the moral in his *Adagia*:

> *Asinus ad Lyram. Recte torquebitur in
> eos, qui indecore tentant artificium, cuius
> sunt imperiti, & à quo natura abhorrent.*
>
> An ass to a lyre. This proverb can properly
> be applied to people who undertake to
> practise some art or craft in which they
> have no skill and for which they are by
> nature totally unfitted.

Wyatt's use of *harp* suggests that he knew the
proverb in Chaucer's terms:

> Art thou lyke an asse to the harpe?

as we find it when Pandarus reproached Troilus
in the First Book:

> And sayd awake/ ful wonderlyche & sharpe
> What slombrest thou/ as in a lytargye?
> Or arte thou lyke an asse to the harpe
> That hereth soun/ whan men the stringes ply
> But in his mynde/ of that no melodye
> Maye synke him to gladen/ for that he
> So dull is/ in his bestyalite.

sacks of dirt]

The violence of this language recalls the *abbey-*

lubbers of Starkey [*A dialogue between Cardinal
Pole and Thomas Lupset* c.1538], the *bely-gods*
of Brinkelow [*The complaint of Roderyck Mors,*
1542?], and this passage from Tyndale's *Obedience*, fo: cxxvi, *recto*:

> vnto monkes, freres, and to the other of
> oure holy spiritualte the bely is all in all
> ... So ys cloyster love bely love ... Their
> longinge is to fyll their panch whom they
> serve ...

The most outspoken language was used in the
general satire *Rede me*, which may have been the
work of two ex-monks, Roye and Barlow. Here
is a specimen from *sig*. f.2 *verso*:

> It is of a trueth they are dedde/
> For they are in no vse nor stedde/
>   To christen mens consolacion.
> And as a dedde stynkynge carkace/
> Vnproffitably cloyeth a space/
>   Yf it be kepte above grownde
> So in their lyfe supersticious/
> Of wicked crymes enormious/
>   No maner proffitablenes is fownde/

The thought here was concentrated in one word,
draffsack. For Wyatt's contemporaries the word
stood literally for the sack containing solid refuse
destined for pigs' food. As some of this refuse was
offal, the word was extended to mean a fat paunch.
This was used by the Reformers to designate the
pampered clergy. A striking specimen may be
found in the works of an itinerant preacher,
forced to live abroad during the reign of Queen
Mary, but able on his return in 1558 to add to
his denunciation the following from an extended
comparison of Mary and Jezebel:

> As in the dayes of wycked Queene Jezabel
> the faythful Prophetes of God lyued wyth
> bread and water, when the Priestes of Baal
> fared most deliciously, and pampred their
> idle draffesackebellies with all kynde of
> pleasaunt wynes and deynty dyshes: euen
> so nowe the true ministers suffer both hunger
> and thirst, whyle the Idolatrous bishops and
> massing Priestes of England lyue lyke hogges
> of Epicures flocke in al kynde of pleasure

and delicate fare.
(Thomas Becon, *An humble supplication*
in *The Workes*: the thyrd parte, 1563,
Folio .xxiiii. *recto*.)

lean and dry] In Tottel's *Miscellany*, *sig*. T.i. *verso* there is a poem beginning:
It is no fire that geues no heate
Though it appeare neuer so hotte:
And they that runne and can not sweate,
Are very leane and dry God wot.

live to feed] Auct. Her. 4/28/39 Diog. Laert. 2/34:
Esse oportet ut uiuas non uiuere ut edas
Richard Taverner *Flores aliquot sig*. B v. *recto*:
[Socrates] sayde, manye lyued to eate and drynke, but he contrarily dyd eate and drynke to lyue . . .
This 'opposition' may have provoked the E scribe to write:
So I may fede to lyve

paunch] *Ep. . . . ad Romanos* 16.18:
Huiuscemodi enim Christo Domino nostro non seruiunt, sed suo uentri . . .
For they that are such serue not the Lorde Iesus Christ: but their awne bellyes . . .

be missed] If, as it seems, this was not idiomatic English in Wyatt's day, it may be a translation of *ne quid silentio praetereatur*, 'passed over in silence'.

hark . . . intend] 'Listen to what I take to be the truth'.

truth . . . offend] This proverbial expression was taken from Terence *Andria* Act I scene i/38:
SI.   *ita ut facillume*
sine inuidia laudem inuenias et amicos pares.
SO.   *sapienter uitam instituit; namque hoc tem-*
pore
obsequium amicos, ueritas odium parit.
SI.   . . . in such a way that very easily and without exciting envy you get praise and win friends.
SO.   His way of life has been commendable, for nowadays the only way to get friends is to

use flattery: telling the truth generates hatred.

See also the note on Favell in *Mine own J.P.*

It is both]   Avoiding truth is the way to secure ...

praise ... misease]   Wyatt may have had in mind Juvenal *Sat.* I/74:

> *probitas laudatur et alget*
> honesty is praised and freezes

and the sense may be 'Truth suffers when it comes close to the wind of praise.' This thought is close to that he expressed in his poem *Throughout the world*, particularly in the phrase, *words are but wind*. This same poem was in his mind in the following lines, particularly in the contrast between say well and do well.

far unmeet]   'Completely unfit'.

Taverner *Prouerbes* (1569) p. 32 *recto*:

> that craft is ... far vnmete for Christen persons

Surrey *Each beast*/14:

> And with a beck full low he bowed at her
>   feet
> In humble wise, as who would say, 'I am too
>   far unmeet'.

Udall *Apophthegmes* p. 84:

> A man voide of phylosophie is ferre vnmete for al good occupacions.

each thing]   'Every thing'.

bare feet]   Could the meaning be, 'relying solely on your own resources'?

Unless ... least]   The general nature of the fraudulent exchange Wyatt is ironically recommending is to be found in Gower's *Confessio Amantis* II/2344ff., where his Supplantator comes off best in a bargain:

> He reccheth noght, be so he winne,
> Of that an other man schal lese,
> And thus fulofte chalk for chese
> He changeth with ful litel cost,
> Whereof an other hath the lost
> And he the profit schal receive.

It may be only a coincidence of thought that a similar phrase occurs in Juvenal's Fourteenth

Satire/200:
pares quod uendere possis
pluris dimido
> You could buy merchandise and resell it
> at a fifty per cent profit or half as much
> again as you paid for it.

At any rate, *return* seems to stand for what you get back on the deal, as does *cant*, if it is connected with *cantle*, a slice of bread or cheese.

lose]

Wyatt wrote *lese*.

Learn at]

'Learn from'.

Kitson]

A very plausible candidate is a Thomas Kytson (1485-1540), who began commercial life as a mercer's apprentice and, by joining the Merchant Adventurers, rose rapidly to wealth, which he used to purchase land of a nobleman and build a magnificent house on it, Hengrave Hall in Suffolk (1525-1538). In 1533 Kitson became Sheriff of London and was knighted. This poem may have been circulated in his life-time, for in two extant versions the name Kitson has been replaced by *ladde*.

lands or fees]

That is to say, he had no landed estates for which he would have to obtain legitimation from the King. The expression *lands and fees* arose in feudal times, and was regularly used when a new heir sued to the King for possession and paid what was known as the *relief*. An illustration may be found in Lord Berners' *Huon of Bordeaux* p. 274/25:
> After that kynge Charlemayn was departyd
> fro Burdex & that Huon was retournyd, he
> assembled all his barons, to whom he made
> good chere, and there they toke there londes
> & fees of hym & made there homage . . .
> p. 20/3:
> we are goyng to Parys to the kynges court,
> to releue our londys and our foos, and to
> serue hym . . .

Sometime . . . dote]

This is one of the topics in Horace's Satire. He speaks of *senem delirum* 'an old dotard'.

Stay]

'Support physically by lending hand or arm'.

Wyatt may have been taking this hint from Horace:
                        ne tamen illi
tu comes exterior, si postulet, ire recuses
if he asks you to take a walk with him, see
that you do not refuse to take the outer
side.

OED 1630:
A Water-man many times hath his Soueraigne
by the hand, to stay him in and out the Barge.

the arm]   To be treated as one syllable.

if he cough]   Horace *Sat.* II/5/106:

                        si quis
forte coheredum senior male tussiet
if one of the other heirs with you is older
than you and has a hacking cough . . .

tread out]   'step on the spot'; *Hugh Rhodes's Boke of Nurture*,
If thou must spit, or blow thy nose, keep
                        thou it out of sight,
Let it not lye vpon the ground, but treade
                        thou it out right.

picks . . . purse]   A *Pick-purse* was a common expression for a thief.

withouten mo]   'Without more ado'.

Executor]   Probably 'a person appointed by a testator to
execute of carry into effect his will after his
decease'.

what . . . worse?]   'How can it hurt him?'
Skelton's *Magnyfycence*/1782:
It is the gyse nowe, I say, ouer all;
Largesse in wordes, for rewardes are but small:
To make fayre promyse, what are ye the
                        worse?
Sir T. Elyot *Pasquil* p. 16 *verso*:
what art thou the warse, that I name thee
herein for an example?

charge]   In Wyatt this usually means 'trouble', 'labour'
or 'inconvenience'.

deburse]   Though less common than *disburse*, the form was
not rare in Wyatt's day.

rivelled]   'Wrinkled', as in Heywood *The fyrst hundred* No.
66:

A widower riche, with riueld face old

Lydgate *Pilgr.* 24273:

> and by ryuels of my visage,
> How that I am called 'Age' . . .

Tyndale tr. *Enchiridion* sig. Q.vj. *recto*:

> ryueled & yuell favoured age

gold . . . good]

It is possible that Wyatt knew the anecdote of Titus reproaching his father Vespasian with making money out of urine. The Emperor, according to Suetonius,

> *pecuniam . . . admouit ad nares, sciscitans, "num odore offenderetur" . . .*

raising a coin to his nostrils he asked him whether he detected an offensive smell.

Juvenal coined a phrase from this story:

> *lucri bonus est odor ex re qualibet . . .*

money smells sweet whatever the source. . .

curse or ban]

The two verbs are synonyms. *Curse and ban* was a fixed phrase like our *curse and swear.* Wyatt often alters these doublets by putting *or* for *and.* In this case he was not alone, for we find in Barclay's *Shyp of Folys* Vol. I p. 234:

> Thus oft tyme chyldren haue cause to curse or ban . . .

old mule]

A coarse expression for a superannuated whore. In French, *vielle mulle.* Wyatt pronounced it *moyle* with two syllables. See the poem beginning *Ye old mule.*

bite . . . bridle]

'Show impatience'. Barclay, *Seconde Egloge* 821–822:

> these courtiers . . . Smelling those dishes,
> they bite vpon the bridle . . .

Heywood *A dialogue*, The seconde part, The viii chapiter: (of a woman)

> Where I shuld haue bridled her fyrst with rough byt
> To haue made hir chowe on the brydell
> one fyt . . .

Erasmus *Adagia: Frenum mordere.*

Cooper offered the following translations:

> To bite on the bridle; to murmur at his subiection; to signifie griefe of hys keeping vnder . . .

her middle]

   * exquisite, well-made
   * slender

'Waist', as in the *Romaunt of the Rose*/1030:
> For yonge she was and hewed bright,
> Sore plesaunt and fetys* with all,
> Gent* and in her myddell small . . .

If thy better]

Two closely allied thoughts are presented here. One's *better* is one's social superior. That superior's request was equivalent to a command. These two ideas come together in a translation of one of Erasmus' dialogues, *Polyphemus*, by Edmonde Becke. In his Preface to the Reader he quotes from Seneca:

> *Rogando cogit qui rogat superior*

which he glosses as follows:

> And in effecte, is thus moch to say, yf a mannes superior or his better desyre any thinge . . .

It is probable that Wyatt thought of *thy better* as a translation of *potiori* in Horace's Satire:

> *scortator erit: caue te roget: ultro/ Penelopam facilis potiori trade . . .*
> Does the whoremonger lust after your own wedded lady? Oblige him by making him a present of her before he brings the subject up. After all, he is your better . . .

R. Burrant *Preceptes of Cato* 1560 *sig.* B.vj.*verso*: *Maiori cede*]

> When thou haste to doe with one then thy
>   selfe greater,
> Yelde vnto hym mekelye as vnto thy better. . .

for her love besought]

A similar phrase is found in Dyboski p. 115:

> Here beside dwellith a riche barons dowghter
> She wold haue no man that for her love had
>   sought her
>   So nyse she was . . .

turn . . . laughter]

This appears to have been a common phrase. Erasmus *Epicureus* tr. Philip Gerrard: *A Very pleasaunt & fruitful Diologe called the Epicure* (1545) *sig.* C. viij. *verso*:

> suche folishe phansies that turne not afterwarde in too a laughter, but into euerlasting lamentation . . .

N. Udall tr. of Erasmus *Apoph.* p. 324 *verso*:

> Where he noteth that when a cryme is laied to ones charge, whiche he can by no meanes coulour ne auoide, one poore helpe and one poincte of shifte it is, to make a ieste of it, & to turne it (if one maye) to a matier of laughter.

These are all versions of the Latin *in iocum vertere* or *seria ludo vertere.*

gold] Ironic substitution for 'God', as in the phrase 'God speed thee!'

Pandare] To remedy the defective scansion we might suppose that Wyatt wrote *Pandarus.*

In Chaucer's *Troylus and Criseyde* Pandarus twice protests that his motives in acting as a go-between were not mercenary, e.g. Book III/260:

> But God, that al wotteth, take I to wytnesse,
> That never I this for couetyse wrought.

and Troilus assures him in lines 400ff:

> But he that gothe for golde or for rychesse
> On suche messages call hym what ye lyste
> And this that thou doest cal it gentylnesse . . .

Wyatt's remark is satirical, since Chaucer's figure is not regarded as morally blameworthy; on the contrary, he was acting in the name of friendship.

such a like] 'Similar.'

nice] 'Excessively scrupulous'.

next] 'Nearest'. Cooper has a quotation from Terence *Andria* IV/1/12:

> *proximus sum egomet mihi*

which he translated:

> I am nighest friende to my selfe: no man is neerer friende to my selfe then I am.

The sentiment was well brought out by Erasmus in his edition of *Catonis Disticha* (1525 ed. *sig.* B 5. *recto*:)

> *semper tibi proximus esto:*
> *Et ita amicis sis amicus ut tibi ipsi sis ami-*
> *cissimus.*
> Doe so to thy fiendes that thou be most frende vnto thy self.

bears no price] 'Stands low in public estimation'.

laughest thou]

This turn is taken from Horace's satire. e.g. line 3:
> *quid rides*? Why do you laugh at me?
> 58   *num furis? an prudens ludis me?*
> Have you gone off your head, or are you
> cold-bloodedly making a fool of me?

change . . . for gold]

Given Wyatt's evident acquaintance with those
essays by Plutarch which had been put into Latin
by Erasmus, it is possible that he had read a
passionate outburst on this topic in an essay on
deriving advantage from one's enemies. [*Moralia*
92D.]:
> Whenever our enemies appear to have suc-
> ceeded by flattery or base tricks, by bribery
> or corruption, in acquiring disgraceful and
> tyrannical power at court or in government,
> they shall not annoy us. Rather shall they
> put heart into us as we oppose to their vices
> our antithetical virtues of true liberty,
> political purity and decency. All the gold
> both in the earth and on the earth, said
> Plato, cannot pay the price of virtue. And let
> us always have at our elbows that saying of
> Solon's, 'we shall never take their wealth in
> exchange for our virtue'.

This quotation from Solon was repeated by
Plutarch in his essay on true quiet of mind, where
it was translated by Wyatt as:
> We wyll nat chaunge with you/ saith the
> same man/ vertue for riches . . .

godly things]

Gerrard in *The Epicure* [C8] has:
> And as I think the commune sort of men ar
> muche more too bee laught at, whiche in
> steede of Godlye thynges, chose vaine and
> transitory shadowes . . .

honest name]

In the *Book of Proverbs* 22/1 we find:
> *Melius est nomen bonum quam diuitiae*
>   *multae:*
> *super argentum & aurum gratia bona.*
> Betere is a good name, than manye richessis.

This was reduced to a homely proverb: good name
is gold worth. (*How the goode wif taught hir
doughter*) A good name many folde ys more
worthe then golde (*Babees Book*).

farewell]	Horace ends his Satire with *uiue ualeque*: Good-bye!
care . . . shame]	Both words would be easier to understand if translated into Latin! e.g. *si tibi curae . . . pudor* 'If a regard for decency and a fear of losing your good name weigh with you'.
honest poverty]	The point was made by Horace. When Ulysses protested that he, a front fighter at Troy, should have to kowtow to a dirty slave, Tiresias tells him:

> *Ergo pauper eris.*
> Very well, but you will remain poor.

The actual phrase may have been taken from Ode 29 in Book III:

> *probamque*
> *Pauperiem sine dote quaero.*
> I am looking for an honest maiden of modest means even though she brings me no dowry.

gift . . . give]	The poem beginning *Since love is such* has the phrase:

> Thanked be Fortune that me gave
> So fair a gift . . .

in a sieve]	A common proverb. Erasmus *Adagia* col. 174:

> *Cribro aquam haurire*
> To draw water with a sieve.

Wyatt may have known the 'source' in Plato's *Gorgias* 493B.

Fortune doth frown

The poem appears to be making a distinction between fate and fortune similar to that we find in *The pillar perished*, where Wyatt contrasted his *unhap* with his destiny:

> But since that thus it is by destiny,
> What can I more . . .?

The *locus classicus* in this century for the two faces of fortune is Arthur Brooke's *The Tragicall Historie of Romeus and Iuliet* (1562):

> The blindfyld goddess that
>   with frowning face doth fraye,*   frighten*
> And from theyr seate the mighty kinges
>   throwes downe with headlong sway,
> Begynneth now to turne
>   to these her smyling face . . .

he, too, sums up the doctrine of Fortune's wheel:

> For Fortune chaungeth more
>   then fickel fantasie.
> In nothing Fortune constant is
>   saue in vnconstancie.
> Her hasty ronning wheele,
>   is of a restless coorse,
> That turnes the clymers hedlong downe
>   from better to the woorse,
> And those that are beneth
>   she heaueth vp agayne.

This doctrine is found in the poem beginning *Once in your grace* in the lines:

> Though fortune so hath turned my case,
>   That I am down, and he full high . . .

Fortune . . . frown]   In his *Legend of Robert, Duke of Normandie* Drayton described Fortune as:
> Changing her Feature often in an howre . . . .
> Soone would she smile, and suddenly would
>   lowre . . .

What remedy?]   When this phrase was used in connection with Fortune, it meant something like 'what can't be cured must be endured' or 'it is useless to make a fuss', as we see from this passage from the end of a poem by Dunbar:
> Suppois the seruand be long vnquit,
> The lord sumtyme reward will it.
> Gife he does not, quhat remedy?
> To fecht with fortoun is no wit . . .

This meaning is well brought out at the close of Shakespeare's *Merry Wiues of Windsor* when Master Fenton announces that Anne Page and he are irrevocably married:
> *Ford.* Stand not amaz'd, here is no remedie:
> In Loue, the heauens themselues do guide
>   the state,

> Money buyes Lands, and wiues are sold by
> fate . . .
> *Page.* Well, what remedy? *Fenton*, heauen
> giue thee ioy, what cannot be eschew'd,
> must be embrac'd.

Surrey praised Wyatt for having the grace *to smile at Fortune's choice.*

down]

That is, at the bottom of Fortune's wheel. There is a proverb in Drayton's *Legend of Robert, Duke of Normandie*:

> Who can rayse him, that *Fortune* will haue
> downe?

Wyatt's case was worse, for Destiny was God's implacable, inexorable will. An expression of a thought, similar to Wyatt's, it to be found in Dowland's *Second Booke of Songs or Ayres*, 1600 in the close of *Sorow sorow stay*:

> . . . alas I am condempn'd, I am condempnéd
> euer, no hope, no help there doth remaine,
> but downe, downe, downe, downe I fall,
> downe and arise I neuer shall, but downe,
> downe, downe, downe I fall, downe and
> arise, I neuer shall.